Cuba Recent Economic and Political Developments Yearbook

by Cram101

Textbook NOT Included

Table of Contents

Title Page

Copyright

Foundations of Business

Management

Business law

Finance

Human resource management

Information systems

Marketing

Manufacturing

Commerce

Business ethics

Accounting

Index: Answers

Just The Facts101

Exam Prep for

Cuba Recent Economic and Political Developments Yearbook

Just The Facts101 Exam Prep is your link from
the textbook and lecture to your exams.

**Just The Facts101 Exam Preps are unauthorized and comprehensive reviews
of your textbooks.**

All material provided by CTI Publications (c) 2019

Textbook publishers and textbook authors do not participate in or contribute to these reviews.

Just The Facts101 Exam Prep

Copyright © 2019 by CTI Publications. All rights reserved.

eAIN 449533

Foundations of Business

A business, also known as an enterprise, agency or a firm, is an entity involved in the provision of goods and/or services to consumers. Businesses are prevalent in capitalist economies, where most of them are privately owned and provide goods and services to customers in exchange for other goods, services, or money.

:: Project management ::

A _____ is a source or supply from which a benefit is produced and it has some utility. _____ s can broadly be classified upon their availability—they are classified into renewable and non-renewable _____ s. Examples of non renewable _____ s are coal, crude oil natural gas nuclear energy etc. Examples of renewable _____ s are air, water, wind, solar energy etc. They can also be classified as actual and potential on the basis of level of development and use, on the basis of origin they can be classified as biotic and abiotic, and on the basis of their distribution, as ubiquitous and localized. An item becomes a _____ with time and developing technology. Typically, _____ s are materials, energy, services, staff, knowledge, or other assets that are transformed to produce benefit and in the process may be consumed or made unavailable. Benefits of _____ utilization may include increased wealth, proper functioning of a system, or enhanced well-being. From a human perspective a natural _____ is anything obtained from the environment to satisfy human needs and wants. From a broader biological or ecological perspective a _____ satisfies the needs of a living organism.

Exam Probability: **High**

1. *Answer choices:*

(see index for correct answer)

- a. Enterprise project management
- b. Indian Institute of Project Management
- c. Financial plan
- d. A Guide to the Project Management Body of Knowledge

Guidance: level 1

:: Real estate ::

_____ s serve several societal needs – primarily as shelter from weather, security, living space, privacy, to store belongings, and to comfortably live and work. A _____ as a shelter represents a physical division of the human habitat and the outside .

Exam Probability: **High**

2. *Answer choices:*

(see index for correct answer)

- a. Form-based code
- b. Buyer brokerage
- c. Building
- d. Conditional sale

Guidance: level 1

:: Competition (economics) ::

_____ arises whenever at least two parties strive for a goal which cannot be shared: where one`s gain is the other`s loss .

Exam Probability: **High**

3. *Answer choices:*

(see index for correct answer)

- a. Currency competition
- b. Blindspots analysis
- c. Transfer pricing
- d. Competition

Guidance: level 1

:: International trade ::

_____ or globalisation is the process of interaction and integration among people, companies, and governments worldwide. As a complex and multifaceted phenomenon, _____ is considered by some as a form of capitalist expansion which entails the integration of local and national economies into a global, unregulated market economy. _____ has grown due to advances in transportation and communication technology. With the increased global interactions comes the growth of international trade, ideas, and culture. _____ is primarily an economic process of interaction and integration that's associated with social and cultural aspects. However, conflicts and diplomacy are also large parts of the history of _____ , and modern _____ .

Exam Probability: **High**

4. *Answer choices:*

(see index for correct answer)

- a. Globalization
- b. Banyan merchants
- c. David Ricardo

- d. Dollar hegemony

Guidance: level 1

:: Infographics ::

A _____ is a symbolic representation of information according to visualization technique. _____ s have been used since ancient times, but became more prevalent during the Enlightenment. Sometimes, the technique uses a three-dimensional visualization which is then projected onto a two-dimensional surface. The word graph is sometimes used as a synonym for _____ .

Exam Probability: **Medium**

5. *Answer choices:*
(see index for correct answer)

- a. State diagram
- b. Diagram
- c. Staircase model
- d. Graphic organizer

Guidance: level 1

:: Employment ::

The _____ is an individual's metaphorical "journey" through learning, work and other aspects of life. There are a number of ways to define _____ and the term is used in a variety of ways.

Exam Probability: **High**

6. *Answer choices:*

(see index for correct answer)

- a. Working holiday visa
- b. Career
- c. Employment Development Department
- d. Shift work sleep disorder

Guidance: level 1

:: Project management ::

Some scenarios associate "this kind of planning" with learning "life skills". _____ s are necessary, or at least useful, in situations where individuals need to know what time they must be at a specific location to receive a specific service, and where people need to accomplish a set of goals within a set time period.

Exam Probability: **Medium**

7. *Answer choices:*

(see index for correct answer)

- a. Advanced Integrated Practice
- b. RationalPlan
- c. Mandated lead arranger
- d. Project Management South Africa

Guidance: level 1

:: Management ::

In organizational studies, _____ is the efficient and effective development of an organization's resources when they are needed. Such resources may include financial resources, inventory, human skills, production resources, or information technology and natural resources.

Exam Probability: **Low**

8. *Answer choices:*

(see index for correct answer)

- a. Power to the edge
- b. Formula for change
- c. Resource management
- d. Concept of the Corporation

Guidance: level 1

:: Strategic management ::

_____ is a strategic planning technique used to help a person or organization identify strengths, weaknesses, opportunities, and threats related to business competition or project planning. It is intended to specify the objectives of the business venture or project and identify the internal and external factors that are favorable and unfavorable to achieving those objectives. Users of a _____ often ask and answer questions to generate meaningful information for each category to make the tool useful and identify their competitive advantage. SWOT has been described as the tried-and-true tool of strategic analysis.

Exam Probability: **Low**

9. *Answer choices:*

(see index for correct answer)

- a. E-learning Maturity Model
- b. BSC SWOT
- c. SWOT analysis
- d. Strategic control

Guidance: level 1

:: Association of Southeast Asian Nations ::

The Association of Southeast Asian Nations is a regional intergovernmental organization comprising ten countries in Southeast Asia, which promotes intergovernmental cooperation and facilitates economic, political, security, military, educational, and sociocultural integration among its members and other countries in Asia. It also regularly engages other countries in the Asia-Pacific region and beyond. A major partner of Shanghai Cooperation Organisation, _____ maintains a global network of alliances and dialogue partners and is considered by many as a global powerhouse, the central union for cooperation in Asia-Pacific, and a prominent and influential organization. It is involved in numerous international affairs, and hosts diplomatic missions throughout the world.

Exam Probability: **High**

10. *Answer choices:*

(see index for correct answer)

- a. ASEAN Intergovernmental Commission on Human Rights
- b. ASEAN
- c. Flag of the Association of Southeast Asian Nations
- d. Emblem of the Association of Southeast Asian Nations

Guidance: level 1

:: Critical thinking ::

An _____ is a set of statements usually constructed to describe a set of facts which clarifies the causes, context, and consequences of those facts. This description of the facts et cetera may establish rules or laws, and may clarify the existing rules or laws in relation to any objects, or phenomena examined. The components of an _____ can be implicit, and interwoven with one another.

Exam Probability: **Medium**

11. *Answer choices:*

(see index for correct answer)

- a. Higher-order thinking
- b. Precising definition
- c. Explanatory power
- d. Proof

Guidance: level 1

:: Management ::

_____ is the practice of initiating, planning, executing, controlling, and closing the work of a team to achieve specific goals and meet specific success criteria at the specified time.

Exam Probability: **Medium**

12. Answer choices:

(see index for correct answer)

- a. Automated decision support
- b. Performance management
- c. Power to the edge
- d. Project management

Guidance: level 1

:: International relations ::

A _____ is any event that is going to lead to an unstable and dangerous situation affecting an individual, group, community, or whole society. Crises are deemed to be negative changes in the security, economic, political, societal, or environmental affairs, especially when they occur abruptly, with little or no warning. More loosely, it is a term meaning "a testing time" or an "emergency event".

Exam Probability: **High**

13. Answer choices:

(see index for correct answer)

- a. Crisis
- b. Nation-building
- c. Centre of Excellence on Public Security
- d. Democracy building

Guidance: level 1

:: Rhetoric ::

_____ is the pattern of narrative development that aims to make vivid a place, object, character, or group. _____ is one of four rhetorical modes, along with exposition, argumentation, and narration. In practice it would be difficult to write literature that drew on just one of the four basic modes.

Exam Probability: **Low**

14. *Answer choices:*

(see index for correct answer)

- a. Sarcasm
- b. Satire
- c. Description
- d. Euphuism

Guidance: level 1

:: Financial statements ::

In financial accounting, a _____ or statement of financial position or statement of financial condition is a summary of the financial balances of an individual or organization, whether it be a sole proprietorship, a business partnership, a corporation, private limited company or other organization such as Government or not-for-profit entity. Assets, liabilities and ownership equity are listed as of a specific date, such as the end of its financial year. A _____ is often described as a "snapshot of a company's financial condition". Of the four basic financial statements, the _____ is the only statement which applies to a single point in time of a business' calendar year.

Exam Probability: **Low**

15. *Answer choices:*

(see index for correct answer)

- a. Government financial statements
- b. Balance sheet
- c. Quarterly finance report
- d. Statement of retained earnings

Guidance: level 1

:: Reputation management ::

_____ or image of a social entity is an opinion about that entity, typically as a result of social evaluation on a set of criteria.

Exam Probability: **Medium**

16. *Answer choices:*

(see index for correct answer)

- a. ClaimID
- b. Lithium Technologies
- c. Reputation
- d. Star

Guidance: level 1

:: Graphic design ::

An _____ is an artifact that depicts visual perception, such as a photograph or other two-dimensional picture, that resembles a subject—usually a physical object—and thus provides a depiction of it. In the context of signal processing, an _____ is a distributed amplitude of color.

Exam Probability: **Medium**

17. *Answer choices:*

(see index for correct answer)

- a. Rich black
- b. AndreaMosaic
- c. Letterpress printing

- d. Image

Guidance: level 1

:: Business ethics ::

_____ is a type of harassment technique that relates to a sexual nature and the unwelcome or inappropriate promise of rewards in exchange for sexual favors. _____ includes a range of actions from mild transgressions to sexual abuse or assault. Harassment can occur in many different social settings such as the workplace, the home, school, churches, etc. Harassers or victims may be of any gender.

Exam Probability: **High**

18. *Answer choices:*

(see index for correct answer)

- a. Corporate sustainable profitability
- b. Global Reporting Initiative
- c. Sexual harassment
- d. Corporate Knights

Guidance: level 1

:: Mathematical finance ::

In economics and finance, _____ , also known as present discounted value, is the value of an expected income stream determined as of the date of valuation. The _____ is always less than or equal to the future value because money has interest-earning potential, a characteristic referred to as the time value of money, except during times of negative interest rates, when the _____ will be more than the future value. Time value can be described with the simplified phrase, "A dollar today is worth more than a dollar tomorrow". Here, `worth more` means that its value is greater. A dollar today is worth more than a dollar tomorrow because the dollar can be invested and earn a day`s worth of interest, making the total accumulate to a value more than a dollar by tomorrow. Interest can be compared to rent. Just as rent is paid to a landlord by a tenant without the ownership of the asset being transferred, interest is paid to a lender by a borrower who gains access to the money for a time before paying it back. By letting the borrower have access to the money, the lender has sacrificed the exchange value of this money, and is compensated for it in the form of interest. The initial amount of the borrowed funds is less than the total amount of money paid to the lender.

Exam Probability: **Low**

19. *Answer choices:*

(see index for correct answer)

- a. Consumer math
- b. Inverse demand function
- c. Implied volatility
- d. QuantLib

Guidance: level 1

:: Stock market ::

The _____ of a corporation is all of the shares into which ownership of the corporation is divided. In American English, the shares are commonly known as "_____ s". A single share of the _____ represents fractional ownership of the corporation in proportion to the total number of shares. This typically entitles the _____ holder to that fraction of the company's earnings, proceeds from liquidation of assets, or voting power, often dividing these up in proportion to the amount of money each _____ holder has invested. Not all _____ is necessarily equal, as certain classes of _____ may be issued for example without voting rights, with enhanced voting rights, or with a certain priority to receive profits or liquidation proceeds before or after other classes of shareholders.

Exam Probability: **High**

20. *Answer choices:*

(see index for correct answer)

- a. Stock
- b. Seeking Alpha
- c. Wash trade
- d. Central securities depository

Guidance: level 1

:: Management ::

_____ is the process of thinking about the activities required to achieve a desired goal. It is the first and foremost activity to achieve desired results. It involves the creation and maintenance of a plan, such as psychological aspects that require conceptual skills. There are even a couple of tests to measure someone's capability of _____ well. As such, _____ is a fundamental property of intelligent behavior. An important further meaning, often just called "_____" is the legal context of permitted building developments.

Exam Probability: **High**

21. *Answer choices:*

(see index for correct answer)

- a. Social risk management
- b. Integrated master plan
- c. Business process improvement
- d. Planning

Guidance: level 1

:: Decision theory ::

A _____ is a deliberate system of principles to guide decisions and achieve rational outcomes. A _____ is a statement of intent, and is implemented as a procedure or protocol. Policies are generally adopted by a governance body within an organization. Policies can assist in both subjective and objective decision making. Policies to assist in subjective decision making usually assist senior management with decisions that must be based on the relative merits of a number of factors, and as a result are often hard to test objectively, e.g. work-life balance _____. In contrast policies to assist in objective decision making are usually operational in nature and can be objectively tested, e.g. password _____.

Exam Probability: **High**

22. *Answer choices:*

(see index for correct answer)

- a. Two-moment decision model
- b. Outcome primacy
- c. Probabilistic prognosis
- d. There are known knowns

Guidance: level 1

:: Management accounting ::

_____ s are costs that change as the quantity of the good or service that a business produces changes. _____ s are the sum of marginal costs over all units produced. They can also be considered normal costs. Fixed costs and _____ s make up the two components of total cost. Direct costs are costs that can easily be associated with a particular cost object. However, not all _____ s are direct costs. For example, variable manufacturing overhead costs are _____ s that are indirect costs, not direct costs. _____ s are sometimes called unit-level costs as they vary with the number of units produced.

Exam Probability: **Low**

23. *Answer choices:*

(see index for correct answer)

- a. activity based costing
- b. Fixed assets management
- c. Variable cost
- d. Owner earnings

Guidance: level 1

:: Income ::

_____ is a ratio between the net profit and cost of investment resulting from an investment of some resources. A high ROI means the investment's gains favorably to its cost. As a performance measure, ROI is used to evaluate the efficiency of an investment or to compare the efficiencies of several different investments. In purely economic terms, it is one way of relating profits to capital invested. _____ is a performance measure used by businesses to identify the efficiency of an investment or number of different investments.

Exam Probability: **Low**

24. *Answer choices:*

(see index for correct answer)

- a. bottom line
- b. Return on investment
- c. Stipend
- d. Gratuity

Guidance: level 1

:: Management ::

A _____ is an idea of the future or desired result that a person or a group of people envisions, plans and commits to achieve. People endeavor to reach _____ s within a finite time by setting deadlines.

Exam Probability: **High**

25. Answer choices:

(see index for correct answer)

- a. Process-based management
- b. Planning fallacy
- c. Project stakeholder
- d. Goal

Guidance: level 1

:: Alchemical processes ::

In chemistry, a _____ is a special type of homogeneous mixture composed of two or more substances. In such a mixture, a solute is a substance dissolved in another substance, known as a solvent. The mixing process of a _____ happens at a scale where the effects of chemical polarity are involved, resulting in interactions that are specific to solvation. The _____ assumes the phase of the solvent when the solvent is the larger fraction of the mixture, as is commonly the case. The concentration of a solute in a _____ is the mass of that solute expressed as a percentage of the mass of the whole _____ . The term aqueous _____ is when one of the solvents is water.

Exam Probability: **Medium**

26. Answer choices:

(see index for correct answer)

- a. Putrefaction
- b. Corporification

- c. Unity of opposites
- d. Putrefying bacteria

Guidance: level 1

:: Business law ::

A _____ is an arrangement where parties, known as partners, agree to cooperate to advance their mutual interests. The partners in a _____ may be individuals, businesses, interest-based organizations, schools, governments or combinations. Organizations may partner to increase the likelihood of each achieving their mission and to amplify their reach. A _____ may result in issuing and holding equity or may be only governed by a contract.

Exam Probability: **Low**

27. *Answer choices:*
(see index for correct answer)

- a. Free agent
- b. Double ticketing
- c. Vehicle leasing
- d. Managed service company

Guidance: level 1

:: Business terms ::

A _____ is a short statement of why an organization exists, what its overall goal is, identifying the goal of its operations: what kind of product or service it provides, its primary customers or market, and its geographical region of operation. It may include a short statement of such fundamental matters as the organization's values or philosophies, a business's main competitive advantages, or a desired future state—the "vision".

Exam Probability: **Low**

28. *Answer choices:*

(see index for correct answer)

- a. churn rate
- b. noncommercial
- c. customer base
- d. Mission statement

Guidance: level 1

:: Insolvency ::

_____ is a legal process through which people or other entities who cannot repay debts to creditors may seek relief from some or all of their debts. In most jurisdictions, _____ is imposed by a court order, often initiated by the debtor.

Exam Probability: **High**

29. *Answer choices:*

(see index for correct answer)

- a. United Kingdom insolvency law
- b. George Samuel Ford
- c. Bankruptcy
- d. Insolvency

Guidance: level 1

:: Financial regulatory authorities of the United States ::

The _____ is the revenue service of the United States federal government. The government agency is a bureau of the Department of the Treasury, and is under the immediate direction of the Commissioner of Internal Revenue, who is appointed to a five-year term by the President of the United States. The IRS is responsible for collecting taxes and administering the Internal Revenue Code, the main body of federal statutory tax law of the United States. The duties of the IRS include providing tax assistance to taxpayers and pursuing and resolving instances of erroneous or fraudulent tax filings. The IRS has also overseen various benefits programs, and enforces portions of the Affordable Care Act.

Exam Probability: **Low**

30. *Answer choices:*

(see index for correct answer)

- a. Office of Thrift Supervision

- b. National Futures Association
- c. Securities Investor Protection Corporation
- d. Consumer Financial Protection Bureau

Guidance: level 1

:: ::

A _____ is an organization, usually a group of people or a company, authorized to act as a single entity and recognized as such in law. Early incorporated entities were established by charter. Most jurisdictions now allow the creation of new _____ s through registration.

Exam Probability: **Medium**

31. *Answer choices:*
(see index for correct answer)

- a. hierarchical perspective
- b. open system
- c. imperative
- d. cultural

Guidance: level 1

:: Business ::

The seller, or the provider of the goods or services, completes a sale in response to an acquisition, appropriation, requisition or a direct interaction with the buyer at the point of sale. There is a passing of title of the item, and the settlement of a price, in which agreement is reached on a price for which transfer of ownership of the item will occur. The seller, not the purchaser typically executes the sale and it may be completed prior to the obligation of payment. In the case of indirect interaction, a person who sells goods or service on behalf of the owner is known as a salesman or saleswoman or salesperson, but this often refers to someone _____ goods in a store/shop, in which case other terms are also common, including salesclerk, shop assistant, and retail clerk.

Exam Probability: **High**

32. *Answer choices:*

(see index for correct answer)

- a. Organizational life cycle
- b. Employee experience management
- c. Selling
- d. Ansoff Matrix

Guidance: level 1

:: Stock market ::

_____ is a form of corporate equity ownership, a type of security. The terms voting share and ordinary share are also used frequently in other parts of the world; "_____" being primarily used in the United States. They are known as Equity shares or Ordinary shares in the UK and other Commonwealth realms. This type of share gives the stockholder the right to share in the profits of the company, and to vote on matters of corporate policy and the composition of the members of the board of directors.

Exam Probability: **Medium**

33. *Answer choices:*

(see index for correct answer)

- a. Pattern day trader
- b. Common stock
- c. Long squeeze
- d. SPI 200 futures contract

Guidance: level 1

:: ::

_____ is the means to see, hear, or become aware of something or someone through our fundamental senses. The term _____ derives from the Latin word perceptio, and is the organization, identification, and interpretation of sensory information in order to represent and understand the presented information, or the environment.

Exam Probability: **High**

34. *Answer choices:*

(see index for correct answer)

- a. similarity-attraction theory
- b. functional perspective
- c. Perception
- d. hierarchical

Guidance: level 1

:: Management ::

_____ is the identification, evaluation, and prioritization of risks followed by coordinated and economical application of resources to minimize, monitor, and control the probability or impact of unfortunate events or to maximize the realization of opportunities.

Exam Probability: **Low**

35. *Answer choices:*

(see index for correct answer)

- a. Risk management
- b. Community of practice
- c. Profitable growth

- d. Jarratt report

Guidance: level 1

:: Training ::

_____ is teaching, or developing in oneself or others, any skills and knowledge that relate to specific useful competencies. _____ has specific goals of improving one's capability, capacity, productivity and performance. It forms the core of apprenticeships and provides the backbone of content at institutes of technology . In addition to the basic _____ required for a trade, occupation or profession, observers of the labor-market recognize as of 2008 the need to continue _____ beyond initial qualifications: to maintain, upgrade and update skills throughout working life. People within many professions and occupations may refer to this sort of _____ as professional development.

Exam Probability: **High**

36. *Answer choices:*

(see index for correct answer)

- a. Training
- b. Facila
- c. Instructor-led training
- d. Youth Training Scheme

Guidance: level 1

:: Scientific method ::

In the social sciences and life sciences, a _____ is a research method involving an up-close, in-depth, and detailed examination of a subject of study, as well as its related contextual conditions.

Exam Probability: **Low**

37. *Answer choices:*
(see index for correct answer)

- a. Causal research
- b. pilot project
- c. Case study
- d. Preference test

Guidance: level 1

:: Interest rates ::

An _____ is the amount of interest due per period, as a proportion of the amount lent, deposited or borrowed. The total interest on an amount lent or borrowed depends on the principal sum, the _____ , the compounding frequency, and the length of time over which it is lent, deposited or borrowed.

Exam Probability: **Low**

38. Answer choices:

(see index for correct answer)

- a. London Interbank Bid Rate
- b. Inflation derivative
- c. Interest rate
- d. Bank rate

Guidance: level 1

:: Loans ::

In finance, a _____ is the lending of money by one or more individuals, organizations, or other entities to other individuals, organizations etc. The recipient incurs a debt, and is usually liable to pay interest on that debt until it is repaid, and also to repay the principal amount borrowed.

Exam Probability: **Medium**

39. Answer choices:

(see index for correct answer)

- a. Loan
- b. Installment loan
- c. Bridge loan
- d. Loan modification company

Guidance: level 1

:: Industrial design ::

In physics and mathematics, the _____ of a mathematical space is informally defined as the minimum number of coordinates needed to specify any point within it. Thus a line has a _____ of one because only one coordinate is needed to specify a point on it for example, the point at 5 on a number line. A surface such as a plane or the surface of a cylinder or sphere has a _____ of two because two coordinates are needed to specify a point on it for example, both a latitude and longitude are required to locate a point on the surface of a sphere. The inside of a cube, a cylinder or a sphere is three- _____ al because three coordinates are needed to locate a point within these spaces.

Exam Probability: **Medium**

40. *Answer choices:*
(see index for correct answer)

- a. Objectified
- b. Solid Ground Curing
- c. World Design Capital
- d. Dimension

Guidance: level 1

:: ::

_____ is the collection of mechanisms, processes and relations by which corporations are controlled and operated. Governance structures and principles identify the distribution of rights and responsibilities among different participants in the corporation and include the rules and procedures for making decisions in corporate affairs. _____ is necessary because of the possibility of conflicts of interests between stakeholders, primarily between shareholders and upper management or among shareholders.

Exam Probability: **Low**

41. *Answer choices:*
(see index for correct answer)

- a. levels of analysis
- b. deep-level diversity
- c. hierarchical perspective
- d. corporate values

Guidance: level 1

:: Non-profit technology ::

Instituto del Tercer Mundo is a Non-Governmental Organization that performs information, communication and education activities. _____, which was established in 1989, shares the same secretariat and coordinating personnel as Social Watch and is based in Montevideo, Uruguay.

Exam Probability: **Medium**

42. Answer choices:

(see index for correct answer)

- a. Software Patent Institute
- b. Cougar Mountain Software
- c. INeedAPencil
- d. ITeM

Guidance: level 1

:: Organizational behavior ::

_____ is the state or fact of exclusive rights and control over property, which may be an object, land/real estate or intellectual property. _____ involves multiple rights, collectively referred to as title, which may be separated and held by different parties.

Exam Probability: **Low**

43. Answer choices:

(see index for correct answer)

- a. Positive organizational behavior
- b. Organizational Expedience
- c. Civic virtue
- d. Ownership

Guidance: level 1

:: Real estate valuation ::

_____ or OMV is the price at which an asset would trade in a competitive auction setting. _____ is often used interchangeably with open _____, fair value or fair _____, although these terms have distinct definitions in different standards, and may or may not differ in some circumstances.

Exam Probability: **High**

44. *Answer choices:*
(see index for correct answer)

- a. E.surv
- b. Uniform Standards of Professional Appraisal Practice
- c. Market value
- d. Zoopla

Guidance: level 1

:: International trade ::

_____ involves the transfer of goods or services from one person or entity to another, often in exchange for money. A system or network that allows _____ is called a market.

Exam Probability: **Medium**

45. *Answer choices:*

(see index for correct answer)

- a. Kennedy Round
- b. Trade creation
- c. Trade
- d. Commercial invoice

Guidance: level 1

:: Credit cards ::

A _____ is a payment card issued to users to enable the cardholder to pay a merchant for goods and services based on the cardholder's promise to the card issuer to pay them for the amounts plus the other agreed charges. The card issuer creates a revolving account and grants a line of credit to the cardholder, from which the cardholder can borrow money for payment to a merchant or as a cash advance.

Exam Probability: **Low**

46. Answer choices:

(see index for correct answer)

- a. HSBC
- b. Palladium Card
- c. American Express
- d. Credit card

Guidance: level 1

:: Costs ::

In microeconomic theory, the _____, or alternative cost, of making a particular choice is the value of the most valuable choice out of those that were not taken. In other words, opportunity that will require sacrifices.

Exam Probability: **High**

47. Answer choices:

(see index for correct answer)

- a. Cost curve
- b. Average cost
- c. Opportunity cost
- d. Cost of poor quality

Guidance: level 1

:: Organizational structure ::

An _____ defines how activities such as task allocation, coordination, and supervision are directed toward the achievement of organizational aims.

Exam Probability: **Low**

48. *Answer choices:*

(see index for correct answer)

- a. Blessed Unrest
- b. Unorganisation
- c. The Starfish and the Spider
- d. Organizational structure

Guidance: level 1

:: Legal terms ::

An _____ is an action which is inaccurate or incorrect. In some usages, an _____ is synonymous with a mistake. In statistics, "_____" refers to the difference between the value which has been computed and the correct value. An _____ could result in failure or in a deviation from the intended performance or behaviour.

Exam Probability: **Medium**

49. *Answer choices:*

(see index for correct answer)

- a. Negative pledge
- b. Principal case
- c. Error
- d. Injunction

Guidance: level 1

:: Macroeconomics ::

_____ is the increase in the inflation-adjusted market value of the goods and services produced by an economy over time. It is conventionally measured as the percent rate of increase in real gross domestic product, or real GDP.

Exam Probability: **Low**

50. *Answer choices:*

(see index for correct answer)

- a. Job guarantee
- b. Country attractiveness
- c. Ordoliberalism

- d. Economic growth

Guidance: level 1

:: Summary statistics ::

_____ is the number of occurrences of a repeating event per unit of time. It is also referred to as temporal _____ , which emphasizes the contrast to spatial _____ and angular _____ . The period is the duration of time of one cycle in a repeating event, so the period is the reciprocal of the _____ . For example: if a newborn baby's heart beats at a _____ of 120 times a minute, its period—the time interval between beats—is half a second . _____ is an important parameter used in science and engineering to specify the rate of oscillatory and vibratory phenomena, such as mechanical vibrations, audio signals , radio waves, and light.

Exam Probability: **Low**

51. *Answer choices:*

(see index for correct answer)

- a. Higher-order statistics
- b. Summary statistics
- c. Frequency
- d. Quartile

Guidance: level 1

:: ::

_____ is an abstract concept of management of complex systems according to a set of rules and trends. In systems theory, these types of rules exist in various fields of biology and society, but the term has slightly different meanings according to context. For example.

Exam Probability: **Medium**

52. *Answer choices:*

(see index for correct answer)

- a. deep-level diversity
- b. surface-level diversity
- c. co-culture
- d. process perspective

Guidance: level 1

:: Statistical terminology ::

_____ is the ability to avoid wasting materials, energy, efforts, money, and time in doing something or in producing a desired result. In a more general sense, it is the ability to do things well, successfully, and without waste. In more mathematical or scientific terms, it is a measure of the extent to which input is well used for an intended task or function. It often specifically comprises the capability of a specific application of effort to produce a specific outcome with a minimum amount or quantity of waste, expense, or unnecessary effort. _____ refers to very different inputs and outputs in different fields and industries.

Exam Probability: **Medium**

53. *Answer choices:*

(see index for correct answer)

- a. Efficiency
- b. Likelihood
- c. Nuisance parameter
- d. Skewness risk

Guidance: level 1

:: Corporate crime ::

_____ LLP, based in Chicago, was an American holding company. Formerly one of the "Big Five" accounting firms, the firm had provided auditing, tax, and consulting services to large corporations. By 2001, it had become one of the world's largest multinational companies.

Exam Probability: **Medium**

54. *Answer choices:*

(see index for correct answer)

- a. FirstEnergy
- b. Tip and Trade
- c. New England Compounding Center
- d. Ovson Egg

Guidance: level 1

:: Marketing ::

_____ or stock is the goods and materials that a business holds for the ultimate goal of resale .

Exam Probability: **Medium**

55. *Answer choices:*

(see index for correct answer)

- a. Price umbrella
- b. Cyberdoc
- c. Price point
- d. Gimmick

Guidance: level 1

:: Unemployment ::

In economics, a _____ is a business cycle contraction when there is a general decline in economic activity. Macroeconomic indicators such as GDP, investment spending, capacity utilization, household income, business profits, and inflation fall, while bankruptcies and the unemployment rate rise. In the United Kingdom, it is defined as a negative economic growth for two consecutive quarters.

Exam Probability: **High**

56. *Answer choices:*

(see index for correct answer)

- a. Natural rate of unemployment
- b. Employment Promotion and Protection against Unemployment Convention, 1988
- c. Functional finance
- d. Recession

Guidance: level 1

:: Generally Accepted Accounting Principles ::

Expenditure is an outflow of money to another person or group to pay for an item or service, or for a category of costs. For a tenant, rent is an _____. For students or parents, tuition is an _____. Buying food, clothing, furniture or an automobile is often referred to as an _____. An _____ is a cost that is "paid" or "remitted", usually in exchange for something of value. Something that seems to cost a great deal is "expensive". Something that seems to cost little is "inexpensive". "_____ s of the table" are _____ s of dining, refreshments, a feast, etc.

Exam Probability: **Low**

57. *Answer choices:*
(see index for correct answer)

- a. Shares outstanding
- b. Deferred income
- c. Paid in capital
- d. Chinese accounting standards

Guidance: level 1

:: Consumer theory ::

A _____ is a technical term in psychology, economics and philosophy usually used in relation to choosing between alternatives. For example, someone prefers A over B if they would rather choose A than B.

Exam Probability: **Medium**

58. *Answer choices:*

(see index for correct answer)

- a. End-of-life
- b. Preference
- c. Marginal rate of substitution
- d. intertemporal substitution

Guidance: level 1

:: Retailing ::

_____ is the process of selling consumer goods or services to customers through multiple channels of distribution to earn a profit. _____ ers satisfy demand identified through a supply chain. The term " _____ er" is typically applied where a service provider fills the small orders of a large number of individuals, who are end-users, rather than large orders of a small number of wholesale, corporate or government clientele. Shopping generally refers to the act of buying products. Sometimes this is done to obtain final goods, including necessities such as food and clothing; sometimes it takes place as a recreational activity. Recreational shopping often involves window shopping and browsing: it does not always result in a purchase.

Exam Probability: **Medium**

59. *Answer choices:*

(see index for correct answer)

- a. Aaramshop

- b. Wardrobing
- c. Retail
- d. Tack shop

Guidance: level 1

Management

Management is the administration of an organization, whether it is a business, a not-for-profit organization, or government body. Management includes the activities of setting the strategy of an organization and coordinating the efforts of its employees (or of volunteers) to accomplish its objectives through the application of available resources, such as financial, natural, technological, and human resources.

:: Employment compensation ::

_____ refers to various incentive plans introduced by businesses that provide direct or indirect payments to employees that depend on company's profitability in addition to employees' regular salary and bonuses. In publicly traded companies these plans typically amount to allocation of shares to employees. One of the earliest pioneers of _____ was Englishman Theodore Cooke Taylor, who is known to have introduced the practice in his woollen mills during the late 1800s.

Exam Probability: **High**

1. *Answer choices:*

(see index for correct answer)

- a. Salary cap
- b. Equal Pay Act 1970
- c. Corporate child care
- d. Profit sharing

Guidance: level 1

:: ::

_____ is the assignment of any responsibility or authority to another person to carry out specific activities. It is one of the core concepts of management leadership. However, the person who delegated the work remains accountable for the outcome of the delegated work. _____ empowers a subordinate to make decisions, i.e. it is a shifting of decision-making authority from one organizational level to a lower one. _____ , if properly done, is not fabrication. The opposite of effective _____ is micromanagement, where a manager provides too much input, direction, and review of delegated work. In general, _____ is good and can save money and time, help in building skills, and motivate people. On the other hand, poor _____ might cause frustration and confusion to all the involved parties. Some agents, however, do not favour a _____ and consider the power of making a decision rather burdensome.

Exam Probability: **High**

2. *Answer choices:*

(see index for correct answer)

- a. Character
- b. Delegation
- c. open system
- d. surface-level diversity

Guidance: level 1

:: Project management ::

Some scenarios associate "this kind of planning" with learning "life skills". _____ s are necessary, or at least useful, in situations where individuals need to know what time they must be at a specific location to receive a specific service, and where people need to accomplish a set of goals within a set time period.

Exam Probability: **Medium**

3. *Answer choices:*

(see index for correct answer)

- a. Rolling Wave planning
- b. Work package
- c. Resource
- d. Schedule

Guidance: level 1

:: Training ::

_____ is teaching, or developing in oneself or others, any skills and knowledge that relate to specific useful competencies. _____ has specific goals of improving one's capability, capacity, productivity and performance. It forms the core of apprenticeships and provides the backbone of content at institutes of technology. In addition to the basic _____ required for a trade, occupation or profession, observers of the labor-market recognize as of 2008 the need to continue _____ beyond initial qualifications: to maintain, upgrade and update skills throughout working life. People within many professions and occupations may refer to this sort of _____ as professional development.

Exam Probability: **High**

4. *Answer choices:*
(see index for correct answer)

- a. Training
- b. National sports team
- c. Practicum
- d. Arts-based training

Guidance: level 1

:: ::

A _____ is an individual or institution that legally owns one or more shares of stock in a public or private corporation. _____ s may be referred to as members of a corporation. Legally, a person is not a _____ in a corporation until their name and other details are entered in the corporation's register of _____ s or members.

Exam Probability: **High**

5. *Answer choices:*

(see index for correct answer)

- a. surface-level diversity
- b. Character
- c. empathy
- d. personal values

Guidance: level 1

:: Summary statistics ::

_____ is the number of occurrences of a repeating event per unit of time. It is also referred to as temporal _____ , which emphasizes the contrast to spatial _____ and angular _____ . The period is the duration of time of one cycle in a repeating event, so the period is the reciprocal of the _____ . For example: if a newborn baby's heart beats at a _____ of 120 times a minute, its period—the time interval between beats—is half a second . _____ is an important parameter used in science and engineering to specify the rate of oscillatory and vibratory phenomena, such as mechanical vibrations, audio signals , radio waves, and light.

Exam Probability: **Low**

6. *Answer choices:*

(see index for correct answer)

- a. Quantile
- b. Multiple of the median
- c. Mean percentage error
- d. Percentile

Guidance: level 1

:: Project management ::

A _____ is a team whose members usually belong to different groups, functions and are assigned to activities for the same project. A team can be divided into sub-teams according to need. Usually _____ s are only used for a defined period of time. They are disbanded after the project is deemed complete. Due to the nature of the specific formation and disbandment, _____ s are usually in organizations.

Exam Probability: **Low**

7. *Answer choices:*

(see index for correct answer)

- a. Project team
- b. Product flow diagram

- c. TimeTac
- d. Pmhub

Guidance: level 1

:: ::

A _____ is a type of job aid used to reduce failure by compensating for potential limits of human memory and attention. It helps to ensure consistency and completeness in carrying out a task. A basic example is the "to do list". A more advanced _____ would be a schedule, which lays out tasks to be done according to time of day or other factors. A primary task in _____ is documentation of the task and auditing against the documentation.

Exam Probability: **Low**

8. *Answer choices:*

(see index for correct answer)

- a. hierarchical perspective
- b. Sarbanes-Oxley act of 2002
- c. interpersonal communication
- d. Checklist

Guidance: level 1

:: Human resource management ::

An organizational chart is a diagram that shows the structure of an organization and the relationships and relative ranks of its parts and positions/jobs. The term is also used for similar diagrams, for example ones showing the different elements of a field of knowledge or a group of languages.

Exam Probability: **Low**

9. *Answer choices:*

(see index for correct answer)

- a. Performance domain
- b. Human resource management
- c. Organization chart
- d. Work activity management

Guidance: level 1

:: Workplace ::

A _____ is a process through which feedback from an employee's subordinates, colleagues, and supervisor, as well as a self-evaluation by the employee themselves is gathered. Such feedback can also include, when relevant, feedback from external sources who interact with the employee, such as customers and suppliers or other interested stakeholders. _____ is so named because it solicits feedback regarding an employee's behavior from a variety of points of view. It therefore may be contrasted with "downward feedback", or "upward feedback" delivered to supervisory or management employees by subordinates only.

Exam Probability: **High**

10. *Answer choices:*

(see index for correct answer)

- a. Rat race
- b. Workplace conflict
- c. 360-degree feedback
- d. Evaluation

Guidance: level 1

:: ::

_____ is the reason for people's actions, willingness and goals. _____ is derived from the word motive in the English language which is defined as a need that requires satisfaction. These needs could also be wants or desires that are acquired through influence of culture, society, lifestyle, etc. or generally innate. _____ is one's direction to behaviour, or what causes a person to want to repeat a behaviour, a set of force that acts behind the motives. An individual's _____ may be inspired by others or events or it may come from within the individual. _____ has been considered as one of the most important reasons that inspires a person to move forward in life. _____ results from the interaction of both conscious and unconscious factors. Mastering _____ to allow sustained and deliberate practice is central to high levels of achievement e.g. in the worlds of elite sport, medicine or music.

Exam Probability: **Low**

11. *Answer choices:*

(see index for correct answer)

- a. surface-level diversity
- b. deep-level diversity
- c. process perspective
- d. open system

Guidance: level 1

:: Cognitive biases ::

The _____ is a type of immediate judgement discrepancy, or cognitive bias, where a person making an initial assessment of another person, place, or thing will assume ambiguous information based upon concrete information. A simplified example of the _____ is when an individual noticing that the person in the photograph is attractive, well groomed, and properly attired, assumes, using a mental heuristic, that the person in the photograph is a good person based upon the rules of that individual's social concept. This constant error in judgment is reflective of the individual's preferences, prejudices, ideology, aspirations, and social perception. The _____ is an evaluation by an individual and can affect the perception of a decision, action, idea, business, person, group, entity, or other whenever concrete data is generalized or influences ambiguous information.

Exam Probability: **Medium**

12. *Answer choices:*

(see index for correct answer)

- a. Overjustification effect
- b. Cognitive distortion
- c. Familiarity heuristic
- d. Halo effect

Guidance: level 1

:: Industry ::

_____ describes various measures of the efficiency of production. Often , a _____ measure is expressed as the ratio of an aggregate output to a single input or an aggregate input used in a production process, i.e. output per unit of input. Most common example is the labour _____ measure, e.g., such as GDP per worker. There are many different definitions of _____ and the choice among them depends on the purpose of the _____ measurement and/or data availability. The key source of difference between various _____ measures is also usually related to how the outputs and the inputs are aggregated into scalars to obtain such a ratio-type measure of _____ .

Exam Probability: **High**

13. *Answer choices:*
(see index for correct answer)

- a. Tertiary sector of the economy
- b. Mass production
- c. Industrial society
- d. Metal expansion joint

Guidance: level 1

:: ::

_____ is a form of development in which a person called a coach supports a learner or client in achieving a specific personal or professional goal by providing training and guidance. The learner is sometimes called a coachee. Occasionally, _____ may mean an informal relationship between two people, of whom one has more experience and expertise than the other and offers advice and guidance as the latter learns; but _____ differs from mentoring in focusing on specific tasks or objectives, as opposed to more general goals or overall development.

Exam Probability: **High**

14. *Answer choices:*

(see index for correct answer)

- a. hierarchical perspective
- b. process perspective
- c. personal values
- d. cultural

Guidance: level 1

:: Evaluation ::

_____ solving consists of using generic or ad hoc methods in an orderly manner to find solutions to _____ s. Some of the _____ -solving techniques developed and used in philosophy, artificial intelligence, computer science, engineering, mathematics, or medicine are related to mental _____ -solving techniques studied in psychology.

Exam Probability: **Medium**

15. *Answer choices:*
(see index for correct answer)

- a. Princeton Application Repository for Shared-Memory Computers
- b. Program evaluation
- c. Problem
- d. Educational assessment

Guidance: level 1

:: Human resource management ::

_____ expands the capacity of individuals to perform in leadership roles within organizations. Leadership roles are those that facilitate execution of a company's strategy through building alignment, winning mindshare and growing the capabilities of others. Leadership roles may be formal, with the corresponding authority to make decisions and take responsibility, or they may be informal roles with little official authority.

Exam Probability: **High**

16. *Answer choices:*

(see index for correct answer)

- a. Mergers and acquisitions
- b. Employment testing
- c. Adaptive performance
- d. Focal Point Review

Guidance: level 1

:: Socialism ::

In sociology, _____ is the process of internalizing the norms and ideologies of society. _____ encompasses both learning and teaching and is thus "the means by which social and cultural continuity are attained".

Exam Probability: **High**

17. *Answer choices:*

(see index for correct answer)

- a. Immiseration thesis
- b. Soviet republic
- c. Socialization
- d. Gucci socialist

Guidance: level 1

:: Life skills ::

_____ , emotional leadership , emotional quotient and _____ quotient , is the capability of individuals to recognize their own emotions and those of others, discern between different feelings and label them appropriately, use emotional information to guide thinking and behavior, and manage and/or adjust emotions to adapt to environments or achieve one`s goal.

Exam Probability: **High**

18. *Answer choices:*

(see index for correct answer)

- a. emotion work
- b. coping mechanism
- c. Social intelligence
- d. multiple intelligence

Guidance: level 1

:: Labor rights ::

A _____ is a wrong or hardship suffered, real or supposed, which forms legitimate grounds of complaint. In the past, the word meant the infliction or cause of hardship.

Exam Probability: **Medium**

19. *Answer choices:*

(see index for correct answer)

- a. Labor rights
- b. Swift raids
- c. Kate Mullany House
- d. Grievance

Guidance: level 1

:: ::

Business is the activity of making one's living or making money by producing or buying and selling products . Simply put, it is "any activity or enterprise entered into for profit. It does not mean it is a company, a corporation, partnership, or have any such formal organization, but it can range from a street peddler to General Motors."

Exam Probability: **High**

20. *Answer choices:*

(see index for correct answer)

- a. deep-level diversity
- b. functional perspective

- c. similarity-attraction theory
- d. Firm

Guidance: level 1

:: Statistical terminology ::

_____ es can be learned implicitly within cultural contexts. People may develop _____ es toward or against an individual, an ethnic group, a sexual or gender identity, a nation, a religion, a social class, a political party, theoretical paradigms and ideologies within academic domains, or a species. _____ ed means one-sided, lacking a neutral viewpoint, or not having an open mind. _____ can come in many forms and is related to prejudice and intuition.

Exam Probability: **High**

21. *Answer choices:*

(see index for correct answer)

- a. Iterated conditional modes
- b. Bias
- c. probability function
- d. Noncentrality parameter

Guidance: level 1

:: Autonomy ::

In developmental psychology and moral, political, and bioethical philosophy, _____ is the capacity to make an informed, uncoerced decision. Autonomous organizations or institutions are independent or self-governing. _____ can also be defined from a human resources perspective, where it denotes a level of discretion granted to an employee in his or her work. In such cases, _____ is known to generally increase job satisfaction. _____ is a term that is also widely used in the field of medicine — personal _____ is greatly recognized and valued in health care.

Exam Probability: **High**

22. *Answer choices:*

(see index for correct answer)

- a. Quebec autonomism
- b. Autonomy
- c. Autonomous robot
- d. Self-determination theory

Guidance: level 1

:: Time management ::

_____ is the process of planning and exercising conscious control of time spent on specific activities, especially to increase effectiveness, efficiency, and productivity. It involves a juggling act of various demands upon a person relating to work, social life, family, hobbies, personal interests and commitments with the finiteness of time. Using time effectively gives the person "choice" on spending/managing activities at their own time and expediency.

Exam Probability: **Medium**

23. *Answer choices:*

(see index for correct answer)

- a. Time management
- b. Getting Things Done
- c. HabitRPG
- d. waiting room

Guidance: level 1

:: ::

The _____ or just chief executive, is the most senior corporate, executive, or administrative officer in charge of managing an organization especially an independent legal entity such as a company or nonprofit institution. CEOs lead a range of organizations, including public and private corporations, non-profit organizations and even some government organizations. The CEO of a corporation or company typically reports to the board of directors and is charged with maximizing the value of the entity, which may include maximizing the share price, market share, revenues or another element. In the non-profit and government sector, CEOs typically aim at achieving outcomes related to the organization's mission, such as reducing poverty, increasing literacy, etc.

Exam Probability: **High**

24. *Answer choices:*

(see index for correct answer)

- a. open system
- b. Chief executive officer
- c. Sarbanes-Oxley act of 2002
- d. corporate values

Guidance: level 1

:: Evaluation methods ::

In social psychology, _____ is the process of looking at oneself in order to assess aspects that are important to one's identity. It is one of the motives that drive self-evaluation, along with self-verification and self-enhancement. Sedikides suggests that the _____ motive will prompt people to seek information to confirm their uncertain self-concept rather than their certain self-concept and at the same time people use _____ to enhance their certainty of their own self-knowledge. However, the _____ motive could be seen as quite different from the other two self-evaluation motives. Unlike the other two motives through _____ people are interested in the accuracy of their current self view, rather than improving their self-view. This makes _____ the only self-evaluative motive that may cause a person's self-esteem to be damaged.

Exam Probability: **Medium**

25. *Answer choices:*
(see index for correct answer)

- a. Fixtureless in-circuit test
- b. quasi-experimental
- c. Self-assessment
- d. Position weight matrix

Guidance: level 1

:: E-commerce ::

_____ is the activity of buying or selling of products on online services or over the Internet. Electronic commerce draws on technologies such as mobile commerce, electronic funds transfer, supply chain management, Internet marketing, online transaction processing, electronic data interchange, inventory management systems, and automated data collection systems.

Exam Probability: **Medium**

26. *Answer choices:*

(see index for correct answer)

- a. Mobilpenge
- b. Electronic trading
- c. PapiNet
- d. E-commerce

Guidance: level 1

:: Management ::

In organizational studies, _____ is the efficient and effective development of an organization's resources when they are needed. Such resources may include financial resources, inventory, human skills, production resources, or information technology and natural resources.

Exam Probability: **High**

27. Answer choices:

(see index for correct answer)

- a. Business economics
- b. Stewardship theory
- c. Resource management
- d. Dominant design

Guidance: level 1

:: Elementary mathematics ::

_____ is a numerical measurement of how far apart objects are. In physics or everyday usage, _____ may refer to a physical length or an estimation based on other criteria . In most cases, " _____ from A to B" is interchangeable with " _____ from B to A". In mathematics, a _____ function or metric is a generalization of the concept of physical _____ . A metric is a function that behaves according to a specific set of rules, and is a way of describing what it means for elements of some space to be "close to" or "far away from" each other.

Exam Probability: **Low**

28. Answer choices:

(see index for correct answer)

- a. Arg max
- b. Distance

- c. Unary numeral system
- d. Distinct

Guidance: level 1

:: ::

_____ is the process of making predictions of the future based on past and present data and most commonly by analysis of trends. A commonplace example might be estimation of some variable of interest at some specified future date. Prediction is a similar, but more general term. Both might refer to formal statistical methods employing time series, cross-sectional or longitudinal data, or alternatively to less formal judgmental methods. Usage can differ between areas of application: for example, in hydrology the terms "forecast" and "_____" are sometimes reserved for estimates of values at certain specific future times, while the term "prediction" is used for more general estimates, such as the number of times floods will occur over a long period.

Exam Probability: **High**

29. *Answer choices:*

(see index for correct answer)

- a. hierarchical
- b. information systems assessment
- c. Forecasting
- d. Sarbanes-Oxley act of 2002

Guidance: level 1

:: ::

_____ comprises all of the processes of governing – whether undertaken by the government of a state, by a market or by a network – over a social system and whether through the laws, norms, power or language of an organized society. It relates to "the processes of interaction and decision-making among the actors involved in a collective problem that lead to the creation, reinforcement, or reproduction of social norms and institutions". In lay terms, it could be described as the political processes that exist in and between formal institutions.

Exam Probability: **High**

30. *Answer choices:*

(see index for correct answer)

- a. deep-level diversity
- b. interpersonal communication
- c. corporate values
- d. imperative

Guidance: level 1

:: Production economics ::

_____ is the joint use of a resource or space. It is also the process of dividing and distributing. In its narrow sense, it refers to joint or alternating use of inherently finite goods, such as a common pasture or a shared residence. Still more loosely, "_____" can actually mean giving something as an outright gift: for example, to "share" one's food really means to give some of it as a gift. _____ is a basic component of human interaction, and is responsible for strengthening social ties and ensuring a person's well-being.

Exam Probability: **High**

31. *Answer choices:*

(see index for correct answer)

- a. Marginal rate of technical substitution
- b. Foundations of Economic Analysis
- c. Producer's risk
- d. Split-off point

Guidance: level 1

:: Credit cards ::

The _____ Company, also known as Amex, is an American multinational financial services corporation headquartered in Three World Financial Center in New York City. The company was founded in 1850 and is one of the 30 components of the Dow Jones Industrial Average. The company is best known for its charge card, credit card, and traveler's cheque businesses.

Exam Probability: **Medium**

32. *Answer choices:*

(see index for correct answer)

- a. American Express
- b. Barclaycard
- c. BC Card
- d. Payments as a service

Guidance: level 1

:: Marketing techniques ::

In industry, product lifecycle management is the process of managing the entire lifecycle of a product from inception, through engineering design and manufacture, to service and disposal of manufactured products. PLM integrates people, data, processes and business systems and provides a product information backbone for companies and their extended enterprise.

Exam Probability: **Medium**

33. *Answer choices:*

(see index for correct answer)

- a. Unique selling language
- b. Market segmentation

- c. Product life cycle
- d. Elevator pitch

Guidance: level 1

:: ::

In a supply chain, a _____, or a seller, is an enterprise that contributes goods or services. Generally, a supply chain _____ manufactures inventory/stock items and sells them to the next link in the chain. Today, these terms refer to a supplier of any good or service.

Exam Probability: **Low**

34. *Answer choices:*

(see index for correct answer)

- a. personal values
- b. hierarchical
- c. imperative
- d. cultural

Guidance: level 1

:: ::

_____ s and acquisitions are transactions in which the ownership of companies, other business organizations, or their operating units are transferred or consolidated with other entities. As an aspect of strategic management, M&A can allow enterprises to grow or downsize, and change the nature of their business or competitive position.

Exam Probability: **Low**

35. *Answer choices:*

(see index for correct answer)

- a. process perspective
- b. Merger
- c. imperative
- d. corporate values

Guidance: level 1

:: Marketing ::

_____ or stock control can be broadly defined as "the activity of checking a shop's stock." However, a more focused definition takes into account the more science-based, methodical practice of not only verifying a business' inventory but also focusing on the many related facets of inventory management "within an organisation to meet the demand placed upon that business economically." Other facets of _____ include supply chain management, production control, financial flexibility, and customer satisfaction. At the root of _____ , however, is the _____ problem, which involves determining when to order, how much to order, and the logistics of those decisions.

Exam Probability: **Medium**

36. *Answer choices:*

(see index for correct answer)

- a. Art Infusion
- b. Inventory control
- c. Marketing spending
- d. Corporate capabilities package

Guidance: level 1

_____ refers to the overall process of attracting, shortlisting, selecting and appointing suitable candidates for jobs within an organization. _____ can also refer to processes involved in choosing individuals for unpaid roles. Managers, human resource generalists and _____ specialists may be tasked with carrying out _____ , but in some cases public-sector employment agencies, commercial _____ agencies, or specialist search consultancies are used to undertake parts of the process. Internet-based technologies which support all aspects of _____ have become widespread.

Exam Probability: **High**

37. *Answer choices:*

(see index for correct answer)

- a. co-culture
- b. deep-level diversity
- c. Recruitment
- d. hierarchical

Guidance: level 1

:: ::

_____ is the exchange of capital, goods, and services across international borders or territories.

Exam Probability: **Low**

38. *Answer choices:*

(see index for correct answer)

- a. co-culture
- b. International trade
- c. empathy
- d. Character

Guidance: level 1

:: Management accounting ::

In economics, _____ s, indirect costs or overheads are business expenses that are not dependent on the level of goods or services produced by the business. They tend to be time-related, such as interest or rents being paid per month, and are often referred to as overhead costs. This is in contrast to variable costs, which are volume-related and unknown at the beginning of the accounting year. For a simple example, such as a bakery, the monthly rent for the baking facilities, and the monthly payments for the security system and basic phone line are _____ s, as they do not change according to how much bread the bakery produces and sells. On the other hand, the wage costs of the bakery are variable, as the bakery will have to hire more workers if the production of bread increases. Economists reckon _____ as a entry barrier for new entrepreneurs.

Exam Probability: **High**

39. *Answer choices:*

(see index for correct answer)

- a. Constraints accounting
- b. Semi-variable cost
- c. Fixed cost
- d. Corporate travel management

Guidance: level 1

:: ::

In mathematics, a _____ is a relationship between two numbers indicating how many times the first number contains the second. For example, if a bowl of fruit contains eight oranges and six lemons, then the _____ of oranges to lemons is eight to six. Similarly, the _____ of lemons to oranges is 6:8 and the _____ of oranges to the total amount of fruit is 8:14.

Exam Probability: **Low**

40. *Answer choices:*

(see index for correct answer)

- a. similarity-attraction theory
- b. process perspective
- c. information systems assessment
- d. Ratio

Guidance: level 1

:: Project management ::

_____ is the right to exercise power, which can be formalized by a state and exercised by way of judges, appointed executives of government, or the ecclesiastical or priestly appointed representatives of a God or other deities.

Exam Probability: **High**

41. *Answer choices:*

(see index for correct answer)

- a. Product-based planning
- b. Collaborative planning software
- c. Authority
- d. Front-end loading

Guidance: level 1

:: Project management ::

_____ and Theory Y are theories of human work motivation and management. They were created by Douglas McGregor while he was working at the MIT Sloan School of Management in the 1950s, and developed further in the 1960s. McGregor's work was rooted in motivation theory alongside the works of Abraham Maslow, who created the hierarchy of needs. The two theories proposed by McGregor describe contrasting models of workforce motivation applied by managers in human resource management, organizational behavior, organizational communication and organizational development. _____ explains the importance of heightened supervision, external rewards, and penalties, while Theory Y highlights the motivating role of job satisfaction and encourages workers to approach tasks without direct supervision. Management use of _____ and Theory Y can affect employee motivation and productivity in different ways, and managers may choose to implement strategies from both theories into their practices.

Exam Probability: **Medium**

42. *Answer choices:*

(see index for correct answer)

- a. Outcomes theory
- b. Resource leveling
- c. The International Association of Project and Program Management
- d. Theory X

Guidance: level 1

:: ::

_____ is the capacity of consciously making sense of things, establishing and verifying facts, applying logic, and changing or justifying practices, institutions, and beliefs based on new or existing information. It is closely associated with such characteristically human activities as philosophy, science, language, mathematics and art, and is normally considered to be a distinguishing ability possessed by humans. _____ , or an aspect of it, is sometimes referred to as rationality.

Exam Probability: **Low**

43. *Answer choices:*

(see index for correct answer)

- a. cultural
- b. surface-level diversity
- c. similarity-attraction theory
- d. Reason

Guidance: level 1

:: Types of marketing ::

In microeconomics and management, _____ is an arrangement in which the supply chain of a company is owned by that company. Usually each member of the supply chain produces a different product or service, and the products combine to satisfy a common need. It is contrasted with horizontal integration, wherein a company produces several items which are related to one another. _____ has also described management styles that bring large portions of the supply chain not only under a common ownership, but also into one corporation .

Exam Probability: **Low**

44. *Answer choices:*

(see index for correct answer)

- a. Figure of merit
- b. Share of voice
- c. Project SCUM
- d. Vertical integration

Guidance: level 1

:: Organizational behavior ::

_____ is the state or fact of exclusive rights and control over property, which may be an object, land/real estate or intellectual property. _____ involves multiple rights, collectively referred to as title, which may be separated and held by different parties.

Exam Probability: **Medium**

45. *Answer choices:*

(see index for correct answer)

- a. Organizational Expedience
- b. Ownership
- c. Micro-initiative

- d. Burnout

Guidance: level 1

:: Monopoly (economics) ::

_____ is a category of property that includes intangible creations of the human intellect. _____ encompasses two types of rights: industrial property rights and copyright. It was not until the 19th century that the term " _____ " began to be used, and not until the late 20th century that it became commonplace in the majority of the world.

Exam Probability: **Medium**

46. *Answer choices:*

(see index for correct answer)

- a. Cost per procedure
- b. Copyright law of the European Union
- c. Regulatory economics
- d. Intellectual property

Guidance: level 1

:: Critical thinking ::

An _____ is a set of statements usually constructed to describe a set of facts which clarifies the causes, context, and consequences of those facts. This description of the facts et cetera may establish rules or laws, and may clarify the existing rules or laws in relation to any objects, or phenomena examined. The components of an _____ can be implicit, and interwoven with one another.

Exam Probability: **High**

47. *Answer choices:*
(see index for correct answer)

- a. SEE-I
- b. Project Reason
- c. Topical logic
- d. Explanation

Guidance: level 1

:: ::

_____ , known in Europe as research and technological development , refers to innovative activities undertaken by corporations or governments in developing new services or products, or improving existing services or products. _____ constitutes the first stage of development of a potential new service or the production process.

Exam Probability: **Low**

48. Answer choices:

(see index for correct answer)

- a. deep-level diversity
- b. interpersonal communication
- c. functional perspective
- d. Research and development

Guidance: level 1

:: Evaluation ::

_____ is the practice of being honest and showing a consistent and uncompromising adherence to strong moral and ethical principles and values. In ethics, _____ is regarded as the honesty and truthfulness or accuracy of one's actions. _____ can stand in opposition to hypocrisy, in that judging with the standards of _____ involves regarding internal consistency as a virtue, and suggests that parties holding within themselves apparently conflicting values should account for the discrepancy or alter their beliefs. The word _____ evolved from the Latin adjective integer, meaning whole or complete. In this context, _____ is the inner sense of "wholeness" deriving from qualities such as honesty and consistency of character. As such, one may judge that others "have _____ " to the extent that they act according to the values, beliefs and principles they claim to hold.

Exam Probability: **High**

49. Answer choices:

(see index for correct answer)

- a. Educational assessment
- b. Encomium
- c. Joint Committee on Standards for Educational Evaluation
- d. XTS-400

Guidance: level 1

:: Legal terms ::

_____ is a type of meaning in which a phrase, statement or resolution is not explicitly defined, making several interpretations plausible. A common aspect of _____ is uncertainty. It is thus an attribute of any idea or statement whose intended meaning cannot be definitively resolved according to a rule or process with a finite number of steps.

Exam Probability: **Low**

50. *Answer choices:*
(see index for correct answer)

- a. Ambiguity
- b. Prohibited degree of kinship
- c. Incidental damages
- d. Dissenting opinion

Guidance: level 1

:: Training ::

_____ is action or inaction that is regulated to be in accordance with a particular system of governance. _____ is commonly applied to regulating human and animal behavior, and furthermore, it is applied to each activity-branch in all branches of organized activity, knowledge, and other fields of study and observation. _____ can be a set of expectations that are required by any governing entity including the self, groups, classes, fields, industries, or societies.

Exam Probability: **High**

51. *Answer choices:*

(see index for correct answer)

- a. Makers Academy
- b. American Council on Exercise
- c. Safety Services Company
- d. Discipline

Guidance: level 1

:: Export and import control ::

"_____" means the Government Service which is responsible for the administration of _____ law and the collection of duties and taxes and which also has the responsibility for the application of other laws and regulations relating to the importation, exportation, movement or storage of goods.

Exam Probability: **Low**

52. *Answer choices:*

(see index for correct answer)

- a. Riding officer
- b. GOST R Conformity Declaration
- c. Neutron scanner
- d. Export Control Classification Number

Guidance: level 1

:: ::

_____ is the amount of time someone works beyond normal working hours. The term is also used for the pay received for this time. Normal hours may be determined in several ways.

Exam Probability: **Medium**

53. *Answer choices:*

(see index for correct answer)

- a. corporate values
- b. Overtime
- c. deep-level diversity
- d. imperative

Guidance: level 1

:: ::

In organizational behavior and industrial/organizational psychology, proactivity or _____ behavior by individuals refers to anticipatory, change-oriented and self-initiated behavior in situations. _____ behavior involves acting in advance of a future situation, rather than just reacting. It means taking control and making things happen rather than just adjusting to a situation or waiting for something to happen. _____ employees generally do not need to be asked to act, nor do they require detailed instructions.

Exam Probability: **Medium**

54. *Answer choices:*

(see index for correct answer)

- a. cultural
- b. open system
- c. co-culture
- d. imperative

Guidance: level 1

:: Systems thinking ::

Systems theory is the interdisciplinary study of systems. A system is a cohesive conglomeration of interrelated and interdependent parts that is either natural or man-made. Every system is delineated by its spatial and temporal boundaries, surrounded and influenced by its environment, described by its structure and purpose or nature and expressed in its functioning. In terms of its effects, a system can be more than the sum of its parts if it expresses synergy or emergent behavior. Changing one part of the system usually affects other parts and the whole system, with predictable patterns of behavior. For systems that are self-learning and self-adapting, the positive growth and adaptation depend upon how well the system is adjusted with its environment. Some systems function mainly to support other systems by aiding in the maintenance of the other system to prevent failure. The goal of systems theory is systematically discovering a system's dynamics, constraints, conditions and elucidating principles that can be discerned and applied to systems at every level of nesting, and in every field for achieving optimized equifinality.

Exam Probability: **High**

55. *Answer choices:*
(see index for correct answer)

- a. The Energy and Resources Institute
- b. Thought leader
- c. IBZL
- d. Ray Hammond

Guidance: level 1

:: ::

A _____ is a fund into which a sum of money is added during an employee's employment years, and from which payments are drawn to support the person's retirement from work in the form of periodic payments. A _____ may be a "defined benefit plan" where a fixed sum is paid regularly to a person, or a "defined contribution plan" under which a fixed sum is invested and then becomes available at retirement age. _____ s should not be confused with severance pay; the former is usually paid in regular installments for life after retirement, while the latter is typically paid as a fixed amount after involuntary termination of employment prior to retirement.

Exam Probability: **High**

56. *Answer choices:*

(see index for correct answer)

- a. personal values
- b. hierarchical perspective
- c. Pension
- d. levels of analysis

Guidance: level 1

:: Security compliance ::

A _____ is a communicated intent to inflict harm or loss on another person. A _____ is considered an act of coercion. _____ s are widely observed in animal behavior, particularly in a ritualized form, chiefly in order to avoid the unnecessary physical violence that can lead to physical damage or the death of both conflicting parties.

Exam Probability: **Medium**

57. *Answer choices:*

(see index for correct answer)

- a. Vulnerability
- b. Threat
- c. Attack
- d. Vulnerability management

Guidance: level 1

:: Costs ::

In economics, _____ is the total economic cost of production and is made up of variable cost, which varies according to the quantity of a good produced and includes inputs such as labour and raw materials, plus fixed cost, which is independent of the quantity of a good produced and includes inputs that cannot be varied in the short term: fixed costs such as buildings and machinery, including sunk costs if any. Since cost is measured per unit of time, it is a flow variable.

Exam Probability: **High**

58. *Answer choices:*

(see index for correct answer)

- a. Psychic cost
- b. Flyaway cost
- c. Implicit cost
- d. Total cost

Guidance: level 1

:: Planning ::

_____ is a high level plan to achieve one or more goals under conditions of uncertainty. In the sense of the "art of the general," which included several subsets of skills including tactics, siegecraft, logistics etc., the term came into use in the 6th century C.E. in East Roman terminology, and was translated into Western vernacular languages only in the 18th century. From then until the 20th century, the word "_____" came to denote "a comprehensive way to try to pursue political ends, including the threat or actual use of force, in a dialectic of wills" in a military conflict, in which both adversaries interact.

Exam Probability: **Medium**

59. *Answer choices:*

(see index for correct answer)

- a. Disruption
- b. Strategic communication
- c. Enterprise architecture planning
- d. Reproductive life plan

Guidance: level 1

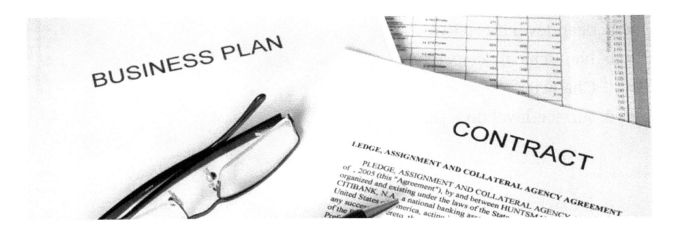

Business law

Corporate law (also known as business law) is the body of law governing the rights, relations, and conduct of persons, companies, organizations and businesses. It refers to the legal practice relating to, or the theory of corporations. Corporate law often describes the law relating to matters which derive directly from the life-cycle of a corporation. It thus encompasses the formation, funding, governance, and death of a corporation.

:: ::

The _____ is the central philosophical concept in the deontological moral philosophy of Immanuel Kant. Introduced in Kant's 1785 Groundwork of the Metaphysics of Morals, it may be defined as a way of evaluating motivations for action.

Exam Probability: **Medium**

1. *Answer choices:*

(see index for correct answer)

- a. deep-level diversity
- b. hierarchical perspective
- c. Character
- d. surface-level diversity

Guidance: level 1

:: Criminal procedure ::

In law, a verdict is the formal finding of fact made by a jury on matters or questions submitted to the jury by a judge. In a bench trial, the judge's decision near the end of the trial is simply referred to as a finding. In England and Wales, a coroner's findings are called verdicts.

Exam Probability: **Medium**

2. *Answer choices:*

(see index for correct answer)

- a. criminal procedure
- b. Directed verdict

Guidance: level 1

:: ::

The Sherman Antitrust Act of 1890 was a United States antitrust law that regulates competition among enterprises, which was passed by Congress under the presidency of Benjamin Harrison.

Exam Probability: **Low**

3. *Answer choices:*

(see index for correct answer)

- a. Character
- b. interpersonal communication
- c. similarity-attraction theory
- d. process perspective

Guidance: level 1

:: ::

In law, a _____ is a coming together of parties to a dispute, to present information in a tribunal, a formal setting with the authority to adjudicate claims or disputes. One form of tribunal is a court. The tribunal, which may occur before a judge, jury, or other designated trier of fact, aims to achieve a resolution to their dispute.

Exam Probability: **High**

4. *Answer choices:*

(see index for correct answer)

- a. Trial
- b. functional perspective
- c. imperative
- d. surface-level diversity

Guidance: level 1

:: United States securities law ::

_____ is a legal term for intent or knowledge of wrongdoing. An offending party then has knowledge of the "wrongness" of an act or event prior to committing it.

Exam Probability: **Medium**

5. *Answer choices:*

(see index for correct answer)

- a. Blue sky law
- b. Scienter
- c. General Securities Principal Exam
- d. Uniform Securities Agent State Law Exam

Guidance: level 1

:: Decision theory ::

A _____ is a deliberate system of principles to guide decisions and achieve rational outcomes. A _____ is a statement of intent, and is implemented as a procedure or protocol. Policies are generally adopted by a governance body within an organization. Policies can assist in both subjective and objective decision making. Policies to assist in subjective decision making usually assist senior management with decisions that must be based on the relative merits of a number of factors, and as a result are often hard to test objectively, e.g. work-life balance _____ . In contrast policies to assist in objective decision making are usually operational in nature and can be objectively tested, e.g. password _____ .

Exam Probability: **Low**

6. *Answer choices:*

(see index for correct answer)

- a. Ophelimity
- b. Policy
- c. ELECTRE
- d. Consensus decision-making

Guidance: level 1

:: Business ethics ::

Banking secrecy, alternately known as _____ , banking discretion, or bank safety, is a conditional agreement between a bank and its clients that all foregoing activities remain secure, confidential, and private. While some banking institutions voluntarily impose banking secrecy institutionally, others operate in regions where the practice is legally mandated and protected . Almost all banking secrecy standards prohibit the disclosure of client information to third parties without consent or an accepted criminal complaint. Additional privacy is provided to select clients via numbered bank accounts or underground bank vaults. Most often associated with banking in Switzerland, banking secrecy is prevalent in Luxembourg, Monaco, Hong Kong, Singapore, Ireland, Lebanon and the Cayman Islands, among other off-shore banking institutions.

Exam Probability: **Low**

7. *Answer choices:*

(see index for correct answer)

- a. Financial privacy
- b. Proceedings of the International Association for Business and Society
- c. Unfree labour
- d. Institute of Business Ethics

Guidance: level 1

:: ::

A _____, in common law jurisdictions, is a civil wrong that causes a claimant to suffer loss or harm resulting in legal liability for the person who commits the _____ious act. It can include the intentional infliction of emotional distress, negligence, financial losses, injuries, invasion of privacy, and many other things.

Exam Probability: **Medium**

8. *Answer choices:*

(see index for correct answer)

- a. open system
- b. deep-level diversity
- c. process perspective
- d. empathy

Guidance: level 1

:: Statutory law ::

_____ is a principal's approval of an act of its agent that lacked the authority to bind the principal legally. _____ defines the international act in which a state indicates its consent to be bound to a treaty if the parties intended to show their consent by such an act. In the case of bilateral treaties, _____ is usually accomplished by exchanging the requisite instruments, and in the case of multilateral treaties, the usual procedure is for the depositary to collect the _____s of all states, keeping all parties informed of the situation.

Exam Probability: **High**

9. *Answer choices:*

(see index for correct answer)

- a. statute law
- b. incorporation by reference
- c. Statutory law
- d. Ratification

Guidance: level 1

:: ::

_____ , in law, is a transaction or action that is valid but may be annulled by one of the parties to the transaction. _____ is usually used in distinction to void ab initio and unenforceable.

Exam Probability: **Low**

10. *Answer choices:*

(see index for correct answer)

- a. Character
- b. corporate values
- c. information systems assessment
- d. Voidable

Guidance: level 1

:: ::

A _____ is monetary compensation paid by an employer to an employee in exchange for work done. Payment may be calculated as a fixed amount for each task completed, or at an hourly or daily rate, or based on an easily measured quantity of work done.

Exam Probability: **High**

11. *Answer choices:*

(see index for correct answer)

- a. open system
- b. Wage
- c. personal values
- d. process perspective

Guidance: level 1

:: Business law ::

In the United States, the United Kingdom, Australia, Canada and South Africa, _____ relates to the doctrines of the law of agency. It is relevant particularly in corporate law and constitutional law. _____ refers to a situation where a reasonable third party would understand that an agent had authority to act. This means a principal is bound by the agent's actions, even if the agent had no actual authority, whether express or implied. It raises an estoppel because the third party is given an assurance, which he relies on and would be inequitable for the principal to deny the authority given. _____ can legally be found, even if actual authority has not been given.

Exam Probability: **Medium**

12. *Answer choices:*

(see index for correct answer)

- a. Limited liability limited partnership
- b. Apparent authority
- c. Free agent
- d. Finance lease

Guidance: level 1

:: ::

_____ is the act or practice of forbidding something by law; more particularly the term refers to the banning of the manufacture, storage, transportation, sale, possession, and consumption of alcoholic beverages. The word is also used to refer to a period of time during which such bans are enforced.

Exam Probability: **High**

13. *Answer choices:*

(see index for correct answer)

- a. levels of analysis
- b. Prohibition
- c. hierarchical perspective
- d. Character

Guidance: level 1

:: Money market instruments ::

_____ , in the global financial market, is an unsecured promissory note with a fixed maturity of not more than 270 days.

Exam Probability: **Low**

14. *Answer choices:*

(see index for correct answer)

- a. Banker's acceptance
- b. Commercial Paper

Guidance: level 1

:: Abuse of the legal system ::

_____ occurs when a person is restricted in their personal movement within any area without justification or consent. Actual physical restraint is not necessary for _____ to occur. A _____ claim may be made based upon private acts, or upon wrongful governmental detention. For detention by the police, proof of _____ provides a basis to obtain a writ of habeas corpus.

Exam Probability: **Low**

15. *Answer choices:*
(see index for correct answer)

- a. False imprisonment
- b. Obstruction of Justice
- c. Forum shopping

Guidance: level 1

:: ::

The U.S. _____ is an independent agency of the United States federal government. The SEC holds primary responsibility for enforcing the federal securities laws, proposing securities rules, and regulating the securities industry, the nation's stock and options exchanges, and other activities and organizations, including the electronic securities markets in the United States.

Exam Probability: **High**

16. *Answer choices:*

(see index for correct answer)

- a. Securities and Exchange Commission
- b. Character
- c. functional perspective
- d. open system

Guidance: level 1

:: Legal terms ::

_____, or non-absolute contributory negligence outside the United States, is a partial legal defense that reduces the amount of damages that a plaintiff can recover in a negligence-based claim, based upon the degree to which the plaintiff's own negligence contributed to cause the injury. When the defense is asserted, the factfinder, usually a jury, must decide the degree to which the plaintiff's negligence and the combined negligence of all other relevant actors all contributed to cause the plaintiff's damages. It is a modification of the doctrine of contributory negligence that disallows any recovery by a plaintiff whose negligence contributed even minimally to causing the damages.

Exam Probability: **Low**

17. *Answer choices:*

(see index for correct answer)

- a. Holding
- b. Comparative negligence
- c. Allonge
- d. Law of the land

Guidance: level 1

:: Sexual harassment in the United States ::

In law, a _____, reasonable man, or the man on the Clapham omnibus is a hypothetical person of legal fiction crafted by the courts and communicated through case law and jury instructions.

Exam Probability: **Low**

18. *Answer choices:*

(see index for correct answer)

- a. War Zone
- b. Sandy Gallin
- c. Puerto Rican Day Parade attacks
- d. Reasonable person

Guidance: level 1

:: Business law ::

A _____ is a legal right granted by a debtor to a creditor over the debtor's property which enables the creditor to have recourse to the property if the debtor defaults in making payment or otherwise performing the secured obligations. One of the most common examples of a _____ is a mortgage: When person, by the action of an expressed conveyance, pledges by a promise to pay a certain sum of money, with certain conditions, on a said date or dates for a said period, that action on the page with wet ink applied on the part of the one wishing the exchange creates the original funds and negotiable Instrument. That action of pledging conveys a promise binding upon the mortgagee which creates a face value upon the Instrument of the amount of currency being asked for in exchange. It is therein in good faith offered to the Bank in exchange for local currency from the Bank to buy a house. The particular country's Bank Acts usually requires the Banks to deliver such fund bearing negotiable instruments to the Countries Main Bank such as is the case in Canada. This creates a _____ in the land the house sits on for the Bank and they file a caveat at land titles on the house as evidence of that _____ . If the mortgagee fails to pay defaulting in his promise to repay the exchange, the bank then applies to the court to for-close on your property to eventually sell the house and apply the proceeds to the outstanding exchange.

Exam Probability: **Low**

19. *Answer choices:*

(see index for correct answer)

- a. Security interest
- b. Tax patent
- c. Business.gov
- d. Participation

Guidance: level 1

:: Contract law ::

A _____ cannot be enforced by law. _____ s are different from voidable contracts, which are contracts that may be nullified. However, when a contract is being written and signed, there is no automatic mechanism available in every situation that can be utilized to detect the validity or enforceability of that contract. Practically, a contract can be declared to be void by a court of law. So the main question is that under what conditions can a contract be deemed as void

Exam Probability: **Low**

20. *Answer choices:*
(see index for correct answer)

- a. Collateral warranty
- b. Title-transfer theory of contract
- c. Void contract
- d. Offeror

Guidance: level 1

:: ::

_____ , or auditory perception, is the ability to perceive sounds by detecting vibrations, changes in the pressure of the surrounding medium through time, through an organ such as the ear. The academic field concerned with _____ is auditory science.

Exam Probability: **Low**

21. *Answer choices:*

(see index for correct answer)

- a. co-culture
- b. Character
- c. Hearing
- d. imperative

Guidance: level 1

:: ::

_____ is the production of products for use or sale using labour and machines, tools, chemical and biological processing, or formulation. The term may refer to a range of human activity, from handicraft to high tech, but is most commonly applied to industrial design, in which raw materials are transformed into finished goods on a large scale. Such finished goods may be sold to other manufacturers for the production of other, more complex products, such as aircraft, household appliances, furniture, sports equipment or automobiles, or sold to wholesalers, who in turn sell them to retailers, who then sell them to end users and consumers.

Exam Probability: **Low**

22. *Answer choices:*

(see index for correct answer)

- a. Sarbanes-Oxley act of 2002
- b. interpersonal communication
- c. process perspective
- d. Manufacturing

Guidance: level 1

:: Insurance law ::

_____ exists when an insured person derives a financial or other kind of benefit from the continuous existence, without repairment or damage, of the insured object. A person has an _____ in something when loss of or damage to that thing would cause the person to suffer a financial or other kind of loss. Normally, _____ is established by ownership, possession, or direct relationship. For example, people have _____ s in their own homes and vehicles, but not in their neighbors' homes and vehicles, and almost certainly not those of strangers.

Exam Probability: **Medium**

23. *Answer choices:*
(see index for correct answer)

- a. QC clause
- b. Insurable interest
- c. Uberrima fides
- d. California Insurance Code

Guidance: level 1

:: ::

_____ is a type of government support for the citizens of that society. _____ may be provided to people of any income level, as with social security, but it is usually intended to ensure that the poor can meet their basic human needs such as food and shelter. _____ attempts to provide poor people with a minimal level of well-being, usually either a free- or a subsidized-supply of certain goods and social services, such as healthcare, education, and vocational training.

Exam Probability: **Medium**

24. *Answer choices:*

(see index for correct answer)

- a. Welfare
- b. functional perspective
- c. process perspective
- d. interpersonal communication

Guidance: level 1

:: Utilitarianism ::

_____ is a family of consequentialist ethical theories that promotes actions that maximize happiness and well-being for the majority of a population. Although different varieties of _____ admit different characterizations, the basic idea behind all of them is to in some sense maximize utility, which is often defined in terms of well-being or related concepts. For instance, Jeremy Bentham, the founder of _____, described utility as

Exam Probability: **Low**

25. *Answer choices:*

(see index for correct answer)

- a. Utilitarianism
- b. Preference utilitarianism
- c. Utility monster
- d. Felicific calculus

Guidance: level 1

:: Marketing ::

A _____ is an overall experience of a customer that distinguishes an organization or product from its rivals in the eyes of the customer. _____ s are used in business, marketing, and advertising. Name _____ s are sometimes distinguished from generic or store _____ s.

Exam Probability: **Medium**

26. *Answer choices:*

(see index for correct answer)

- a. Leverage
- b. Online ethnography
- c. Brand
- d. Green market

Guidance: level 1

:: Business law ::

A _____ is a business entity created by two or more parties, generally characterized by shared ownership, shared returns and risks, and shared governance. Companies typically pursue _____ s for one of four reasons: to access a new market, particularly emerging markets; to gain scale efficiencies by combining assets and operations; to share risk for major investments or projects; or to access skills and capabilities.

Exam Probability: **Low**

27. *Answer choices:*

(see index for correct answer)

- a. Joint venture
- b. Uniform Partnership Act
- c. General assignment
- d. License

Guidance: level 1

:: ::

A _____ is a request to do something, most commonly addressed to a government official or public entity. _____ s to a deity are a form of prayer called supplication.

Exam Probability: **Low**

28. *Answer choices:*

(see index for correct answer)

- a. Character
- b. corporate values
- c. Petition
- d. information systems assessment

Guidance: level 1

:: Mereology ::

_____, in the abstract, is what belongs to or with something, whether as an attribute or as a component of said thing. In the context of this article, it is one or more components, whether physical or incorporeal, of a person's estate; or so belonging to, as in being owned by, a person or jointly a group of people or a legal entity like a corporation or even a society. Depending on the nature of the _____, an owner of _____ has the right to consume, alter, share, redefine, rent, mortgage, pawn, sell, exchange, transfer, give away or destroy it, or to exclude others from doing these things, as well as to perhaps abandon it; whereas regardless of the nature of the _____, the owner thereof has the right to properly use it, or at the very least exclusively keep it.

Exam Probability: **Low**

29. *Answer choices:*

(see index for correct answer)

- a. Simple
- b. Property
- c. Mereotopology
- d. Mereological nihilism

Guidance: level 1

_____ is the study and management of exchange relationships. _____ is the business process of creating relationships with and satisfying customers. With its focus on the customer, _____ is one of the premier components of business management.

Exam Probability: **High**

30. *Answer choices:*

(see index for correct answer)

- a. Marketing
- b. imperative
- c. hierarchical
- d. Sarbanes-Oxley act of 2002

Guidance: level 1

:: Business law ::

The _____ , first published in 1952, is one of a number of Uniform Acts that have been established as law with the goal of harmonizing the laws of sales and other commercial transactions across the United States of America through UCC adoption by all 50 states, the District of Columbia, and the Territories of the United States.

Exam Probability: **High**

31. *Answer choices:*

(see index for correct answer)

- a. Uniform Commercial Code
- b. Vehicle leasing
- c. Copyright transfer agreement
- d. Stick licensing

Guidance: level 1

:: ::

A federation is a political entity characterized by a union of partially self-governing provinces, states, or other regions under a central _____ . In a federation, the self-governing status of the component states, as well as the division of power between them and the central government, is typically constitutionally entrenched and may not be altered by a unilateral decision of either party, the states or the federal political body. Alternatively, federation is a form of government in which sovereign power is formally divided between a central authority and a number of constituent regions so that each region retains some degree of control over its internal affairs. It is often argued that federal states where the central government has the constitutional authority to suspend a constituent state's government by invoking gross mismanagement or civil unrest, or to adopt national legislation that overrides or infringe on the constituent states' powers by invoking the central government's constitutional authority to ensure "peace and good government" or to implement obligations contracted under an international treaty, are not truly federal states.

Exam Probability: **High**

32. Answer choices:

(see index for correct answer)

- a. deep-level diversity
- b. empathy
- c. Federal government
- d. information systems assessment

Guidance: level 1

:: Anti-competitive behaviour ::

Restraints of trade is a common law doctrine relating to the enforceability of contractual restrictions on freedom to conduct business. It is a precursor of modern competition law. In an old leading case of Mitchel v Reynolds Lord Smith LC said,

Exam Probability: **High**

33. Answer choices:

(see index for correct answer)

- a. Competition regulator
- b. Radius clause
- c. Killer bees
- d. Restraint of trade

Guidance: level 1

:: Ethically disputed business practices ::

_____ is the trading of a public company's stock or other securities by individuals with access to nonpublic information about the company. In various countries, some kinds of trading based on insider information is illegal. This is because it is seen as unfair to other investors who do not have access to the information, as the investor with insider information could potentially make larger profits than a typical investor could make. The rules governing _____ are complex and vary significantly from country to country. The extent of enforcement also varies from one country to another. The definition of insider in one jurisdiction can be broad, and may cover not only insiders themselves but also any persons related to them, such as brokers, associates and even family members. A person who becomes aware of non-public information and trades on that basis may be guilty of a crime.

Exam Probability: **Low**

34. *Answer choices:*
(see index for correct answer)

- a. at-will
- b. Spiv
- c. Creative accounting
- d. Insider trading

Guidance: level 1

:: Business law ::

A _____ is a group of people who jointly supervise the activities of an organization, which can be either a for-profit business, nonprofit organization, or a government agency. Such a board's powers, duties, and responsibilities are determined by government regulations and the organization's own constitution and bylaws. These authorities may specify the number of members of the board, how they are to be chosen, and how often they are to meet.

Exam Probability: **Low**

35. *Answer choices:*
(see index for correct answer)

- a. Arbitration clause
- b. Hundi
- c. Board of directors
- d. Principal

Guidance: level 1

:: Contract law ::

An _____, or simply option, is defined as "a promise which meets the requirements for the formation of a contract and limits the promisor's power to revoke an offer."

Exam Probability: **Low**

36. *Answer choices:*

(see index for correct answer)

- a. Illusory promise
- b. Option contract
- c. Doctrine of concurrent delay
- d. Personal contract purchase

Guidance: level 1

:: ::

_____ is the practical authority granted to a legal body to administer justice within a defined field of responsibility, e.g., Michigan tax law. In federations like the United States, areas of _____ apply to local, state, and federal levels; e.g. the court has _____ to apply federal law.

Exam Probability: **Medium**

37. *Answer choices:*

(see index for correct answer)

- a. similarity-attraction theory
- b. Jurisdiction
- c. Sarbanes-Oxley act of 2002

- d. functional perspective

Guidance: level 1

:: ::

A _____ is an aggregate of fundamental principles or established precedents that constitute the legal basis of a polity, organisation or other type of entity, and commonly determine how that entity is to be governed.

Exam Probability: **Low**

38. *Answer choices:*

(see index for correct answer)

- a. interpersonal communication
- b. Constitution
- c. personal values
- d. cultural

Guidance: level 1

:: ::

According to the philosopher Piyush Mathur, "Tangibility is the property that a phenomenon exhibits if it has and/or transports mass and/or energy and/or momentum".

Exam Probability: **Medium**

39. *Answer choices:*
(see index for correct answer)

- a. cultural
- b. hierarchical perspective
- c. similarity-attraction theory
- d. Sarbanes-Oxley act of 2002

Guidance: level 1

:: Contract law ::

_____ is a doctrine in contract law that describes terms that are so extremely unjust, or overwhelmingly one-sided in favor of the party who has the superior bargaining power, that they are contrary to good conscience. Typically, an unconscionable contract is held to be unenforceable because no reasonable or informed person would otherwise agree to it. The perpetrator of the conduct is not allowed to benefit, because the consideration offered is lacking, or is so obviously inadequate, that to enforce the contract would be unfair to the party seeking to escape the contract.

Exam Probability: **Medium**

40. Answer choices:

(see index for correct answer)

- a. Unconscionability
- b. Accommodation
- c. Forum selection clause
- d. Pirate code

Guidance: level 1

:: Notes (finance) ::

A _____, sometimes referred to as a note payable, is a legal instrument, in which one party promises in writing to pay a determinate sum of money to the other, either at a fixed or determinable future time or on demand of the payee, under specific terms.

Exam Probability: **Low**

41. Answer choices:

(see index for correct answer)

- a. note payable
- b. Circular note
- c. Promissory note
- d. Surplus note

Guidance: level 1

:: Business law ::

A _____, also known as the sole trader, individual entrepreneurship or proprietorship, is a type of enterprise that is owned and run by one person and in which there is no legal distinction between the owner and the business entity. A sole trader does not necessarily work 'alone'—it is possible for the sole trader to employ other people.

Exam Probability: **Low**

42. *Answer choices:*

(see index for correct answer)

- a. Sole proprietorship
- b. Oppression remedy
- c. Contract A
- d. Enhanced use lease

Guidance: level 1

:: Business ethics ::

_____ is a type of harassment technique that relates to a sexual nature and the unwelcome or inappropriate promise of rewards in exchange for sexual favors. _____ includes a range of actions from mild transgressions to sexual abuse or assault. Harassment can occur in many different social settings such as the workplace, the home, school, churches, etc. Harassers or victims may be of any gender.

Exam Probability: **High**

43. *Answer choices:*

(see index for correct answer)

- a. Minority business enterprise
- b. Sweatshop
- c. Sexual harassment
- d. Sherpa

Guidance: level 1

:: Insolvency ::

_____ is the process in accounting by which a company is brought to an end in the United Kingdom, Republic of Ireland and United States. The assets and property of the company are redistributed. _____ is also sometimes referred to as winding-up or dissolution, although dissolution technically refers to the last stage of _____. The process of _____ also arises when customs, an authority or agency in a country responsible for collecting and safeguarding customs duties, determines the final computation or ascertainment of the duties or drawback accruing on an entry.

Exam Probability: **Medium**

44. *Answer choices:*

(see index for correct answer)

- a. Liquidator
- b. Official Committee of Equity Security Holders
- c. United Kingdom insolvency law
- d. Liquidation

Guidance: level 1

:: ::

A _____ is a person who holds a legal or ethical relationship of trust with one or more other parties . Typically, a _____ prudently takes care of money or other assets for another person. One party, for example, a corporate trust company or the trust department of a bank, acts in a _____ capacity to another party, who, for example, has entrusted funds to the _____ for safekeeping or investment. Likewise, financial advisers, financial planners, and; asset managers, including managers of pension plans, endowments, and other tax-exempt assets, are considered fiduciaries under applicable statutes and laws. In a _____ relationship, one person, in a position of vulnerability, justifiably vests confidence, good faith, reliance, and trust in another whose aid, advice, or protection is sought in some matter. In such a relation good conscience requires the _____ to act at all times for the sole benefit and interest of the one who trusts.

Exam Probability: **Medium**

45. *Answer choices:*

(see index for correct answer)

- a. functional perspective
- b. process perspective
- c. Fiduciary
- d. Sarbanes-Oxley act of 2002

Guidance: level 1

:: Manufactured goods ::

A _____ or final good is any commodity that is produced or consumed by the consumer to satisfy current wants or needs. _____ s are ultimately consumed, rather than used in the production of another good. For example, a microwave oven or a bicycle that is sold to a consumer is a final good or _____ , but the components that are sold to be used in those goods are intermediate goods. For example, textiles or transistors can be used to make some further goods.

Exam Probability: **Low**

46. *Answer choices:*

(see index for correct answer)

- a. Tarpaulin
- b. Final good
- c. Bespoke

- d. Consumer Good

Guidance: level 1

:: Shareholders ::

A _____ is a payment made by a corporation to its shareholders, usually as a distribution of profits. When a corporation earns a profit or surplus, the corporation is able to re-invest the profit in the business and pay a proportion of the profit as a _____ to shareholders. Distribution to shareholders may be in cash or, if the corporation has a _____ reinvestment plan, the amount can be paid by the issue of further shares or share repurchase. When _____ s are paid, shareholders typically must pay income taxes, and the corporation does not receive a corporate income tax deduction for the _____ payments.

Exam Probability: **Low**

47. *Answer choices:*

(see index for correct answer)

- a. Institutional Shareholder Services
- b. Majority interest
- c. Dividend
- d. Shareholder oppression

Guidance: level 1

:: ::

_____ or accountancy is the measurement, processing, and communication of financial information about economic entities such as businesses and corporations. The modern field was established by the Italian mathematician Luca Pacioli in 1494. _____ , which has been called the "language of business", measures the results of an organization's economic activities and conveys this information to a variety of users, including investors, creditors, management, and regulators. Practitioners of _____ are known as accountants. The terms "_____" and "financial reporting" are often used as synonyms.

Exam Probability: **High**

48. *Answer choices:*

(see index for correct answer)

- a. imperative
- b. personal values
- c. open system
- d. empathy

Guidance: level 1

:: Legal doctrines and principles ::

In the common law of torts, _____ loquitur is a doctrine that infers negligence from the very nature of an accident or injury in the absence of direct evidence on how any defendant behaved. Although modern formulations differ by jurisdiction, common law originally stated that the accident must satisfy the necessary elements of negligence: duty, breach of duty, causation, and injury. In _____ loquitur, the elements of duty of care, breach, and causation are inferred from an injury that does not ordinarily occur without negligence.

Exam Probability: **High**

49. *Answer choices:*

(see index for correct answer)

- a. Duty to rescue
- b. Res ipsa
- c. Unilateral mistake
- d. compulsory acquisition

Guidance: level 1

:: Legal doctrines and principles ::

_____, land acquisition, compulsory purchase, resumption, resumption/compulsory acquisition, or expropriation is the power of a state, provincial, or national government to take private property for public use. However, this power can be legislatively delegated by the state to municipalities, government subdivisions, or even to private persons or corporations, when they are authorized by the legislature to exercise the functions of public character.

Exam Probability: **Medium**

50. *Answer choices:*

(see index for correct answer)

- a. Act of state doctrine
- b. negligence
- c. Unilateral mistake
- d. Assumption of risk

Guidance: level 1

:: ::

A _____, or trial by jury, is a lawful proceeding in which a jury makes a decision or findings of fact. It is distinguished from a bench trial in which a judge or panel of judges makes all decisions.

Exam Probability: **High**

51. Answer choices:

(see index for correct answer)

- a. interpersonal communication
- b. hierarchical perspective
- c. Jury Trial
- d. Sarbanes-Oxley act of 2002

Guidance: level 1

:: Real property law ::

A _____ is the grant of authority or rights, stating that the granter formally recognizes the prerogative of the recipient to exercise the rights specified. It is implicit that the granter retains superiority, and that the recipient admits a limited status within the relationship, and it is within that sense that _____ s were historically granted, and that sense is retained in modern usage of the term.

Exam Probability: **High**

52. Answer choices:

(see index for correct answer)

- a. Charter
- b. Life estate
- c. Latent defect
- d. Escheat

Guidance: level 1

:: Business law ::

A _____ is a contractual arrangement calling for the lessee to pay the lessor for use of an asset. Property, buildings and vehicles are common assets that are _____ d. Industrial or business equipment is also _____ d.

Exam Probability: **High**

53. *Answer choices:*

(see index for correct answer)

- a. Lease
- b. Teck Corp. Ltd. v. Millar
- c. WIPO Copyright Treaty
- d. Retroactive overtime

Guidance: level 1

:: ::

In law, a _____ is the formal finding of fact made by a jury on matters or questions submitted to the jury by a judge. In a bench trial, the judge's decision near the end of the trial is simply referred to as a finding. In England and Wales, a coroner's findings are called _____ s.

Exam Probability: **Medium**

54. *Answer choices:*

(see index for correct answer)

- a. co-culture
- b. hierarchical
- c. similarity-attraction theory
- d. Verdict

Guidance: level 1

:: Clauses of the United States Constitution ::

The _____ describes an enumerated power listed in the United States Constitution. The clause states that the United States Congress shall have power "To regulate Commerce with foreign Nations, and among the several States, and with the Indian Tribes." Courts and commentators have tended to discuss each of these three areas of commerce as a separate power granted to Congress. It is common to see the individual components of the _____ referred to under specific terms: the Foreign _____, the Interstate _____, and the Indian _____.

Exam Probability: **Low**

55. *Answer choices:*

(see index for correct answer)

- a. Commerce Clause
- b. Double Jeopardy Clause
- c. Full faith and credit

Guidance: level 1

:: Legal terms ::

_____ is the set of laws that governs how members of a society are to behave. It is contrasted with procedural law, which is the set of procedures for making, administering, and enforcing _____ . _____ defines rights and responsibilities in civil law, and crimes and punishments in criminal law. It may be codified in statutes or exist through precedent in common law.

Exam Probability: **Medium**

56. *Answer choices:*

(see index for correct answer)

- a. Error
- b. Substantive law
- c. Obiter dictum

- d. Condonation

Guidance: level 1

:: Commercial crimes ::

_____ is the process of concealing the origins of money obtained illegally by passing it through a complex sequence of banking transfers or commercial transactions. The overall scheme of this process returns the money to the launderer in an obscure and indirect way.

Exam Probability: **Medium**

57. *Answer choices:*
(see index for correct answer)

- a. Fence
- b. Money laundering
- c. Terrorism financing
- d. Fraudulent conveyance

Guidance: level 1

:: Legal terms ::

_____ , a form of alternative dispute resolution , is a way to resolve disputes outside the courts. The dispute will be decided by one or more persons , which renders the " _____ award". An _____ award is legally binding on both sides and enforceable in the courts.

Exam Probability: **Low**

58. *Answer choices:*

(see index for correct answer)

- a. Dissent aversion
- b. Misdemeanor
- c. Commandeering
- d. Arbitration

Guidance: level 1

:: ::

In legal terminology, a _____ is any formal legal document that sets out the facts and legal reasons that the filing party or parties believes are sufficient to support a claim against the party or parties against whom the claim is brought that entitles the plaintiff to a remedy . For example, the Federal Rules of Civil Procedure that govern civil litigation in United States courts provide that a civil action is commenced with the filing or service of a pleading called a _____ . Civil court rules in states that have incorporated the Federal Rules of Civil Procedure use the same term for the same pleading.

Exam Probability: **High**

59. *Answer choices:*

(see index for correct answer)

- a. Sarbanes-Oxley act of 2002
- b. interpersonal communication
- c. process perspective
- d. co-culture

Guidance: level 1

Finance

Finance is a field that is concerned with the allocation (investment) of assets and liabilities over space and time, often under conditions of risk or uncertainty. Finance can also be defined as the science of money management. Participants in the market aim to price assets based on their risk level, fundamental value, and their expected rate of return. Finance can be split into three sub-categories: public finance, corporate finance and personal finance.

:: Financial accounting ::

In accounting, _____ is the value of an asset according to its balance sheet account balance. For assets, the value is based on the original cost of the asset less any depreciation, amortization or impairment costs made against the asset. Traditionally, a company's _____ is its total assets minus intangible assets and liabilities. However, in practice, depending on the source of the calculation, _____ may variably include goodwill, intangible assets, or both. The value inherent in its workforce, part of the intellectual capital of a company, is always ignored. When intangible assets and goodwill are explicitly excluded, the metric is often specified to be "tangible _____ ".

Exam Probability: **Medium**

1. *Answer choices:*

(see index for correct answer)

- a. Financial Condition Report
- b. Book value
- c. Finance charge
- d. Working capital

Guidance: level 1

:: Management accounting ::

_____, or dollar contribution per unit, is the selling price per unit minus the variable cost per unit. "Contribution" represents the portion of sales revenue that is not consumed by variable costs and so contributes to the coverage of fixed costs. This concept is one of the key building blocks of break-even analysis.

Exam Probability: **High**

2. *Answer choices:*

(see index for correct answer)

- a. Contribution margin
- b. Indirect costs
- c. Direct material price variance
- d. Certified Management Accountant

Guidance: level 1

:: Mereology ::

_____ , in the abstract, is what belongs to or with something, whether as an attribute or as a component of said thing. In the context of this article, it is one or more components , whether physical or incorporeal, of a person's estate; or so belonging to, as in being owned by, a person or jointly a group of people or a legal entity like a corporation or even a society. Depending on the nature of the _____ , an owner of _____ has the right to consume, alter, share, redefine, rent, mortgage, pawn, sell, exchange, transfer, give away or destroy it, or to exclude others from doing these things, as well as to perhaps abandon it; whereas regardless of the nature of the _____ , the owner thereof has the right to properly use it , or at the very least exclusively keep it.

Exam Probability: **High**

3. *Answer choices:*

(see index for correct answer)

- a. Non-wellfounded mereology
- b. Property
- c. Mereological nihilism
- d. Gunk

Guidance: level 1

:: Capital (economics) ::

In Economics and Accounting, the _____ is the cost of a company's funds , or, from an investor's point of view "the required rate of return on a portfolio company's existing securities". It is used to evaluate new projects of a company. It is the minimum return that investors expect for providing capital to the company, thus setting a benchmark that a new project has to meet.

Exam Probability: **High**

4. *Answer choices:*

(see index for correct answer)

- a. operating capital
- b. required rate of return
- c. Information capital
- d. financial capital

Guidance: level 1

:: Fixed income market ::

In finance, the _____ is a curve showing several yields or interest rates across different contract lengths for a similar debt contract. The curve shows the relation between the interest rate and the time to maturity, known as the "term", of the debt for a given borrower in a given currency. For example, the U.S. dollar interest rates paid on U.S. Treasury securities for various maturities are closely watched by many traders, and are commonly plotted on a graph such as the one on the right which is informally called "the _____". More formal mathematical descriptions of this relation are often called the term structure of interest rates.

Exam Probability: **High**

5. *Answer choices:*

(see index for correct answer)

- a. Bond Exchange of South Africa
- b. Basis point
- c. Pool factor
- d. Yield curve

Guidance: level 1

:: Human resource management ::

_____ is the corporate management term for the act of reorganizing the legal, ownership, operational, or other structures of a company for the purpose of making it more profitable, or better organized for its present needs. Other reasons for _____ include a change of ownership or ownership structure, demerger, or a response to a crisis or major change in the business such as bankruptcy, repositioning, or buyout. _____ may also be described as corporate _____, debt _____ and financial _____.

Exam Probability: **High**

6. *Answer choices:*

(see index for correct answer)

- a. Dr. Marri Channa Reddy Human Resource Development Institute of Andhra Pradesh
- b. Workforce management
- c. Restructuring
- d. SLT Human Capital Solutions

Guidance: level 1

:: Goods ::

In most contexts, the concept of _____ denotes the conduct that should be preferred when posed with a choice between possible actions. _____ is generally considered to be the opposite of evil, and is of interest in the study of morality, ethics, religion and philosophy. The specific meaning and etymology of the term and its associated translations among ancient and contemporary languages show substantial variation in its inflection and meaning depending on circumstances of place, history, religious, or philosophical context.

Exam Probability: **Medium**

7. *Answer choices:*

(see index for correct answer)

- a. Experience good
- b. Composite good
- c. Good
- d. Merit good

Guidance: level 1

:: ::

In accounting, the _____ is a measure of the number of times inventory is sold or used in a time period such as a year. It is calculated to see if a business has an excessive inventory in comparison to its sales level. The equation for _____ equals the cost of goods sold divided by the average inventory. _____ is also known as inventory turns, merchandise turnover, stockturn, stock turns, turns, and stock turnover.

Exam Probability: **High**

8. *Answer choices:*

(see index for correct answer)

- a. imperative
- b. Inventory turnover
- c. personal values
- d. co-culture

Guidance: level 1

:: Financial risk ::

_____ is the risk that arises for bond owners from fluctuating interest rates. How much _____ a bond has depends on how sensitive its price is to interest rate changes in the market. The sensitivity depends on two things, the bond's time to maturity, and the coupon rate of the bond.

Exam Probability: **Low**

9. *Answer choices:*

(see index for correct answer)

- a. Risk metric
- b. Government risk
- c. Time consistency

- d. Interest rate risk

Guidance: level 1

:: Business law ::

The expression "_____" is somewhat confusing as it has a different meaning based on the context that is under consideration. From a product characteristic stand point, this type of a lease, as distinguished from a finance lease, is one where the lessor takes residual risk. As such, the lease is non full payout. From an accounting stand point, this type of lease results in off balance sheet financing.

Exam Probability: **Low**

10. *Answer choices:*

(see index for correct answer)

- a. Operating lease
- b. Country of origin
- c. Negotiable instrument
- d. Novation

Guidance: level 1

:: Portfolio theories ::

In finance, the _____ is a model used to determine a theoretically appropriate required rate of return of an asset, to make decisions about adding assets to a well-diversified portfolio.

Exam Probability: **Low**

11. *Answer choices:*

(see index for correct answer)

- a. Intertemporal portfolio choice
- b. Post-modern portfolio theory
- c. Behavioral portfolio theory
- d. Capital asset pricing model

Guidance: level 1

:: Leasing ::

A finance lease is a type of lease in which a finance company is typically the legal owner of the asset for the duration of the lease, while the lessee not only has operating control over the asset, but also has a some share of the economic risks and returns from the change in the valuation of the underlying asset.

Exam Probability: **High**

12. *Answer choices:*

(see index for correct answer)

- a. Capital lease
- b. Farmout agreement

Guidance: level 1

:: Stock market ::

_____ is a form of stock which may have any combination of features not possessed by common stock including properties of both an equity and a debt instrument, and is generally considered a hybrid instrument. _____ s are senior to common stock, but subordinate to bonds in terms of claim and may have priority over common stock in the payment of dividends and upon liquidation. Terms of the _____ are described in the issuing company's articles of association or articles of incorporation.

Exam Probability: **High**

13. *Answer choices:*

(see index for correct answer)

- a. Chi-X Global
- b. P chip
- c. Microexchanges
- d. Preferred stock

Guidance: level 1

:: Management accounting ::

_____ s are costs that change as the quantity of the good or service that a business produces changes. _____ s are the sum of marginal costs over all units produced. They can also be considered normal costs. Fixed costs and _____ s make up the two components of total cost. Direct costs are costs that can easily be associated with a particular cost object. However, not all _____ s are direct costs. For example, variable manufacturing overhead costs are _____ s that are indirect costs, not direct costs. _____ s are sometimes called unit-level costs as they vary with the number of units produced.

Exam Probability: **Medium**

14. *Answer choices:*

(see index for correct answer)

- a. Direct material total variance
- b. Process costing
- c. Management accounting in supply chains
- d. Variable cost

Guidance: level 1

:: Consumer theory ::

_____ is the quantity of a good that consumers are willing and able to purchase at various prices during a given period of time.

Exam Probability: **High**

15. *Answer choices:*

(see index for correct answer)

- a. Expenditure function
- b. Rational addiction
- c. Consumer service
- d. Demand

Guidance: level 1

:: ::

The _____ is a private, non-profit organization standard-setting body whose primary purpose is to establish and improve Generally Accepted Accounting Principles within the United States in the public's interest. The Securities and Exchange Commission designated the FASB as the organization responsible for setting accounting standards for public companies in the US. The FASB replaced the American Institute of Certified Public Accountants' Accounting Principles Board on July 1, 1973.

Exam Probability: **Low**

16. Answer choices:

(see index for correct answer)

- a. information systems assessment
- b. Sarbanes-Oxley act of 2002
- c. similarity-attraction theory
- d. hierarchical perspective

Guidance: level 1

:: ::

A tax is a compulsory financial charge or some other type of levy imposed upon a taxpayer by a governmental organization in order to fund various public expenditures. A failure to pay, along with evasion of or resistance to _____ , is punishable by law. Taxes consist of direct or indirect taxes and may be paid in money or as its labour equivalent.

Exam Probability: **Low**

17. Answer choices:

(see index for correct answer)

- a. open system
- b. Taxation
- c. information systems assessment
- d. Sarbanes-Oxley act of 2002

Guidance: level 1

:: ::

A _____ is the process of presenting a topic to an audience. It is typically a demonstration, introduction, lecture, or speech meant to inform, persuade, inspire, motivate, or to build good will or to present a new idea or product. The term can also be used for a formal or ritualized introduction or offering, as with the _____ of a debutante. _____ s in certain formats are also known as keynote address.

Exam Probability: **Low**

18. *Answer choices:*
(see index for correct answer)

- a. Sarbanes-Oxley act of 2002
- b. hierarchical
- c. interpersonal communication
- d. Presentation

Guidance: level 1

:: ::

A _____ is any person who contracts to acquire an asset in return for some form of consideration.

Exam Probability: **Low**

19. *Answer choices:*

(see index for correct answer)

- a. Buyer
- b. Character
- c. information systems assessment
- d. surface-level diversity

Guidance: level 1

:: Management accounting ::

_____ is a managerial accounting cost concept. Under this method, manufacturing overhead is incurred in the period that a product is produced. This addresses the issue of absorption costing that allows income to rise as production rises. Under an absorption cost method, management can push forward costs to the next period when products are sold. This artificially inflates profits in the period of production by incurring less cost than would be incurred under a _____ system. _____ is generally not used for external reporting purposes. Under the Tax Reform Act of 1986, income statements must use absorption costing to comply with GAAP.

Exam Probability: **Medium**

20. *Answer choices:*

(see index for correct answer)

- a. Managerial risk accounting
- b. Variable Costing
- c. Throughput accounting
- d. Customer profitability

Guidance: level 1

:: Business economics ::

A _____ is a term used primarily in cost accounting to describe something to which costs are assigned. Common examples of _____ s are: product lines, geographic territories, customers, departments or anything else for which management would like to quantify cost.

Exam Probability: **Low**

21. *Answer choices:*

(see index for correct answer)

- a. Global strategy
- b. Cost object
- c. Kaizen costing
- d. Corporate ecosystem

Guidance: level 1

:: Commerce ::

Continuation of an entity as a _____ is presumed as the basis for financial reporting unless and until the entity's liquidation becomes imminent. Preparation of financial statements under this presumption is commonly referred to as the _____ basis of accounting. If and when an entity's liquidation becomes imminent, financial statements are prepared under the liquidation basis of accounting.

Exam Probability: **Low**

22. *Answer choices:*

(see index for correct answer)

- a. Emerging Markets Index
- b. Going concern
- c. RFM
- d. Too cheap to meter

Guidance: level 1

:: ::

_____ focuses on ratios, equities and debts. It is useful for portfolio management,distribution of dividend,capital raising,hedging and looking after fluctuations in foreign currency and product cycles.Financial managers are the people who will do research and based on the research, decide what sort of capital to obtain in order to fund the company's assets as well as maximizing the value of the firm for all the stakeholders. It also refers to the efficient and effective management of money in such a manner as to accomplish the objectives of the organization. It is the specialized function directly associated with the top management. The significance of this function is not seen in the `Line` but also in the capacity of the `Staff` in overall of a company. It has been defined differently by different experts in the field.

Exam Probability: **Low**

23. *Answer choices:*

(see index for correct answer)

- a. functional perspective
- b. Financial management
- c. information systems assessment
- d. corporate values

Guidance: level 1

:: Fixed income analysis ::

The _____ , book yield or redemption yield of a bond or other fixed-interest security, such as gilts, is the internal rate of return earned by an investor who buys the bond today at the market price, assuming that the bond is held until maturity, and that all coupon and principal payments are made on schedule. _____ is the discount rate at which the sum of all future cash flows from the bond is equal to the current price of the bond. The YTM is often given in terms of Annual Percentage Rate , but more often market convention is followed. In a number of major markets the convention is to quote annualized yields with semi-annual compounding ; thus, for example, an annual effective yield of 10.25% would be quoted as 10.00%, because 1.05 × 1.05 = 1.1025 and 2 × 5 = 10.

Exam Probability: **High**

24. *Answer choices:*

(see index for correct answer)

- a. Mortgage yield
- b. Day count convention
- c. Option Adjusted Spread
- d. LIBOR market model

Guidance: level 1

:: Cash flow ::

_____ s are narrowly interconnected with the concepts of value, interest rate and liquidity.A _____ that shall happen on a future day tN can be transformed into a _____ of the same value in t0.

Exam Probability: **High**

25. *Answer choices:*

(see index for correct answer)

- a. Free cash flow
- b. Discounted cash flow
- c. Discounted payback period
- d. Factoring

Guidance: level 1

:: Contract law ::

A _____ is a legally-binding agreement which recognises and governs the rights and duties of the parties to the agreement. A _____ is legally enforceable because it meets the requirements and approval of the law. An agreement typically involves the exchange of goods, services, money, or promises of any of those. In the event of breach of _____ , the law awards the injured party access to legal remedies such as damages and cancellation.

Exam Probability: **Low**

26. *Answer choices:*

(see index for correct answer)

- a. Recording contract
- b. Contract

- c. Good faith
- d. Invitation to treat

Guidance: level 1

:: Investment ::

_____ , and investment appraisal, is the planning process used to determine whether an organization's long term investments such as new machinery, replacement of machinery, new plants, new products, and research development projects are worth the funding of cash through the firm's capitalization structure . It is the process of allocating resources for major capital, or investment, expenditures. One of the primary goals of _____ investments is to increase the value of the firm to the shareholders.

Exam Probability: **Low**

27. *Answer choices:*

(see index for correct answer)

- a. Investment Securities
- b. IPM Informed Portfolio Management
- c. Indo Premier Investment Management
- d. Do-it-yourself investing

Guidance: level 1

:: Asset ::

In financial accounting, an _____ is any resource owned by the business. Anything tangible or intangible that can be owned or controlled to produce value and that is held by a company to produce positive economic value is an _____ . Simply stated, _____ s represent value of ownership that can be converted into cash . The balance sheet of a firm records the monetary value of the _____ s owned by that firm. It covers money and other valuables belonging to an individual or to a business.

Exam Probability: **Medium**

28. *Answer choices:*
(see index for correct answer)

- a. Current asset
- b. Fixed asset

Guidance: level 1

:: Pension funds ::

_____s typically have large amounts of money to invest and are the major investors in listed and private companies. They are especially important to the stock market where large institutional investors dominate. The largest 300 _____s collectively hold about $6 trillion in assets. In January 2008, The Economist reported that Morgan Stanley estimates that _____s worldwide hold over US$20 trillion in assets, the largest for any category of investor ahead of mutual funds, insurance companies, currency reserves, sovereign wealth funds, hedge funds, or private equity.

Exam Probability: **High**

29. *Answer choices:*

(see index for correct answer)

- a. Pension buyout
- b. Pension fund
- c. Texas Municipal Retirement System

Guidance: level 1

:: Decision theory ::

Within economics the concept of _____ is used to model worth or value, but its usage has evolved significantly over time. The term was introduced initially as a measure of pleasure or satisfaction within the theory of utilitarianism by moral philosophers such as Jeremy Bentham and John Stuart Mill. But the term has been adapted and reapplied within neoclassical economics, which dominates modern economic theory, as a _____ function that represents a consumer's preference ordering over a choice set. As such, it is devoid of its original interpretation as a measurement of the pleasure or satisfaction obtained by the consumer from that choice.

Exam Probability: **Medium**

30. *Answer choices:*

(see index for correct answer)

- a. Linear partial information
- b. Lock-in
- c. Bulk Dispatch Lapse
- d. Utility

Guidance: level 1

:: ::

_____ is a concept of English common law and is a necessity for simple contracts but not for special contracts. The concept has been adopted by other common law jurisdictions, including the US.

Exam Probability: **High**

31. *Answer choices:*

(see index for correct answer)

- a. process perspective
- b. Character
- c. interpersonal communication
- d. Consideration

Guidance: level 1

:: ::

An _____ is a contingent motivator. Traditional _____ s are extrinsic motivators which reward actions to yield a desired outcome. The effectiveness of traditional _____ s has changed as the needs of Western society have evolved. While the traditional _____ model is effective when there is a defined procedure and goal for a task, Western society started to require a higher volume of critical thinkers, so the traditional model became less effective. Institutions are now following a trend in implementing strategies that rely on intrinsic motivations rather than the extrinsic motivations that the traditional _____ s foster.

Exam Probability: **Medium**

32. *Answer choices:*

(see index for correct answer)

- a. empathy
- b. levels of analysis
- c. deep-level diversity
- d. Incentive

Guidance: level 1

:: Business ::

The seller, or the provider of the goods or services, completes a sale in response to an acquisition, appropriation, requisition or a direct interaction with the buyer at the point of sale. There is a passing of title of the item, and the settlement of a price, in which agreement is reached on a price for which transfer of ownership of the item will occur. The seller, not the purchaser typically executes the sale and it may be completed prior to the obligation of payment. In the case of indirect interaction, a person who sells goods or service on behalf of the owner is known as a salesman or saleswoman or salesperson, but this often refers to someone _____ goods in a store/shop, in which case other terms are also common, including salesclerk, shop assistant, and retail clerk.

Exam Probability: **Medium**

33. *Answer choices:*

(see index for correct answer)

- a. CyberAlert, Inc.
- b. Price-based selling
- c. Vladislav Doronin

- d. Selling

Guidance: level 1

:: Stock market ::

A _____ , equity market or share market is the aggregation of buyers and sellers of stocks , which represent ownership claims on businesses; these may include securities listed on a public stock exchange, as well as stock that is only traded privately. Examples of the latter include shares of private companies which are sold to investors through equity crowdfunding platforms. Stock exchanges list shares of common equity as well as other security types, e.g. corporate bonds and convertible bonds.

Exam Probability: **Medium**

34. *Answer choices:*
(see index for correct answer)

- a. Bear raid
- b. Relative valuation
- c. Ticker symbol
- d. Order book

Guidance: level 1

:: ::

In production, research, retail, and accounting, a _____ is the value of money that has been used up to produce something or deliver a service, and hence is not available for use anymore. In business, the _____ may be one of acquisition, in which case the amount of money expended to acquire it is counted as _____ . In this case, money is the input that is gone in order to acquire the thing. This acquisition _____ may be the sum of the _____ of production as incurred by the original producer, and further _____ s of transaction as incurred by the acquirer over and above the price paid to the producer. Usually, the price also includes a mark-up for profit over the _____ of production.

Exam Probability: **Low**

35. *Answer choices:*

(see index for correct answer)

- a. corporate values
- b. similarity-attraction theory
- c. Cost
- d. process perspective

Guidance: level 1

:: Accounting terminology ::

_____ of something is, in finance, the adding together of interest or different investments over a period of time. It holds specific meanings in accounting, where it can refer to accounts on a balance sheet that represent liabilities and non-cash-based assets used in _____ -based accounting. These types of accounts include, among others, accounts payable, accounts receivable, goodwill, deferred tax liability and future interest expense.

Exam Probability: **Medium**

36. *Answer choices:*

(see index for correct answer)

- a. Checkoff
- b. Chart of accounts
- c. General ledger
- d. Statement of financial position

Guidance: level 1

:: Bonds (finance) ::

A _____ is a type of bond that allows the issuer of the bond to retain the privilege of redeeming the bond at some point before the bond reaches its date of maturity. In other words, on the call date, the issuer has the right, but not the obligation, to buy back the bonds from the bond holders at a defined call price. Technically speaking, the bonds are not really bought and held by the issuer but are instead cancelled immediately.

Exam Probability: **Low**

37. *Answer choices:*

(see index for correct answer)

- a. Callable bond
- b. Bond market index
- c. Methuselah
- d. Floating rate note

Guidance: level 1

:: ::

_____ is the concept of one topic being connected to another topic in a way that makes it useful to consider the second topic when considering the first. The concept of _____ is studied in many different fields, including cognitive sciences, logic, and library and information science. Most fundamentally, however, it is studied in epistemology. Different theories of knowledge have different implications for what is considered relevant and these fundamental views have implications for all other fields as well.

Exam Probability: **Low**

38. *Answer choices:*

(see index for correct answer)

- a. Relevance

- b. Character
- c. personal values
- d. information systems assessment

Guidance: level 1

:: Currency ::

A _____ , in the most specific sense is money in any form when in use or circulation as a medium of exchange, especially circulating banknotes and coins. A more general definition is that a _____ is a system of money in common use, especially for people in a nation. Under this definition, US dollars , pounds sterling , Australian dollars , European euros , Russian rubles and Indian Rupees are examples of currencies. These various currencies are recognized as stores of value and are traded between nations in foreign exchange markets, which determine the relative values of the different currencies. Currencies in this sense are defined by governments, and each type has limited boundaries of acceptance.

Exam Probability: **Low**

39. *Answer choices:*
(see index for correct answer)

- a. Pre-decimal currency
- b. Remonetisation
- c. Currency
- d. Fiat money

Guidance: level 1

:: Financial markets ::

The _____ is the part of the capital market that deals with the issuance and sale of equity-backed securities to investors directly by the issuer. Investor buy securities that were never traded before. _____ s create long term instruments through which corporate entities raise funds from the capital market. It is also known as the New Issue Market.

Exam Probability: **Medium**

40. *Answer choices:*

(see index for correct answer)

- a. Primary market
- b. QuickFIX
- c. Options Price Reporting Authority
- d. Forward market

Guidance: level 1

:: Financial ratios ::

_____ is a financial ratio that indicates the percentage of a company's assets that are provided via debt. It is the ratio of total debt and total assets.

Exam Probability: **High**

41. *Answer choices:*

(see index for correct answer)

- a. return on invested capital
- b. Debt ratio
- c. Rate of return on a portfolio
- d. Cost accrual ratio

Guidance: level 1

:: Inventory ::

Costs are associated with particular goods using one of the several formulas, including specific identification, first-in first-out, or average cost. Costs include all costs of purchase, costs of conversion and other costs that are incurred in bringing the inventories to their present location and condition. Costs of goods made by the businesses include material, labor, and allocated overhead. The costs of those goods which are not yet sold are deferred as costs of inventory until the inventory is sold or written down in value.

Exam Probability: **Low**

42. Answer choices:

(see index for correct answer)

- a. Inventory optimization
- b. Phantom inventory
- c. Inventory control problem
- d. Average cost method

Guidance: level 1

:: ::

An _____ is an asset that lacks physical substance. It is defined in opposition to physical assets such as machinery and buildings. An _____ is usually very hard to evaluate. Patents, copyrights, franchises, goodwill, trademarks, and trade names. The general interpretation also includes software and other intangible computer based assets are all examples of _____ s. _____ s generally—though not necessarily—suffer from typical market failures of non-rivalry and non-excludability.

Exam Probability: **Medium**

43. Answer choices:

(see index for correct answer)

- a. deep-level diversity
- b. hierarchical
- c. Intangible asset

- d. Sarbanes-Oxley act of 2002

Guidance: level 1

:: ::

_____ is the process whereby a business sets the price at which it will sell its products and services, and may be part of the business's marketing plan. In setting prices, the business will take into account the price at which it could acquire the goods, the manufacturing cost, the market place, competition, market condition, brand, and quality of product.

Exam Probability: **Medium**

44. *Answer choices:*

(see index for correct answer)

- a. Character
- b. hierarchical
- c. levels of analysis
- d. process perspective

Guidance: level 1

:: Actuarial science ::

_____ is the addition of interest to the principal sum of a loan or deposit, or in other words, interest on interest. It is the result of reinvesting interest, rather than paying it out, so that interest in the next period is then earned on the principal sum plus previously accumulated interest. _____ is standard in finance and economics.

Exam Probability: **High**

45. *Answer choices:*

(see index for correct answer)

- a. Compound interest
- b. Actuarial present value
- c. Economic capital
- d. Experience modifier

Guidance: level 1

:: Accounting journals and ledgers ::

A _____ , in accounting, is the logging of a transaction in an accounting journal that shows a company's debit and credit balances. The _____ can consist of several recordings, each of which is either a debit or a credit. The total of the debits must equal the total of the credits or the _____ is considered unbalanced. Journal entries can record unique items or recurring items such as depreciation or bond amortization. In accounting software, journal entries are usually entered using a separate module from accounts payable, which typically has its own subledger, that indirectly affects the general ledger. As a result, journal entries directly change the account balances on the general ledger. A properly documented _____ consists of the correct date, amount that will be debited, amount that will be credited, description of transaction, and unique reference number .

Exam Probability: **High**

46. *Answer choices:*

(see index for correct answer)

- a. Subsidiary ledger
- b. General journal
- c. Subledger
- d. Journal entry

Guidance: level 1

:: Accounting source documents ::

A _____ or account statement is a summary of financial transactions which have occurred over a given period on a bank account held by a person or business with a financial institution.

Exam Probability: **High**

47. *Answer choices:*
(see index for correct answer)

- a. Bank statement
- b. Credit memo
- c. Credit memorandum
- d. Air waybill

Guidance: level 1

:: Personal finance ::

_____ is income not spent, or deferred consumption. Methods of _____ include putting money aside in, for example, a deposit account, a pension account, an investment fund, or as cash. _____ also involves reducing expenditures, such as recurring costs. In terms of personal finance, _____ generally specifies low-risk preservation of money, as in a deposit account, versus investment, wherein risk is a lot higher; in economics more broadly, it refers to any income not used for immediate consumption.

Exam Probability: **High**

48. *Answer choices:*

(see index for correct answer)

- a. Downshifting
- b. Bankruptcy risk score
- c. Saving
- d. O2 Money

Guidance: level 1

:: Accounting in the United States ::

_____ is the title of qualified accountants in numerous countries in the English-speaking world. In the United States, the CPA is a license to provide accounting services to the public. It is awarded by each of the 50 states for practice in that state. Additionally, almost every state has passed mobility laws to allow CPAs from other states to practice in their state. State licensing requirements vary, but the minimum standard requirements include passing the Uniform _____ Examination, 150 semester units of college education, and one year of accounting related experience.

Exam Probability: **High**

49. *Answer choices:*

(see index for correct answer)

- a. Federal Accounting Standards Advisory Board
- b. Trueblood Committee

- c. Association of Certified Fraud Examiners
- d. Legal liability of certified public accountants

Guidance: level 1

:: Debt ::

_____ , in finance and economics, is payment from a borrower or deposit-taking financial institution to a lender or depositor of an amount above repayment of the principal sum , at a particular rate. It is distinct from a fee which the borrower may pay the lender or some third party. It is also distinct from dividend which is paid by a company to its shareholders from its profit or reserve, but not at a particular rate decided beforehand, rather on a pro rata basis as a share in the reward gained by risk taking entrepreneurs when the revenue earned exceeds the total costs.

Exam Probability: **Medium**

50. *Answer choices:*

(see index for correct answer)

- a. Recourse debt
- b. Floating charge
- c. Money disorders
- d. Default trap

Guidance: level 1

:: Marketing ::

_____ is a financial mechanism in which a debtor obtains the right to delay payments to a creditor, for a defined period of time, in exchange for a charge or fee. Essentially, the party that owes money in the present purchases the right to delay the payment until some future date. The discount, or charge, is the difference between the original amount owed in the present and the amount that has to be paid in the future to settle the debt.

Exam Probability: **Medium**

51. *Answer choices:*

(see index for correct answer)

- a. Affective design
- b. Pink money
- c. Azerbaijan Marketing Society
- d. Discounting

Guidance: level 1

:: Scheduling (computing) ::

Ageing or _____ is the process of becoming older. The term refers especially to human beings, many animals, and fungi, whereas for example bacteria, perennial plants and some simple animals are potentially biologically immortal. In the broader sense, ageing can refer to single cells within an organism which have ceased dividing or to the population of a species .

Exam Probability: **High**

52. *Answer choices:*

(see index for correct answer)

- a. Affinity mask
- b. Notation for theoretic scheduling problems
- c. Kernel preemption
- d. Idle

Guidance: level 1

:: Money market instruments ::

_____ , in the global financial market, is an unsecured promissory note with a fixed maturity of not more than 270 days.

Exam Probability: **High**

53. *Answer choices:*

(see index for correct answer)

- a. Commercial paper
- b. Commercial paper in India

Guidance: level 1

:: ::

In marketing, a _____ is a ticket or document that can be redeemed for a financial discount or rebate when purchasing a product.

Exam Probability: **Low**

54. *Answer choices:*
(see index for correct answer)

- a. similarity-attraction theory
- b. cultural
- c. process perspective
- d. corporate values

Guidance: level 1

:: Business law ::

_____ is where a person's financial liability is limited to a fixed sum, most commonly the value of a person's investment in a company or partnership. If a company with _____ is sued, then the claimants are suing the company, not its owners or investors. A shareholder in a limited company is not personally liable for any of the debts of the company, other than for the amount already invested in the company and for any unpaid amount on the shares in the company, if any. The same is true for the members of a _____ partnership and the limited partners in a limited partnership. By contrast, sole proprietors and partners in general partnerships are each liable for all the debts of the business.

Exam Probability: **Low**

55. *Answer choices:*

(see index for correct answer)

- a. Ladenschlussgesetz
- b. Uniform Commercial Code
- c. Limited liability
- d. Business method patent

Guidance: level 1

:: Occupations ::

An _____ is a practitioner of accounting or accountancy, which is the measurement, disclosure or provision of assurance about financial information that helps managers, investors, tax authorities and others make decisions about allocating resource.

Exam Probability: **High**

56. *Answer choices:*

(see index for correct answer)

- a. Mixing engineer
- b. Nuclear gypsy
- c. Accountant
- d. Principal teacher

Guidance: level 1

:: Basic financial concepts ::

In finance, maturity or _____ refers to the final payment date of a loan or other financial instrument, at which point the principal is due to be paid.

Exam Probability: **Medium**

57. *Answer choices:*

(see index for correct answer)

- a. Tax shield
- b. Deflation
- c. Short interest
- d. balloon payment

Guidance: level 1

:: Financial economics ::

A _____ is defined to include property of any kind held by an assessee, whether connected with their business or profession or not connected with their business or profession. It includes all kinds of property, movable or immovable, tangible or intangible, fixed or circulating. Thus, land and building, plant and machinery, motorcar, furniture, jewellery, route permits, goodwill, tenancy rights, patents, trademarks, shares, debentures, securities, units, mutual funds, zero-coupon bonds etc. are _____ s.

Exam Probability: **Medium**

58. *Answer choices:*

(see index for correct answer)

- a. Settlement date
- b. Portfolio insurance
- c. Capital asset
- d. Ask price

Guidance: level 1

:: ::

An _____ is a systematic and independent examination of books, accounts, statutory records, documents and vouchers of an organization to ascertain how far the financial statements as well as non-financial disclosures present a true and fair view of the concern. It also attempts to ensure that the books of accounts are properly maintained by the concern as required by law. _____ ing has become such a ubiquitous phenomenon in the corporate and the public sector that academics started identifying an " _____ Society". The _____ or perceives and recognises the propositions before them for examination, obtains evidence, evaluates the same and formulates an opinion on the basis of his judgement which is communicated through their _____ ing report.

Exam Probability: **Low**

59. *Answer choices:*

(see index for correct answer)

- a. personal values
- b. Character
- c. interpersonal communication
- d. Audit

Guidance: level 1

Human resource management

Human resource (HR) management is the strategic approach to the effective management of organization workers so that they help the business gain a competitive advantage. It is designed to maximize employee performance in service of an employer's strategic objectives. HR is primarily concerned with the management of people within organizations, focusing on policies and on systems. HR departments are responsible for overseeing employee-benefits design, employee recruitment, training and development, performance appraisal, and rewarding (e.g., managing pay and benefit systems). HR also concerns itself with organizational change and industrial relations, that is, the balancing of organizational practices with requirements arising from collective bargaining and from governmental laws.

:: Employment compensation ::

A _____ is a type of employee benefit plan offered in the United States pursuant to Section 125 of the Internal Revenue Code. Its name comes from the earliest such plans that allowed employees to choose between different types of benefits, similar to the ability of a customer to choose among available items in a cafeteria. Qualified _____s are excluded from gross income. To qualify, a _____ must allow employees to choose from two or more benefits consisting of cash or qualified benefit plans. The Internal Revenue Code explicitly excludes deferred compensation plans from qualifying as a _____ subject to a gross income exemption. Section 125 also provides two exceptions.

Exam Probability: **High**

1. *Answer choices:*

(see index for correct answer)

- a. Stock appreciation right
- b. Cafeteria plan
- c. Labour law
- d. Employee stock purchase plan

Guidance: level 1

:: Employee relations ::

_____ is a fundamental concept in the effort to understand and describe, both qualitatively and quantitatively, the nature of the relationship between an organization and its employees. An "engaged employee" is defined as one who is fully absorbed by and enthusiastic about their work and so takes positive action to further the organization's reputation and interests. An engaged employee has a positive attitude towards the organization and its values. In contrast, a disengaged employee may range from someone doing the bare minimum at work, up to an employee who is actively damaging the company's work output and reputation.

Exam Probability: **Medium**

2. *Answer choices:*

(see index for correct answer)

- a. Employee morale
- b. Industry Federation of the State of Rio de Janeiro
- c. Employee handbook
- d. Employee engagement

Guidance: level 1

:: Employment ::

_____ is a relationship between two parties, usually based on a contract where work is paid for, where one party, which may be a corporation, for profit, not-for-profit organization, co-operative or other entity is the employer and the other is the employee. Employees work in return for payment, which may be in the form of an hourly wage, by piecework or an annual salary, depending on the type of work an employee does or which sector she or he is working in. Employees in some fields or sectors may receive gratuities, bonus payment or stock options. In some types of _____ , employees may receive benefits in addition to payment. Benefits can include health insurance, housing, disability insurance or use of a gym. _____ is typically governed by _____ laws, regulations or legal contracts.

Exam Probability: **Low**

3. *Answer choices:*

(see index for correct answer)

- a. Local hiring
- b. Goldbricking
- c. Alternative employment arrangements
- d. Employment

Guidance: level 1

:: Persuasion techniques ::

_____ is a psychological technique in which an individual attempts to influence another person by becoming more likeable to their target. This term was coined by social psychologist Edward E. Jones, who further defined _____ as "a class of strategic behaviors illicitly designed to influence a particular other person concerning the attractiveness of one's personal qualities." _____ research has identified some specific tactics of employing _____ .

Exam Probability: **Low**

4. *Answer choices:*

(see index for correct answer)

- a. Ingratiation
- b. Flattery
- c. Apologue
- d. Modes of persuasion

Guidance: level 1

:: Validity (statistics) ::

In psychometrics, criterion or concrete validity is the extent to which a measure is related to an outcome. _____ is often divided into concurrent and predictive validity. Concurrent validity refers to a comparison between the measure in question and an outcome assessed at the same time. In Standards for Educational & Psychological Tests, it states, "concurrent validity reflects only the status quo at a particular time." Predictive validity, on the other hand, compares the measure in question with an outcome assessed at a later time. Although concurrent and predictive validity are similar, it is cautioned to keep the terms and findings separated. "Concurrent validity should not be used as a substitute for predictive validity without an appropriate supporting rationale."

Exam Probability: **Low**

5. *Answer choices:*

(see index for correct answer)

- a. Criterion validity
- b. Internal validity
- c. Incremental validity
- d. Statistical conclusion

Guidance: level 1

:: Human resource management ::

_____ is a continual process used to align the needs and priorities of the organization with those of its workforce to ensure it can meet its legislative, regulatory, service and production requirements and organizational objectives. _____ enables evidence based workforce development strategies.

Exam Probability: **Medium**

6. *Answer choices:*
(see index for correct answer)

- a. Job design
- b. Up or out
- c. Parallel running
- d. Workforce planning

Guidance: level 1

:: Employment ::

A flat organization has an organizational structure with few or no levels of middle management between staff and executives. An organization's structure refers to the nature of the distribution of the units and positions within it, also to the nature of the relationships among those units and positions. Tall and flat organizations differ based on how many levels of management are present in the organization, and how much control managers are endowed with.

Exam Probability: **Medium**

7. Answer choices:

(see index for correct answer)

- a. Customized employment
- b. CRCC Asia
- c. Liaison officer
- d. Numerary

Guidance: level 1

:: ::

_____ is a form of government characterized by strong central power and limited political freedoms. Individual freedoms are subordinate to the state and there is no constitutional accountability and rule of law under an authoritarian regime. Authoritarian regimes can be autocratic with power concentrated in one person or it can be more spread out between multiple officials and government institutions. Juan Linz`s influential 1964 description of _____ characterized authoritarian political systems by four qualities.

Exam Probability: **Low**

8. Answer choices:

(see index for correct answer)

- a. functional perspective
- b. process perspective
- c. personal values

- d. imperative

Guidance: level 1

:: Office work ::

The _____ is a concept in management developed by Laurence J. Peter, which observes that people in a hierarchy tend to rise to their "level of incompetence". In other words, an employee is promoted based on their success in previous jobs until they reach a level at which they are no longer competent, as skills in one job do not necessarily translate to another. The concept was elucidated in the 1969 book The _____ by Peter and Raymond Hull.

Exam Probability: **Low**

9. *Answer choices:*

(see index for correct answer)

- a. Service bureau
- b. Small office/home office
- c. Office of the future
- d. Peter Principle

Guidance: level 1

:: Business law ::

A _____ is an arrangement where parties, known as partners, agree to cooperate to advance their mutual interests. The partners in a _____ may be individuals, businesses, interest-based organizations, schools, governments or combinations. Organizations may partner to increase the likelihood of each achieving their mission and to amplify their reach. A _____ may result in issuing and holding equity or may be only governed by a contract.

Exam Probability: **Low**

10. *Answer choices:*

(see index for correct answer)

- a. Partnership
- b. Unfair business practices
- c. Companies Acts
- d. Voting trust

Guidance: level 1

:: Human resource management ::

_____ or work sharing is an employment arrangement where typically two people are retained on a part-time or reduced-time basis to perform a job normally fulfilled by one person working full-time. Since all positions are shared thus leads to a net reduction in per-employee income. The people sharing the job work as a team to complete the job task and are equally responsible for the job workload. Compensation is apportioned between the workers. Working hours, pay and holidays are divided equally. The pay as you go system helps make deductions for national insurance and superannuations are made as a straightforward percentage.

Exam Probability: **Medium**

11. *Answer choices:*

(see index for correct answer)

- a. Virtual management
- b. Job sharing
- c. Adaptive performance
- d. Employee silence

Guidance: level 1

In business strategy, _____ is establishing a competitive advantage by having the lowest cost of operation in the industry. _____ is often driven by company efficiency, size, scale, scope and cumulative experience. A _____ strategy aims to exploit scale of production, well-defined scope and other economies, producing highly standardized products, using advanced technology. In recent years, more and more companies have chosen a strategic mix to achieve market leadership. These patterns consist of simultaneous _____, superior customer service and product leadership. Walmart has succeeded across the world due to its _____ strategy. The company has cut down on exesses at every point of production and thus are able to provide the consumers with quality products at low prices.

Exam Probability: **High**

12. *Answer choices:*

(see index for correct answer)

- a. co-culture
- b. information systems assessment
- c. Cost leadership
- d. process perspective

Guidance: level 1

:: Human resource management ::

_____ is the corporate management term for the act of reorganizing the legal, ownership, operational, or other structures of a company for the purpose of making it more profitable, or better organized for its present needs. Other reasons for _____ include a change of ownership or ownership structure, demerger, or a response to a crisis or major change in the business such as bankruptcy, repositioning, or buyout. _____ may also be described as corporate _____ , debt _____ and financial _____ .

Exam Probability: **High**

13. *Answer choices:*

(see index for correct answer)

- a. Restructuring
- b. Workforce management
- c. Illness rate
- d. Leadership development

Guidance: level 1

:: Employment ::

Onboarding, also known as _____ , is management jargon first created in 1988 that refers to the mechanism through which new employees acquire the necessary knowledge, skills, and behaviors in order to become effective organizational members and insiders.

Exam Probability: **Low**

14. Answer choices:

(see index for correct answer)

- a. Organizational socialization
- b. Job security
- c. Extreme careerism
- d. Job shadow

Guidance: level 1

:: Labor ::

_____ s are workers whose main capital is knowledge. Examples include programmers, physicians, pharmacists, architects, engineers, scientists, design thinkers, public accountants, lawyers, and academics, and any other white-collar workers, whose line of work requires the one to "think for a living".

Exam Probability: **High**

15. Answer choices:

(see index for correct answer)

- a. Knowledge worker
- b. Haken
- c. Means of production
- d. Affective labor

Guidance: level 1

:: Employment discrimination ::

A _____ is a metaphor used to represent an invisible barrier that keeps a given demographic from rising beyond a certain level in a hierarchy.

Exam Probability: **High**

16. *Answer choices:*

(see index for correct answer)

- a. New South Wales selection bias
- b. MacBride Principles
- c. Glass ceiling
- d. United Kingdom employment equality law

Guidance: level 1

:: Employment ::

A _____ , a concept developed in contemporary research by organizational scholar Denise Rousseau, represents the mutual beliefs, perceptions and informal obligations between an employer and an employee. It sets the dynamics for the relationship and defines the detailed practicality of the work to be done. It is distinguishable from the formal written contract of employment which, for the most part, only identifies mutual duties and responsibilities in a generalized form.

Exam Probability: **High**

17. *Answer choices:*

(see index for correct answer)

- a. Psychological contract
- b. Taleo
- c. ThinkTalk
- d. Workhaven

Guidance: level 1

:: United States federal labor legislation ::

The _____ of 1967 is a US labor law that forbids employment discrimination against anyone at least 40 years of age in the United States. In 1967, the bill was signed into law by President Lyndon B. Johnson. The ADEA prevents age discrimination and provides equal employment opportunity under conditions that were not explicitly covered in Title VII of the Civil Rights Act of 1964. It also applies to the standards for pensions and benefits provided by employers, and requires that information concerning the needs of older workers be provided to the general public.

Exam Probability: **High**

18. *Answer choices:*

(see index for correct answer)

- a. Employment Act of 1946
- b. Hiring Incentives to Restore Employment Act
- c. Drug-Free Workplace Act of 1988
- d. Age Discrimination in Employment Act

Guidance: level 1

:: Employment compensation ::

_____, merit increase or pay for performance, is performance-related pay, most frequently in the context of educational reform or government civil service reform. It provides bonuses for workers who perform their jobs effectively, according to easily measurable criteria. In the United States, policy makers are divided on whether _____ should be offered to public school teachers, and other public employees, as is commonly the case in the United Kingdom.

Exam Probability: **Medium**

19. *Answer choices:*

(see index for correct answer)

- a. Compensation of employees
- b. Merit pay
- c. Labour law
- d. Salary calculator

Guidance: level 1

:: Business planning ::

_____ is an organization's process of defining its strategy, or direction, and making decisions on allocating its resources to pursue this strategy. It may also extend to control mechanisms for guiding the implementation of the strategy. _____ became prominent in corporations during the 1960s and remains an important aspect of strategic management. It is executed by strategic planners or strategists, who involve many parties and research sources in their analysis of the organization and its relationship to the environment in which it competes.

Exam Probability: **Medium**

20. *Answer choices:*
(see index for correct answer)

- a. Joint decision trap
- b. operational planning
- c. Stakeholder management
- d. Exit planning

Guidance: level 1

:: Management ::

The term _____ refers to measures designed to increase the degree of autonomy and self-determination in people and in communities in order to enable them to represent their interests in a responsible and self-determined way, acting on their own authority. It is the process of becoming stronger and more confident, especially in controlling one's life and claiming one's rights. _____ as action refers both to the process of self- _____ and to professional support of people, which enables them to overcome their sense of powerlessness and lack of influence, and to recognize and use their resources. To do work with power.

Exam Probability: **Medium**

21. *Answer choices:*
(see index for correct answer)

- a. Business-oriented architecture
- b. Functional management
- c. Strategic lenses
- d. Empowerment

Guidance: level 1

:: Industrial engineering ::

_____ is the formal process that sits alongside Requirements analysis and focuses on the human elements of the requirements.

Exam Probability: **Medium**

22. Answer choices:

(see index for correct answer)

- a. Needs analysis
- b. Standard data system
- c. Worker-machine activity chart
- d. Industrial ecology

Guidance: level 1

:: Production and manufacturing ::

_____ is a set of techniques and tools for process improvement. Though as a shortened form it may be found written as 6S, it should not be confused with the methodology known as 6S .

Exam Probability: **Medium**

23. Answer choices:

(see index for correct answer)

- a. Advanced Manufacturing Software
- b. Earned value
- c. Alarm fatigue
- d. Six Sigma

Guidance: level 1

:: Training ::

_____ refers to practicing newly acquired skills beyond the point of initial mastery. The term is also often used to refer to the pedagogical theory that this form of practice leads to automaticity or other beneficial consequences.

Exam Probability: **Low**

24. *Answer choices:*
(see index for correct answer)

- a. Overlearning
- b. Facila
- c. Question Writer
- d. Instructor-led training

Guidance: level 1

:: Lean manufacturing ::

_____ is the Sino-Japanese word for "improvement". In business, _____ refers to activities that continuously improve all functions and involve all employees from the CEO to the assembly line workers. It also applies to processes, such as purchasing and logistics, that cross organizational boundaries into the supply chain. It has been applied in healthcare, psychotherapy, life-coaching, government, and banking.

Exam Probability: **Medium**

25. *Answer choices:*

(see index for correct answer)

- a. Agent-assisted automation
- b. Lean enterprise
- c. Continuous improvement
- d. Lean software development

Guidance: level 1

:: ::

_____ is the administration of an organization, whether it is a business, a not-for-profit organization, or government body. _____ includes the activities of setting the strategy of an organization and coordinating the efforts of its employees to accomplish its objectives through the application of available resources, such as financial, natural, technological, and human resources. The term " _____ " may also refer to those people who manage an organization.

Exam Probability: **Low**

26. *Answer choices:*

(see index for correct answer)

- a. Management
- b. deep-level diversity
- c. levels of analysis
- d. hierarchical perspective

Guidance: level 1

:: Employment compensation ::

_____ is time off from work that workers can use to stay home to address their health and safety needs without losing pay. Paid _____ is a statutory requirement in many nations. Most European, many Latin American, a few African and a few Asian countries have legal requirements for paid _____ .

Exam Probability: **High**

27. *Answer choices:*

(see index for correct answer)

- a. Medical Care and Sickness Benefits Convention, 1969
- b. Protection of Wages Convention, 1949

- c. Basic Income Earth Network
- d. executive stock option

Guidance: level 1

:: Survey methodology ::

A _____ is the procedure of systematically acquiring and recording information about the members of a given population. The term is used mostly in connection with national population and housing _____ es; other common _____ es include agriculture, business, and traffic _____ es. The United Nations defines the essential features of population and housing _____ es as "individual enumeration, universality within a defined territory, simultaneity and defined periodicity", and recommends that population _____ es be taken at least every 10 years. United Nations recommendations also cover _____ topics to be collected, official definitions, classifications and other useful information to co-ordinate international practice.

Exam Probability: **High**

28. *Answer choices:*

(see index for correct answer)

- a. Inverse probability weighting
- b. Enterprise feedback management
- c. Survey sampling
- d. Census

Guidance: level 1

:: Sociological terminology ::

In moral and political philosophy, the _____ is a theory or model that originated during the Age of Enlightenment and usually concerns the legitimacy of the authority of the state over the individual. _____ arguments typically posit that individuals have consented, either explicitly or tacitly, to surrender some of their freedoms and submit to the authority in exchange for protection of their remaining rights or maintenance of the social order. The relation between natural and legal rights is often a topic of _____ theory. The term takes its name from The _____ , a 1762 book by Jean-Jacques Rousseau that discussed this concept. Although the antecedents of _____ theory are found in antiquity, in Greek and Stoic philosophy and Roman and Canon Law, the heyday of the _____ was the mid-17th to early 19th centuries, when it emerged as the leading doctrine of political legitimacy.

Exam Probability: **Low**

29. *Answer choices:*

(see index for correct answer)

- a. Anticipatory socialization
- b. Symbolic capital
- c. Social fact
- d. Social contract

Guidance: level 1

:: Management education ::

_____ refers to simulation games that are used as an educational tool for teaching business. _____ s may be carried out for various business training such as: general management, finance, organizational behaviour, human resources, etc. Often, the term "business simulation" is used with the same meaning.

Exam Probability: **Medium**

30. *Answer choices:*

(see index for correct answer)

- a. Association for Business Communication
- b. Master of Business Administration
- c. MBA degree
- d. Business game

Guidance: level 1

:: Business ethics ::

In United States labor law, a _____ exists when one's behavior within a workplace creates an environment that is difficult or uncomfortable for another person to work in, due to discrimination. Common complaints in sexual harassment lawsuits include fondling, suggestive remarks, sexually-suggestive photos displayed in the workplace, use of sexual language, or off-color jokes. Small matters, annoyances, and isolated incidents are usually not considered to be statutory violations of the discrimination laws. For a violation to impose liability, the conduct must create a work environment that would be intimidating, hostile, or offensive to a reasonable person. An employer can be held liable for failing to prevent these workplace conditions, unless it can prove that it attempted to prevent the harassment and that the employee failed to take advantage of existing harassment counter-measures or tools provided by the employer.

Exam Probability: **Low**

31. *Answer choices:*

(see index for correct answer)

- a. Hostile work environment
- b. Whistleblower
- c. Workplace bullying
- d. Corruption of Foreign Public Officials Act

Guidance: level 1

Educational technology is "the study and ethical practice of facilitating learning and improving performance by creating, using, and managing appropriate technological processes and resources".

Exam Probability: **Medium**

32. *Answer choices:*

(see index for correct answer)

- a. E-learning
- b. functional perspective
- c. Sarbanes-Oxley act of 2002
- d. corporate values

Guidance: level 1

:: Organizational theory ::

Decentralisation is the process by which the activities of an organization, particularly those regarding planning and decision making, are distributed or delegated away from a central, authoritative location or group. Concepts of _____ have been applied to group dynamics and management science in private businesses and organizations, political science, law and public administration, economics, money and technology.

Exam Probability: **Medium**

33. Answer choices:

(see index for correct answer)

- a. Organigraph
- b. System 4
- c. Decentralization
- d. Team leader

Guidance: level 1

:: Validity (statistics) ::

_____ is a type of evidence that can be gathered to defend the use of a test for predicting other outcomes. It is a parameter used in sociology, psychology, and other psychometric or behavioral sciences. _____ is demonstrated when a test correlates well with a measure that has previously been validated. The two measures may be for the same construct, but more often used for different, but presumably related, constructs.

Exam Probability: **Low**

34. Answer choices:

(see index for correct answer)

- a. Content validity
- b. Ecological validity
- c. Incremental validity
- d. Construct validity

Guidance: level 1

:: ::

_____ is an experience a person may have when one moves to a cultural environment which is different from one's own; it is also the personal disorientation a person may feel when experiencing an unfamiliar way of life due to immigration or a visit to a new country, a move between social environments, or simply transition to another type of life. One of the most common causes of _____ involves individuals in a foreign environment. _____ can be described as consisting of at least one of four distinct phases: honeymoon, negotiation, adjustment, and adaptation.

Exam Probability: **Medium**

35. *Answer choices:*

(see index for correct answer)

- a. co-culture
- b. Culture shock
- c. process perspective
- d. surface-level diversity

Guidance: level 1

:: Psychometrics ::

Electronic assessment, also known as e-assessment, _____, computer assisted/mediated assessment and computer-based assessment, is the use of information technology in various forms of assessment such as educational assessment, health assessment, psychiatric assessment, and psychological assessment. This may utilize an online computer connected to a network. This definition embraces a wide range of student activity ranging from the use of a word processor to on-screen testing. Specific types of e-assessment include multiple choice, online/electronic submission, computerized adaptive testing and computerized classification testing.

Exam Probability: **Low**

36. *Answer choices:*

(see index for correct answer)

- a. Linear-on-the-fly testing
- b. Psychometrics of racism
- c. Idiographic image
- d. Online assessment

Guidance: level 1

:: ::

_____ is the process of two or more people or organizations working together to complete a task or achieve a goal. _____ is similar to cooperation. Most _____ requires leadership, although the form of leadership can be social within a decentralized and egalitarian group. Teams that work collaboratively often access greater resources, recognition and rewards when facing competition for finite resources.

Exam Probability: **Low**

37. *Answer choices:*

(see index for correct answer)

- a. functional perspective
- b. co-culture
- c. empathy
- d. cultural

Guidance: level 1

:: Human resource management ::

A _____ is a group of people with different functional expertise working toward a common goal. It may include people from finance, marketing, operations, and human resources departments. Typically, it includes employees from all levels of an organization. Members may also come from outside an organization.

Exam Probability: **Medium**

38. *Answer choices:*

(see index for correct answer)

- a. Cross-functional team
- b. Employee relationship management
- c. Functional job analysis
- d. Employee silence

Guidance: level 1

:: ::

_____ is a form of development in which a person called a coach supports a learner or client in achieving a specific personal or professional goal by providing training and guidance. The learner is sometimes called a coachee. Occasionally, _____ may mean an informal relationship between two people, of whom one has more experience and expertise than the other and offers advice and guidance as the latter learns; but _____ differs from mentoring in focusing on specific tasks or objectives, as opposed to more general goals or overall development.

Exam Probability: **Low**

39. *Answer choices:*

(see index for correct answer)

- a. surface-level diversity
- b. Coaching

- c. process perspective
- d. similarity-attraction theory

Guidance: level 1

:: ::

The _____ of 1938 29 U.S.C. § 203 is a United States labor law that creates the right to a minimum wage, and "time-and-a-half" overtime pay when people work over forty hours a week. It also prohibits most employment of minors in "oppressive child labor". It applies to employees engaged in interstate commerce or employed by an enterprise engaged in commerce or in the production of goods for commerce, unless the employer can claim an exemption from coverage.

Exam Probability: **Low**

40. *Answer choices:*

(see index for correct answer)

- a. Character
- b. Fair Labor Standards Act
- c. imperative
- d. interpersonal communication

Guidance: level 1

:: Human resource management ::

_____ , also known as management by results, was first popularized by Peter Drucker in his 1954 book The Practice of Management. _____ is the process of defining specific objectives within an organization that management can convey to organization members, then deciding on how to achieve each objective in sequence. This process allows managers to take work that needs to be done one step at a time to allow for a calm, yet productive work environment. This process also helps organization members to see their accomplishments as they achieve each objective, which reinforces a positive work environment and a sense of achievement. An important part of MBO is the measurement and comparison of an employee's actual performance with the standards set. Ideally, when employees themselves have been involved with the goal-setting and choosing the course of action to be followed by them, they are more likely to fulfill their responsibilities. According to George S. Odiorne, the system of _____ can be described as a process whereby the superior and subordinate jointly identify common goals, define each individual's major areas of responsibility in terms of the results expected of him or her, and use these measures as guides for operating the unit and assessing the contribution of each of its members.

Exam Probability: **Medium**

41. *Answer choices:*

(see index for correct answer)

- a. Selection ratio
- b. Management by objectives
- c. Mergers and acquisitions
- d. Workforce sciences

Guidance: level 1

:: Unemployment in the United States ::

The _____ is a unit of the United States Department of Labor. It is the principal fact-finding agency for the U.S. government in the broad field of labor economics and statistics and serves as a principal agency of the U.S. Federal Statistical System. The BLS is a governmental statistical agency that collects, processes, analyzes, and disseminates essential statistical data to the American public, the U.S. Congress, other Federal agencies, State and local governments, business, and labor representatives. The BLS also serves as a statistical resource to the United States Department of Labor, and conducts research into how much families need to earn to be able to enjoy a decent standard of living.

Exam Probability: **Medium**

42. *Answer choices:*

(see index for correct answer)

- a. Workforce Innovation and Opportunity Act
- b. Unemployment Action Center
- c. California unemployment statistics
- d. Unemployment Compensation Extension Act of 2010

Guidance: level 1

:: Labour law ::

A _____ is a "shop-floor" organization representing workers that functions as a local/firm-level complement to trade unions but is independent of these at least in some countries. _____ s exist with different names in a variety of related forms in a number of European countries, including Britain ; Germany and Austria ; Luxembourg ; the Netherlands and Flanders in Belgium ; Italy ; France ; Wallonia in Belgium and Spain .

Exam Probability: **Medium**

43. *Answer choices:*

(see index for correct answer)

- a. Emanation of the state
- b. Works council
- c. Unfair dismissal
- d. Vesting

Guidance: level 1

:: Business ethics ::

_____ is a persistent pattern of mistreatment from others in the workplace that causes either physical or emotional harm. It can include such tactics as verbal, nonverbal, psychological, physical abuse and humiliation. This type of workplace aggression is particularly difficult because, unlike the typical school bully, workplace bullies often operate within the established rules and policies of their organization and their society. In the majority of cases, bullying in the workplace is reported as having been by someone who has authority over their victim. However, bullies can also be peers, and occasionally subordinates. Research has also investigated the impact of the larger organizational context on bullying as well as the group-level processes that impact on the incidence and maintenance of bullying behaviour. Bullying can be covert or overt. It may be missed by superiors; it may be known by many throughout the organization. Negative effects are not limited to the targeted individuals, and may lead to a decline in employee morale and a change in organizational culture. It can also take place as overbearing supervision, constant criticism, and blocking promotions.

Exam Probability: **High**

44. *Answer choices:*

(see index for correct answer)

- a. Business Ethics Quarterly
- b. Corporate social entrepreneurship
- c. Marketing ethics
- d. CUC International

Guidance: level 1

:: Human resource management ::

_____ is a process for identifying and developing new leaders who can replace old leaders when they leave, retire or die. _____ increases the availability of experienced and capable employees that are prepared to assume these roles as they become available. Taken narrowly, "replacement planning" for key roles is the heart of _____ .

Exam Probability: **Medium**

45. *Answer choices:*

(see index for correct answer)

- a. Contractor management
- b. TPI-theory
- c. Mergers and acquisitions
- d. Succession planning

Guidance: level 1

:: Project management ::

Some scenarios associate "this kind of planning" with learning "life skills". _____ s are necessary, or at least useful, in situations where individuals need to know what time they must be at a specific location to receive a specific service, and where people need to accomplish a set of goals within a set time period.

Exam Probability: **Medium**

46. Answer choices:

(see index for correct answer)

- a. Precedence diagram method
- b. Project sponsorship
- c. Project manufacturing
- d. Schedule

Guidance: level 1

:: ::

_____ is the moral stance, political philosophy, ideology, or social outlook that emphasizes the moral worth of the individual. Individualists promote the exercise of one's goals and desires and so value independence and self-reliance and advocate that interests of the individual should achieve precedence over the state or a social group, while opposing external interference upon one's own interests by society or institutions such as the government. _____ is often defined in contrast to totalitarianism, collectivism, and more corporate social forms.

Exam Probability: **High**

47. Answer choices:

(see index for correct answer)

- a. personal values
- b. cultural

- c. open system
- d. Individualism

Guidance: level 1

:: Labour relations ::

A _____ , also known as a post-entry closed shop, is a form of a union security clause. Under this, the employer agrees to either only hire labor union members or to require that any new employees who are not already union members become members within a certain amount of time. Use of the _____ varies widely from nation to nation, depending on the level of protection given trade unions in general.

Exam Probability: **Low**

48. *Answer choices:*

(see index for correct answer)

- a. Union shop
- b. Worker center
- c. Whipsaw strike
- d. Acas

Guidance: level 1

:: ::

Refresher/ _____ is the process of learning a new or the same old skill or trade for the same group of personnel. Refresher/ _____ is required to be provided on regular basis to avoid personnel obsolescence due to technological changes & the individuals memory capacity. This short term instruction course shall serve to re-acquaint personnel with skills previously learnt or to bring one's knowledge or skills up-to-date so that skills stay sharp. This kind of training could be provided annually or more frequently as maybe required, based on the importance of consistency of the task of which the skill is involved. Examples of refreshers are cGMP, GDP, HSE trainings. _____ shall also be conducted for an employee, when the employee is rated as 'not qualified' for a skill or knowledge, as determined based on the assessment of answers in the training questionnaire of the employee.

Exam Probability: **Low**

49. *Answer choices:*
(see index for correct answer)

- a. process perspective
- b. Character
- c. hierarchical
- d. cultural

Guidance: level 1

:: Survey methodology ::

_____ is often used to assess thoughts, opinions, and feelings. Surveys can be specific and limited, or they can have more global, widespread goals. Psychologists and sociologists often use surveys to analyze behavior, while it is also used to meet the more pragmatic needs of the media, such as, in evaluating political candidates, public health officials, professional organizations, and advertising and marketing directors. A survey consists of a predetermined set of questions that is given to a sample. With a representative sample, that is, one that is representative of the larger population of interest, one can describe the attitudes of the population from which the sample was drawn. Further, one can compare the attitudes of different populations as well as look for changes in attitudes over time. A good sample selection is key as it allows one to generalize the findings from the sample to the population, which is the whole purpose of _____ .

Exam Probability: **Low**

50. *Answer choices:*

(see index for correct answer)

- a. Public opinion
- b. National Health Interview Survey
- c. Swiss Centre of Expertise in the Social Sciences
- d. Inverse probability weighting

Guidance: level 1

:: Telecommuting ::

_____ , also called telework, teleworking, working from home, mobile work, remote work, and flexible workplace, is a work arrangement in which employees do not commute or travel to a central place of work, such as an office building, warehouse, or store. Teleworkers in the 21st century often use mobile telecommunications technology such as Wi-Fi-equipped laptop or tablet computers and smartphones to work from coffee shops; others may use a desktop computer and a landline phone at their home. According to a Reuters poll, approximately "one in five workers around the globe, particularly employees in the Middle East, Latin America and Asia, telecommute frequently and nearly 10 percent work from home every day." In the 2000s, annual leave or vacation in some organizations was seen as absence from the workplace rather than ceasing work, and some office employees used telework to continue to check work e-mails while on vacation.

Exam Probability: **Low**

51. *Answer choices:*

(see index for correct answer)

- a. Telecommuting
- b. IvanAnywhere
- c. Home Work Convention, 1996
- d. Canadian Telework Association

Guidance: level 1

:: Management ::

A _____ is a method or technique that has been generally accepted as superior to any alternatives because it produces results that are superior to those achieved by other means or because it has become a standard way of doing things, e.g., a standard way of complying with legal or ethical requirements.

Exam Probability: **High**

52. *Answer choices:*

(see index for correct answer)

- a. Topple rate
- b. Best practice
- c. Supply chain optimization
- d. Industrial forensics

Guidance: level 1

:: Validity (statistics) ::

In psychometrics, _____ refers to the extent to which a measure represents all facets of a given construct. For example, a depression scale may lack _____ if it only assesses the affective dimension of depression but fails to take into account the behavioral dimension. An element of subjectivity exists in relation to determining _____, which requires a degree of agreement about what a particular personality trait such as extraversion represents. A disagreement about a personality trait will prevent the gain of a high _____.

Exam Probability: **High**

53. *Answer choices:*

(see index for correct answer)

- a. Statistical conclusion validity
- b. Ecological validity
- c. Content validity
- d. Test validity

Guidance: level 1

:: Project management ::

_____ is a name for various theories of human motivation built on Douglas McGregor's Theory X and Theory Y. Theories X, Y and various versions of Z have been used in human resource management, organizational behavior, organizational communication and organizational development.

Exam Probability: **Low**

54. *Answer choices:*

(see index for correct answer)

- a. Duration
- b. ISO 10006
- c. Theory Z

- d. Dependency

Guidance: level 1

:: Human resource management ::

_____ refers to the anticipation of required human capital for an organization and the planning to meet those needs. The field increased in popularity after McKinsey's 1997 research and the 2001 book on The War for Talent. _____ in this context does not refer to the management of entertainers.

Exam Probability: **High**

55. *Answer choices:*
(see index for correct answer)

- a. IDS HR in Practice
- b. Talent management
- c. Labour is not a commodity
- d. Cross-training

Guidance: level 1

:: Labour relations ::

An _____ is a place of employment at which one is not required to join or financially support a union as a condition of hiring or continued employment. _____ is also known as a merit shop.

Exam Probability: **High**

56. *Answer choices:*

(see index for correct answer)

- a. Worker center
- b. Passfield Memorandum
- c. Union Wallonne des Entreprises
- d. Work Order Act

Guidance: level 1

:: Learning methods ::

_____ is an approach to problem solving. It involves taking action and reflecting upon the results. This helps improve the problem-solving process as well as simplify the solutions developed by the team.

Exam Probability: **Medium**

57. *Answer choices:*

(see index for correct answer)

- a. Collaborative learning
- b. Audience response system
- c. Action learning
- d. double loop learning

Guidance: level 1

:: ::

_____ is the process of collecting, analyzing and/or reporting information regarding the performance of an individual, group, organization, system or component. _____ is not a new concept, some of the earliest records of human activity relate to the counting or recording of activities.

Exam Probability: **High**

58. *Answer choices:*

(see index for correct answer)

- a. Character
- b. hierarchical perspective
- c. Performance measurement
- d. functional perspective

Guidance: level 1

A _____ , covering letter, motivation letter, motivational letter or a letter of motivation is a letter of introduction attached to, or accompanying another document such as a résumé or curriculum vitae.

Exam Probability: **Medium**

59. *Answer choices:*

(see index for correct answer)

- a. Cover letter
- b. corporate values
- c. hierarchical
- d. similarity-attraction theory

Guidance: level 1

Information systems

Information systems (IS) are formal, sociotechnical, organizational systems designed to collect, process, store, and distribute information. In a sociotechnical perspective Information Systems are composed by four components: technology, process, people and organizational structure.

:: Network management ::

_____ is the process of administering and managing computer networks. Services provided by this discipline include fault analysis, performance management, provisioning of networks and maintaining the quality of service. Software that enables network administrators to perform their functions is called _____ software.

Exam Probability: **Low**

1. *Answer choices:*

(see index for correct answer)

- a. Network management
- b. Real user monitoring
- c. IP exchange
- d. EtherApe

Guidance: level 1

:: ::

Collaborative software or _____ is application software designed to help people involved in a common task to achieve their goals. One of the earliest definitions of collaborative software is "intentional group processes plus software to support them".

Exam Probability: **Low**

2. *Answer choices:*

(see index for correct answer)

- a. surface-level diversity
- b. Groupware
- c. levels of analysis

- d. personal values

Guidance: level 1

:: E-commerce ::

_____ is a type of fraud that occurs on the Internet in pay-per-click online advertising. In this type of advertising, the owners of websites that post the ads are paid an amount of money determined by how many visitors to the sites click on the ads. Fraud occurs when a person, automated script or computer program imitates a legitimate user of a web browser, clicking on such an ad without having an actual interest in the target of the ad's link.
_____ is the subject of some controversy and increasing litigation due to the advertising networks being a key beneficiary of the fraud.

Exam Probability: **Medium**

3. *Answer choices:*
(see index for correct answer)

- a. Variable pricing
- b. Ven
- c. Net settlement
- d. Billing and Settlement Plan

Guidance: level 1

:: Credit cards ::

A _____ is a payment card issued to users to enable the cardholder to pay a merchant for goods and services based on the cardholder's promise to the card issuer to pay them for the amounts plus the other agreed charges. The card issuer creates a revolving account and grants a line of credit to the cardholder, from which the cardholder can borrow money for payment to a merchant or as a cash advance.

Exam Probability: **High**

4. *Answer choices:*

(see index for correct answer)

- a. Netbanx
- b. OnePulse
- c. Credit card
- d. Ingenico

Guidance: level 1

:: Google services ::

_____ is a word processor included as part of a free, web-based software office suite offered by Google within its Google Drive service. This service also includes Google Sheets and Google Slides, a spreadsheet and presentation program respectively. _____ is available as a web application, mobile app for Android, iOS, Windows, BlackBerry, and as a desktop application on Google's ChromeOS. The app is compatible with Microsoft Office file formats.The application allows users to create and edit files online while collaborating with other users in real-time. Edits are tracked by user with a revision history presenting changes. An editor's position is highlighted with an editor-specific color and cursor. A permissions system regulates what users can do. Updates have introduced features using machine learning, including "Explore", offering search results based on the contents of a document, and "Action items", allowing users to assign tasks to other users.

Exam Probability: **High**

5. *Answer choices:*

(see index for correct answer)

- a. Google Docs
- b. Google Sites
- c. Google Developers
- d. Google Compute Engine

Guidance: level 1

:: Information systems ::

_____ s are information systems that are developed in response to corporate business initiative. They are intended to give competitive advantage to the organization. They may deliver a product or service that is at a lower cost, that is differentiated, that focuses on a particular market segment, or is innovative.

Exam Probability: **High**

6. *Answer choices:*

(see index for correct answer)

- a. Semantic broker
- b. UK Academy for Information Systems
- c. Information silo
- d. CreditorWatch

Guidance: level 1

:: Economic globalization ::

_____ is an agreement in which one company hires another company to be responsible for a planned or existing activity that is or could be done internally, and sometimes involves transferring employees and assets from one firm to another.

Exam Probability: **High**

7. *Answer choices:*

(see index for correct answer)

- a. Outsourcing
- b. global financial

Guidance: level 1

:: Internet governance ::

A _____ is one of the domains at the highest level in the hierarchical Domain Name System of the Internet. The _____ names are installed in the root zone of the name space. For all domains in lower levels, it is the last part of the domain name, that is, the last label of a fully qualified domain name. For example, in the domain name www.example.com, the _____ is com. Responsibility for management of most _____ s is delegated to specific organizations by the Internet Corporation for Assigned Names and Numbers , which operates the Internet Assigned Numbers Authority , and is in charge of maintaining the DNS root zone.

Exam Probability: **High**

8. *Answer choices:*

(see index for correct answer)

- a. Foretec Seminars
- b. Uniform Domain-Name Dispute-Resolution Policy
- c. Top-level domain
- d. Pathetic dot theory

Guidance: level 1

:: Reputation management ::

A _____ is an astronomical object consisting of a luminous spheroid of plasma held together by its own gravity. The nearest _____ to Earth is the Sun. Many other _____ s are visible to the naked eye from Earth during the night, appearing as a multitude of fixed luminous points in the sky due to their immense distance from Earth. Historically, the most prominent _____ s were grouped into constellations and asterisms, the brightest of which gained proper names. Astronomers have assembled _____ catalogues that identify the known _____ s and provide standardized stellar designations. However, most of the estimated 300 sextillion _____ s in the Universe are invisible to the naked eye from Earth, including all _____ s outside our galaxy, the Milky Way.

Exam Probability: **High**

9. *Answer choices:*

(see index for correct answer)

- a. Conversocial
- b. Star
- c. Hilltop algorithm
- d. Reputation system

Guidance: level 1

:: ::

_____ LLC is an American multinational technology company that specializes in Internet-related services and products, which include online advertising technologies, search engine, cloud computing, software, and hardware. It is considered one of the Big Four technology companies, alongside Amazon, Apple and Facebook.

Exam Probability: **Low**

10. *Answer choices:*

(see index for correct answer)

- a. empathy
- b. Google
- c. corporate values
- d. open system

Guidance: level 1

:: Behavioral and social facets of systemic risk ::

_____ is the difficulty in understanding an issue and effectively making decisions when one has too much information about that issue. Generally, the term is associated with the excessive quantity of daily information. _____ most likely originated from information theory, which are studies in the storage, preservation, communication, compression, and extraction of information. The term, _____ , was first used in Bertram Gross' 1964 book, The Managing of Organizations, and it was further popularized by Alvin Toffler in his bestselling 1970 book Future Shock. Speier et al. stated.

Exam Probability: **Low**

11. *Answer choices:*

(see index for correct answer)

- a. Moral panic
- b. virtuous circle
- c. Information overload
- d. User error

Guidance: level 1

:: Virtual reality ::

_____ is an experience taking place within simulated and immersive environments that can be similar to or completely different from the real world. Applications of _____ can include entertainment and educational purposes. Other, distinct types of VR style technology include augmented reality and mixed reality.

Exam Probability: **High**

12. *Answer choices:*

(see index for correct answer)

- a. NearGlobal
- b. Smeet
- c. Space Shuttle Mission 2007
- d. Circa 1948

Guidance: level 1

:: Advertising techniques ::

The _____ is a story from the Trojan War about the subterfuge that the Greeks used to enter the independent city of Troy and win the war. In the canonical version, after a fruitless 10-year siege, the Greeks constructed a huge wooden horse, and hid a select force of men inside including Odysseus. The Greeks pretended to sail away, and the Trojans pulled the horse into their city as a victory trophy. That night the Greek force crept out of the horse and opened the gates for the rest of the Greek army, which had sailed back under cover of night. The Greeks entered and destroyed the city of Troy, ending the war.

Exam Probability: **High**

13. *Answer choices:*

(see index for correct answer)

- a. Location-based advertising
- b. Roll-in
- c. Soft sell
- d. Testimonial

Guidance: level 1

:: Internet privacy ::

An _____ is a private network accessible only to an organization's staff. Often, a wide range of information and services are available on an organization's internal _____ that are unavailable to the public, unlike the Internet. A company-wide _____ can constitute an important focal point of internal communication and collaboration, and provide a single starting point to access internal and external resources. In its simplest form, an _____ is established with the technologies for local area networks and wide area networks . Many modern _____ s have search engines, user profiles, blogs, mobile apps with notifications, and events planning within their infrastructure.

Exam Probability: **Low**

14. *Answer choices:*

(see index for correct answer)

- a. Do Not Track
- b. I-broker
- c. Geolocation
- d. Intranet

Guidance: level 1

:: Information systems ::

A _____ manages the creation and modification of digital content. It typically supports multiple users in a collaborative environment.

Exam Probability: **High**

15. *Answer choices:*

(see index for correct answer)

- a. Accounting information system
- b. Electronic Case Filing System
- c. Hybrid positioning system
- d. Personal knowledge management

Guidance: level 1

:: Data analysis ::

_____ is a process of inspecting, cleansing, transforming, and modeling data with the goal of discovering useful information, informing conclusions, and supporting decision-making. _____ has multiple facets and approaches, encompassing diverse techniques under a variety of names, and is used in different business, science, and social science domains. In today's business world, _____ plays a role in making decisions more scientific and helping businesses operate more effectively.

Exam Probability: **High**

16. *Answer choices:*

(see index for correct answer)

- a. Principal geodesic analysis
- b. Data analysis
- c. LISREL
- d. Ratio estimator

Guidance: level 1

:: Cryptography ::

In cryptography, _____ is the process of encoding a message or information in such a way that only authorized parties can access it and those who are not authorized cannot. _____ does not itself prevent interference, but denies the intelligible content to a would-be interceptor. In an _____ scheme, the intended information or message, referred to as plaintext, is encrypted using an _____ algorithm – a cipher – generating ciphertext that can be read only if decrypted. For technical reasons, an _____ scheme usually uses a pseudo-random _____ key generated by an algorithm. It is in principle possible to decrypt the message without possessing the key, but, for a well-designed _____ scheme, considerable computational resources and skills are required. An authorized recipient can easily decrypt the message with the key provided by the originator to recipients but not to unauthorized users.

Exam Probability: **Medium**

17. *Answer choices:*

(see index for correct answer)

- a. Electronic Signature
- b. cryptosystem
- c. plaintext
- d. backdoor

Guidance: level 1

:: Policy ::

A _____ is a statement or a legal document that discloses some or all of the ways a party gathers, uses, discloses, and manages a customer or client's data. It fulfills a legal requirement to protect a customer or client's privacy. Personal information can be anything that can be used to identify an individual, not limited to the person's name, address, date of birth, marital status, contact information, ID issue, and expiry date, financial records, credit information, medical history, where one travels, and intentions to acquire goods and services. In the case of a business it is often a statement that declares a party's policy on how it collects, stores, and releases personal information it collects. It informs the client what specific information is collected, and whether it is kept confidential, shared with partners, or sold to other firms or enterprises. Privacy policies typically represent a broader, more generalized treatment, as opposed to data use statements, which tend to be more detailed and specific.

Exam Probability: **High**

18. *Answer choices:*

(see index for correct answer)

- a. Institute of International and European Affairs
- b. Security policy
- c. Privacy policy
- d. Policy transfer

Guidance: level 1

:: Market structure and pricing ::

_____ is a term denoting that a product includes permission to use its source code, design documents, or content. It most commonly refers to the open-source model, in which open-source software or other products are released under an open-source license as part of the open-source-software movement. Use of the term originated with software, but has expanded beyond the software sector to cover other open content and forms of open collaboration.

Exam Probability: **High**

19. *Answer choices:*

(see index for correct answer)

- a. Installed base
- b. Open-source economics
- c. Open source
- d. Market structure

Guidance: level 1

:: Identity management ::

_____ is the ability of an individual or group to seclude themselves, or information about themselves, and thereby express themselves selectively. The boundaries and content of what is considered private differ among cultures and individuals, but share common themes. When something is private to a person, it usually means that something is inherently special or sensitive to them. The domain of _____ partially overlaps with security , which can include the concepts of appropriate use, as well as protection of information. _____ may also take the form of bodily integrity.

Exam Probability: **Medium**

20. *Answer choices:*

(see index for correct answer)

- a. Group
- b. Federated Naming Service
- c. Trombinoscope
- d. Privacy

Guidance: level 1

:: Business process ::

A _____ or business method is a collection of related, structured activities or tasks by people or equipment which in a specific sequence produce a service or product for a particular customer or customers. _____ es occur at all organizational levels and may or may not be visible to the customers. A _____ may often be visualized as a flowchart of a sequence of activities with interleaving decision points or as a process matrix of a sequence of activities with relevance rules based on data in the process. The benefits of using _____ es include improved customer satisfaction and improved agility for reacting to rapid market change. Process-oriented organizations break down the barriers of structural departments and try to avoid functional silos.

Exam Probability: **High**

21. *Answer choices:*

(see index for correct answer)

- a. ProcessEdge
- b. Direct store delivery
- c. Business process
- d. Bonita BPM

Guidance: level 1

:: Production economics ::

_____ is a way of producing goods and services that relies on self-organizing communities of individuals. In such communities, the labor of a large number of people is coordinated towards a shared outcome.

Exam Probability: **Medium**

22. *Answer choices:*
(see index for correct answer)

- a. Productivity Alpha
- b. Multifactor productivity
- c. Marginal cost
- d. Robinson Crusoe economy

Guidance: level 1

:: Financial markets ::

The _____ business model is a business model in which a customer must pay a recurring price at regular intervals for access to a product or service. The model was pioneered by publishers of books and periodicals in the 17th century, and is now used by many businesses and websites.

Exam Probability: **Low**

23. *Answer choices:*
(see index for correct answer)

- a. Derivatives market
- b. Spread trade
- c. Third market
- d. Latino Community Foundation

Guidance: level 1

:: Fraud ::

_____ is the deliberate use of someone else's identity, usually as a method to gain a financial advantage or obtain credit and other benefits in the other person's name, and perhaps to the other person's disadvantage or loss. The person whose identity has been assumed may suffer adverse consequences, especially if they are held responsible for the perpetrator's actions. _____ occurs when someone uses another's personally identifying information, like their name, identifying number, or credit card number, without their permission, to commit fraud or other crimes. The term _____ was coined in 1964. Since that time, the definition of _____ has been statutorily prescribed throughout both the U.K. and the United States as the theft of personally identifying information, generally including a person's name, date of birth, social security number, driver's license number, bank account or credit card numbers, PIN numbers, electronic signatures, fingerprints, passwords, or any other information that can be used to access a person's financial resources.

Exam Probability: **Low**

24. *Answer choices:*

(see index for correct answer)

- a. Corporate scandal
- b. Accreditation mill
- c. Identity theft
- d. Statute of frauds

Guidance: level 1

:: Telecommunications engineering ::

A _____ is a computer processor that incorporates the functions of a central processing unit on a single integrated circuit, or at most a few integrated circuits. The _____ is a multipurpose, clock driven, register based, digital integrated circuit that accepts binary data as input, processes it according to instructions stored in its memory and provides results as output. _____ s contain both combinational logic and sequential digital logic. _____ s operate on numbers and symbols represented in the binary number system.

Exam Probability: **Medium**

25. *Answer choices:*

(see index for correct answer)

- a. network architecture
- b. Computer network

Guidance: level 1

:: Transaction processing ::

In _____, information systems typically facilitate and manage transaction-oriented applications.

Exam Probability: **Low**

26. *Answer choices:*

(see index for correct answer)

- a. Atomic commit
- b. Change vector
- c. Westi
- d. Memory semantics

Guidance: level 1

:: Outsourcing ::

A service-level agreement is a commitment between a service provider and a client. Particular aspects of the service – quality, availability, responsibilities – are agreed between the service provider and the service user. The most common component of SLA is that the services should be provided to the customer as agreed upon in the contract. As an example, Internet service providers and telcos will commonly include _____ s within the terms of their contracts with customers to define the level of service being sold in plain language terms. In this case the SLA will typically have a technical definition in mean time between failures , mean time to repair or mean time to recovery ; identifying which party is responsible for reporting faults or paying fees; responsibility for various data rates; throughput; jitter; or similar measurable details.

Exam Probability: **Medium**

27. *Answer choices:*

(see index for correct answer)

- a. Service-level agreement

- b. Media Process Outsourcing
- c. Affiliated Computer Services
- d. Print and mail outsourcing

Guidance: level 1

:: Sound recording ::

_____ is a medium for magnetic recording, made of a thin, magnetizable coating on a long, narrow strip of plastic film. It was developed in Germany in 1928, based on magnetic wire recording. Devices that record and play back audio and video using _____ are tape recorders and video tape recorders respectively. A device that stores computer data on _____ is known as a tape drive.

Exam Probability: **Low**

28. *Answer choices:*

(see index for correct answer)

- a. British Library Sounds
- b. Laugh track
- c. Low fidelity
- d. Production sound mixer

Guidance: level 1

:: ::

A _____ is a structure / access pattern specific to data warehouse environments, used to retrieve client-facing data. The _____ is a subset of the data warehouse and is usually oriented to a specific business line or team. Whereas data warehouses have an enterprise-wide depth, the information in _____ s pertains to a single department. In some deployments, each department or business unit is considered the owner of its _____ including all the hardware, software and data. This enables each department to isolate the use, manipulation and development of their data. In other deployments where conformed dimensions are used, this business unit ownership will not hold true for shared dimensions like customer, product, etc.

Exam Probability: **High**

29. *Answer choices:*

(see index for correct answer)

- a. hierarchical perspective
- b. levels of analysis
- c. open system
- d. Data mart

Guidance: level 1

:: Data analysis ::

_____ , also referred to as text data mining, roughly equivalent to text analytics, is the process of deriving high-quality information from text. High-quality information is typically derived through the devising of patterns and trends through means such as statistical pattern learning. _____ usually involves the process of structuring the input text , deriving patterns within the structured data, and finally evaluation and interpretation of the output. `High quality' in _____ usually refers to some combination of relevance, novelty, and interest. Typical _____ tasks include text categorization, text clustering, concept/entity extraction, production of granular taxonomies, sentiment analysis, document summarization, and entity relation modeling .

Exam Probability: **High**

30. *Answer choices:*

(see index for correct answer)

- a. Artificial precision
- b. Text mining
- c. Multiscale geometric analysis
- d. Exploratory data analysis

Guidance: level 1

:: Big data ::

_____ refers to the skills, technologies, practices for continuous iterative exploration and investigation of past business performance to gain insight and drive business planning. _____ focuses on developing new insights and understanding of business performance based on data and statistical methods. In contrast, business intelligence traditionally focuses on using a consistent set of metrics to both measure past performance and guide business planning, which is also based on data and statistical methods.

Exam Probability: **Medium**

31. *Answer choices:*

(see index for correct answer)

- a. Social IT
- b. Sumo Logic
- c. CVidya
- d. Hack/reduce

Guidance: level 1

:: Network performance ::

_____ is a distributed computing paradigm which brings computer data storage closer to the location where it is needed. Computation is largely or completely performed on distributed device nodes. _____ pushes applications, data and computing power away from centralized points to locations closer to the user. The target of _____ is any application or general functionality needing to be closer to the source of the action where distributed systems technology interacts with the physical world. _____ does not need contact with any centralized cloud, although it may interact with one. In contrast to cloud computing, _____ refers to decentralized data processing at the edge of the network.

Exam Probability: **High**

32. *Answer choices:*

(see index for correct answer)

- a. Rendezvous delay
- b. Low-latency queuing
- c. Performance tuning
- d. Cross Layer Interaction and Service Mapping

Guidance: level 1

:: Data management ::

" _____ " is a field that treats ways to analyze, systematically extract information from, or otherwise deal with data sets that are too large or complex to be dealt with by traditional data-processing application software. Data with many cases offer greater statistical power, while data with higher complexity may lead to a higher false discovery rate. _____ challenges include capturing data, data storage, data analysis, search, sharing, transfer, visualization, querying, updating, information privacy and data source. _____ was originally associated with three key concepts: volume, variety, and velocity. Other concepts later attributed with _____ are veracity and value.

Exam Probability: **Medium**

33. *Answer choices:*

(see index for correct answer)

- a. Head/tail Breaks
- b. Data archive
- c. Transaction data
- d. Big data

Guidance: level 1

:: Business process ::

Business process re-engineering is a business management strategy, originally pioneered in the early 1990s, focusing on the analysis and design of workflows and business processes within an organization. BPR aimed to help organizations fundamentally rethink how they do their work in order to improve customer service, cut operational costs, and become world-class competitors.

Exam Probability: **Low**

34. *Answer choices:*

(see index for correct answer)

- a. PNMsoft
- b. Business Motivation Model
- c. Business process reengineering
- d. Captive service

Guidance: level 1

:: ::

The _____ , commonly known as the Web, is an information system where documents and other web resources are identified by Uniform Resource Locators , which may be interlinked by hypertext, and are accessible over the Internet. The resources of the WWW may be accessed by users by a software application called a web browser.

Exam Probability: **Medium**

35. *Answer choices:*

(see index for correct answer)

- a. co-culture
- b. levels of analysis
- c. World Wide Web
- d. similarity-attraction theory

Guidance: level 1

:: Information systems ::

_____ is a process used in the life cycle area of the dynamic systems development method to collect business requirements while developing new information systems for a company. "The JAD process also includes approaches for enhancing user participation, expediting development, and improving the quality of specifications." It consists of a workshop where "knowledge workers and IT specialists meet, sometimes for several days, to define and review the business requirements for the system." The attendees include high level management officials who will ensure the product provides the needed reports and information at the end. This acts as "a management process which allows Corporate Information Services departments to work more effectively with users in a shorter time frame".

Exam Probability: **High**

36. *Answer choices:*

(see index for correct answer)

- a. Joint application design
- b. FAO Country Profiles
- c. Expert system
- d. G-Book

Guidance: level 1

:: Information technology management ::

The term _____ is used to refer to periods when a system is unavailable. _____ or outage duration refers to a period of time that a system fails to provide or perform its primary function. Reliability, availability, recovery, and unavailability are related concepts. The unavailability is the proportion of a time-span that a system is unavailable or offline. This is usually a result of the system failing to function because of an unplanned event, or because of routine maintenance.

Exam Probability: **Low**

37. *Answer choices:*

(see index for correct answer)

- a. Mung
- b. Knowledge management software
- c. Digital Fuel
- d. Downtime

Guidance: level 1

:: Human–computer interaction ::

_____ is a database query language for relational databases. It was devised by Moshé M. Zloof at IBM Research during the mid-1970s, in parallel to the development of SQL. It is the first graphical query language, using visual tables where the user would enter commands, example elements and conditions. Many graphical front-ends for databases use the ideas from QBE today. Originally limited only for the purpose of retrieving data, QBE was later extended to allow other operations, such as inserts, deletes and updates, as well as creation of temporary tables.

Exam Probability: **Medium**

38. *Answer choices:*

(see index for correct answer)

- a. Martin M. Wattenberg
- b. Livescribe
- c. Interaction Design Foundation
- d. Retrospective think aloud

Guidance: level 1

:: Computer security standards ::

The _____ for Information Technology Security Evaluation is an international standard for computer security certification. It is currently in version 3.1 revision 5.

Exam Probability: **Low**

39. *Answer choices:*

(see index for correct answer)

- a. AFSSI-5020
- b. IEC 60870-6
- c. S/MIME
- d. ISO 27799

Guidance: level 1

:: ::

A _____, sometimes called a passcode, is a memorized secret used to confirm the identity of a user. Using the terminology of the NIST Digital Identity Guidelines, the secret is memorized by a party called the claimant while the party verifying the identity of the claimant is called the verifier. When the claimant successfully demonstrates knowledge of the _____ to the verifier through an established authentication protocol, the verifier is able to infer the claimant's identity.

Exam Probability: **Low**

40. Answer choices:

(see index for correct answer)

- a. Password
- b. co-culture
- c. imperative
- d. deep-level diversity

Guidance: level 1

:: Industrial design ::

Across the many fields concerned with _____, including information science, computer science, human-computer interaction, communication, and industrial design, there is little agreement over the meaning of the term "_____", although all are related to interaction with computers and other machines with a user interface.

Exam Probability: **Low**

41. Answer choices:

(see index for correct answer)

- a. Pilot experiment
- b. Design Council
- c. World Design Capital
- d. Interactivity

Guidance: level 1

:: Help desk ::

Data center management is the collection of tasks performed by those responsible for managing ongoing operation of a data center This includes Business service management and planning for the future.

Exam Probability: **Medium**

42. *Answer choices:*

(see index for correct answer)

- a. SysAid Technologies
- b. KnowledgeBase Manager Pro
- c. HEAT
- d. AetherPal

Guidance: level 1

:: E-commerce ::

_____ , and its now-deprecated predecessor, Secure Sockets Layer, are cryptographic protocols designed to provide communications security over a computer network. Several versions of the protocols find widespread use in applications such as web browsing, email, instant messaging, and voice over IP . Websites can use TLS to secure all communications between their servers and web browsers.

Exam Probability: **Medium**

43. *Answer choices:*

(see index for correct answer)

- a. Certificate-based encryption
- b. Social commerce
- c. GS1 Sweden
- d. Transport Layer Security

Guidance: level 1

:: E-commerce ::

_____ is the activity of buying or selling of products on online services or over the Internet. Electronic commerce draws on technologies such as mobile commerce, electronic funds transfer, supply chain management, Internet marketing, online transaction processing, electronic data interchange , inventory management systems, and automated data collection systems.

Exam Probability: **High**

44. *Answer choices:*

(see index for correct answer)

- a. ORCA
- b. TRADACOMS
- c. Seja online
- d. Government-to-employees

Guidance: level 1

:: Information technology ::

_____ is the reorientation of product and service designs to focus on the end user as an individual consumer, in contrast with an earlier era of only organization-oriented offerings . Technologies whose first commercialization was at the inter-organization level thus have potential for later _____ . The emergence of the individual consumer as the primary driver of product and service design is most commonly associated with the IT industry, as large business and government organizations dominated the early decades of computer usage and development. Thus the microcomputer revolution, in which electronic computing moved from exclusively enterprise and government use to include personal computing, is a cardinal example of _____ . But many technology-based products, such as calculators and mobile phones, have also had their origins in business markets, and only over time did they become dominated by high-volume consumer usage, as these products commoditized and prices fell. An example of enterprise software that became consumer software is optical character recognition software, which originated with banks and postal systems but eventually became personal productivity software.

Exam Probability: **Medium**

45. Answer choices:

(see index for correct answer)

- a. Zimperium
- b. E-Governance
- c. Software-defined data center
- d. Consumerization

Guidance: level 1

:: ::

Within the Internet, _____ s are formed by the rules and procedures of the _____ System . Any name registered in the DNS is a _____ . _____ s are used in various networking contexts and for application-specific naming and addressing purposes. In general, a _____ represents an Internet Protocol resource, such as a personal computer used to access the Internet, a server computer hosting a web site, or the web site itself or any other service communicated via the Internet. In 2017, 330.6 million _____ s had been registered.

Exam Probability: **Low**

46. Answer choices:

(see index for correct answer)

- a. Domain name
- b. corporate values

- c. co-culture
- d. surface-level diversity

Guidance: level 1

:: Information technology audit ::

_____ is the act of using a computer to take or alter electronic data, or to gain unlawful use of a computer or system. In the United States, _____ is specifically proscribed by the _____ and Abuse Act, which criminalizes computer-related acts under federal jurisdiction. Types of _____ include.

Exam Probability: **Medium**

47. *Answer choices:*

(see index for correct answer)

- a. NCC Group
- b. Information security audit
- c. SekChek Classic
- d. Computer fraud

Guidance: level 1

:: Information science ::

_____ is the resolution of uncertainty; it is that which answers the question of "what an entity is" and thus defines both its essence and nature of its characteristics. _____ relates to both data and knowledge, as data is meaningful _____ representing values attributed to parameters, and knowledge signifies understanding of a concept. _____ is uncoupled from an observer, which is an entity that can access _____ and thus discern what it specifies; _____ exists beyond an event horizon for example. In the case of knowledge, the _____ itself requires a cognitive observer to be obtained.

Exam Probability: **Medium**

48. *Answer choices:*

(see index for correct answer)

- a. Scientific communication
- b. Informatics Corporation of America
- c. Semantic Sensor Web
- d. Information

Guidance: level 1

:: Telecommunication theory ::

In reliability theory and reliability engineering, the term _____ has the following meanings.

Exam Probability: **Low**

49. Answer choices:

(see index for correct answer)

- a. Communication physics
- b. Availability
- c. Harmonic mixer
- d. Filter

Guidance: level 1

:: Information technology organisations ::

The Internet Corporation for Assigned Names and Numbers is a nonprofit organization responsible for coordinating the maintenance and procedures of several databases related to the namespaces and numerical spaces of the Internet, ensuring the network's stable and secure operation. _____ performs the actual technical maintenance work of the Central Internet Address pools and DNS root zone registries pursuant to the Internet Assigned Numbers Authority function contract. The contract regarding the IANA stewardship functions between _____ and the National Telecommunications and Information Administration of the United States Department of Commerce ended on October 1, 2016, formally transitioning the functions to the global multistakeholder community.

Exam Probability: **Medium**

50. Answer choices:

(see index for correct answer)

- a. Australian Federation Against Copyright Theft
- b. UNIGIS
- c. Pangea.org
- d. NASSCOM

Guidance: level 1

:: Information systems ::

_____ are formal, sociotechnical, organizational systems designed to collect, process, store, and distribute information. In a sociotechnical perspective, _____ are composed by four components: task, people, structure , and technology.

Exam Probability: **High**

51. *Answer choices:*

(see index for correct answer)

- a. Information systems
- b. Information Systems Security Association
- c. Vehicle Information and Communication System
- d. Process development execution system

Guidance: level 1

:: Information technology management ::

_____ s or pop-ups are forms of online advertising on the World Wide Web. A pop-up is a graphical user interface display area, usually a small window, that suddenly appears in the foreground of the visual interface. The pop-up window containing an advertisement is usually generated by JavaScript that uses cross-site scripting, sometimes with a secondary payload that uses Adobe Flash. They can also be generated by other vulnerabilities/security holes in browser security.

Exam Probability: **Low**

52. *Answer choices:*

(see index for correct answer)

- a. SFIAPlus
- b. Infrastructure optimization
- c. Software asset management
- d. Pop-up ad

Guidance: level 1

:: Data management ::

_____ is a data management concept concerning the capability that enables an organization to ensure that high data quality exists throughout the complete lifecycle of the data. The key focus areas of _____ include availability, usability, consistency, data integrity and data security and includes establishing processes to ensure effective data management throughout the enterprise such as accountability for the adverse effects of poor data quality and ensuring that the data which an enterprise has can be used by the entire organization.

Exam Probability: **Low**

53. *Answer choices:*

(see index for correct answer)

- a. Data governance
- b. Performance intelligence
- c. RSD
- d. Long-running transaction

Guidance: level 1

:: Virtual economies ::

_____ Inc. is an American social game developer running social video game services founded in April 2007 and headquartered in San Francisco, California, United States. The company primarily focuses on mobile and social networking platforms. _____ states its mission as "connecting the world through games."

Exam Probability: **Low**

54. *Answer choices:*

(see index for correct answer)

- a. Nordeus
- b. Empire Avenue
- c. Zynga
- d. There

Guidance: level 1

:: Fault tolerance ::

_____ is the property that enables a system to continue operating properly in the event of the failure of some of its components. If its operating quality decreases at all, the decrease is proportional to the severity of the failure, as compared to a naively designed system, in which even a small failure can cause total breakdown. _____ is particularly sought after in high-availability or life-critical systems. The ability of maintaining functionality when portions of a system break down is referred to as graceful degradation.

Exam Probability: **High**

55. *Answer choices:*

(see index for correct answer)

- a. Repetition code
- b. Random fault
- c. Fault tolerance
- d. Fly-by-wire

Guidance: level 1

:: Commerce websites ::

_____ is an American classified advertisements website with sections devoted to jobs, housing, for sale, items wanted, services, community service, gigs, résumés, and discussion forums.

Exam Probability: **High**

56. *Answer choices:*

(see index for correct answer)

- a. MobiCart
- b. EatStreet
- c. Optoutprescreen.com
- d. PopSugar

Guidance: level 1

:: Computer data ::

In computer science, _____ is the ability to access an arbitrary element of a sequence in equal time or any datum from a population of addressable elements roughly as easily and efficiently as any other, no matter how many elements may be in the set. It is typically contrasted to sequential access.

Exam Probability: **Medium**

57. *Answer choices:*

(see index for correct answer)

- a. Random access
- b. Leading zero
- c. Lilian date
- d. Persistent data

Guidance: level 1

:: ::

A _____ is a control panel usually located directly ahead of a vehicle's driver, displaying instrumentation and controls for the vehicle's operation.

Exam Probability: **High**

58. *Answer choices:*

(see index for correct answer)

- a. levels of analysis
- b. co-culture
- c. Character
- d. Dashboard

Guidance: level 1

:: ::

The _____ is the global system of interconnected computer networks that use the _____ protocol suite to link devices worldwide. It is a network of networks that consists of private, public, academic, business, and government networks of local to global scope, linked by a broad array of electronic, wireless, and optical networking technologies. The _____ carries a vast range of information resources and services, such as the inter-linked hypertext documents and applications of the World Wide Web , electronic mail, telephony, and file sharing.

Exam Probability: **Medium**

59. *Answer choices:*

(see index for correct answer)

- a. levels of analysis
- b. open system
- c. Sarbanes-Oxley act of 2002

- d. hierarchical

Guidance: level 1

Marketing

Marketing is the study and management of exchange relationships. Marketing is the business process of creating relationships with and satisfying customers. With its focus on the customer, marketing is one of the premier components of business management.

Marketing is defined by the American Marketing Association as "the activity, set of institutions, and processes for creating, communicating, delivering, and exchanging offerings that have value for customers, clients, partners, and society at large."

_____ Company, commonly referred to as _____, is an American multinational corporation headquartered in Detroit that designs, manufactures, markets, and distributes vehicles and vehicle parts, and sells financial services, with global headquarters in Detroit's Renaissance Center. It was originally founded by William C. Durant on September 16, 1908 as a holding company. The company is the largest American automobile manufacturer, and one of the world's largest. As of 2018, _____ is ranked #10 on the Fortune 500 rankings of the largest United States corporations by total revenue.

Exam Probability: **High**

1. *Answer choices:*

(see index for correct answer)

- a. surface-level diversity
- b. information systems assessment
- c. similarity-attraction theory
- d. interpersonal communication

Guidance: level 1

:: Sales ::

_____ is a business discipline which is focused on the practical application of sales techniques and the management of a firm's sales operations. It is an important business function as net sales through the sale of products and services and resulting profit drive most commercial business. These are also typically the goals and performance indicators of _____.

Exam Probability: **Low**

2. *Answer choices:*

(see index for correct answer)

- a. Souvenir
- b. Lead retrieval
- c. Sales management
- d. Leaseback

Guidance: level 1

:: ::

In regulatory jurisdictions that provide for it, _____ is a group of laws and organizations designed to ensure the rights of consumers as well as fair trade, competition and accurate information in the marketplace. The laws are designed to prevent the businesses that engage in fraud or specified unfair practices from gaining an advantage over competitors. They may also provides additional protection for those most vulnerable in society. _____ laws are a form of government regulation that aim to protect the rights of consumers. For example, a government may require businesses to disclose detailed information about products—particularly in areas where safety or public health is an issue, such as food.

Exam Probability: **High**

3. *Answer choices:*

(see index for correct answer)

- a. empathy
- b. levels of analysis
- c. hierarchical perspective
- d. cultural

Guidance: level 1

:: ::

A _____ is an organized collection of data, generally stored and accessed electronically from a computer system. Where _____ s are more complex they are often developed using formal design and modeling techniques.

Exam Probability: **Low**

4. *Answer choices:*

(see index for correct answer)

- a. Database
- b. interpersonal communication
- c. Character
- d. process perspective

Guidance: level 1

:: Information technology ::

_____ is the use of computers to store, retrieve, transmit, and manipulate data, or information, often in the context of a business or other enterprise. IT is considered to be a subset of information and communications technology. An _____ system is generally an information system, a communications system or, more specifically speaking, a computer system – including all hardware, software and peripheral equipment – operated by a limited group of users.

Exam Probability: **Medium**

5. *Answer choices:*

(see index for correct answer)

- a. Information and communication technologies in education
- b. Legal aspects of computing
- c. Collabera
- d. Information and communications technology

Guidance: level 1

:: Market research ::

_____ , an acronym for Information through Disguised Experimentation is an annual market research fair conducted by the students of IIM-Lucknow. Students create games and use various other simulated environments to capture consumers' subconscious thoughts. This innovative method of market research removes the sensitization effect that might bias peoples answers to questions. This ensures that the most truthful answers are captured to research questions. The games are designed in such a way that the observers can elicit all the required information just by observing and noting down the behaviour and the responses of the participants.

Exam Probability: **Medium**

6. *Answer choices:*

(see index for correct answer)

- a. Preference regression
- b. Coolhunting
- c. Virtual store research
- d. Innovation game

Guidance: level 1

:: Brand management ::

_____ is defined as positive feelings towards a brand and dedication to purchase the same product or service repeatedly now and in the future from the same brand, regardless of a competitor's actions or changes in the environment. It can also be demonstrated with other behaviors such as positive word-of-mouth advocacy. _____ is where an individual buys products from the same manufacturer repeatedly rather than from other suppliers. Businesses whose financial and ethical values, for example ESG responsibilities, rest in large part on their _____ are said to use the loyalty business model.

Exam Probability: **Low**

7. *Answer choices:*
(see index for correct answer)

- a. Brand loyalty
- b. Store brand
- c. Umbrella brand
- d. Entertainment Rights

Guidance: level 1

:: Business models ::

A _____ is "an autonomous association of persons united voluntarily to meet their common economic, social, and cultural needs and aspirations through a jointly-owned and democratically-controlled enterprise". _____ s may include.

Exam Probability: **High**

8. *Answer choices:*

(see index for correct answer)

- a. Sustainable business
- b. Cooperative
- c. Component business model
- d. The Community Company

Guidance: level 1

:: Goods ::

In most contexts, the concept of _____ denotes the conduct that should be preferred when posed with a choice between possible actions. _____ is generally considered to be the opposite of evil, and is of interest in the study of morality, ethics, religion and philosophy. The specific meaning and etymology of the term and its associated translations among ancient and contemporary languages show substantial variation in its inflection and meaning depending on circumstances of place, history, religious, or philosophical context.

Exam Probability: **High**

9. *Answer choices:*

(see index for correct answer)

- a. Superior good
- b. Speciality goods
- c. Intermediate good
- d. Good

Guidance: level 1

:: Supply chain management ::

_____ is the removal of intermediaries in economics from a supply chain, or cutting out the middlemen in connection with a transaction or a series of transactions. Instead of going through traditional distribution channels, which had some type of intermediary , companies may now deal with customers directly, for example via the Internet. Hence, the use of factory direct and direct from the factory to mean the same thing.

Exam Probability: **Low**

10. *Answer choices:*

(see index for correct answer)

- a. Delivery Performance
- b. Pharmacode
- c. Disintermediation
- d. Chain of responsibility

Guidance: level 1

:: Health promotion ::

_____ is a form of advertising, it has been a large industry for some time now. Originally with newspapers and billboards, but now we have advanced to huge LCD screens and online advertisement on social medias and websites. The most common use of _____ in today's society is through social media.. It has the primary goal of achieving "social good". Traditional commercial marketing aims are primarily financial, though they can have positive social affects as well. In the context of public health, _____ would promote general health, raise awareness and induce changes in behaviour. To see _____ as only the use of standard commercial marketing practices to achieve non-commercial goals is an oversimplified view.

Exam Probability: **High**

11. *Answer choices:*

(see index for correct answer)

- a. American Frontiers: A Public Lands Journey
- b. Health promotion
- c. Social marketing
- d. Lalonde report

Guidance: level 1

:: Commerce ::

_____ relates to "the exchange of goods and services, especially on a large scale". It includes legal, economic, political, social, cultural and technological systems that operate in a country or in international trade.

Exam Probability: **High**

12. *Answer choices:*

(see index for correct answer)

- a. Commerce
- b. Fixed price
- c. Going concern
- d. Sell-side analyst

Guidance: level 1

:: ::

Employment is a relationship between two parties, usually based on a contract where work is paid for, where one party, which may be a corporation, for profit, not-for-profit organization, co-operative or other entity is the employer and the other is the employee. Employees work in return for payment, which may be in the form of an hourly wage, by piecework or an annual salary, depending on the type of work an employee does or which sector she or he is working in. Employees in some fields or sectors may receive gratuities, bonus payment or stock options. In some types of employment, employees may receive benefits in addition to payment. Benefits can include health insurance, housing, disability insurance or use of a gym. Employment is typically governed by employment laws, regulations or legal contracts.

Exam Probability: **High**

13. *Answer choices:*

(see index for correct answer)

- a. information systems assessment
- b. levels of analysis
- c. Personnel
- d. cultural

Guidance: level 1

:: National accounts ::

_____ is a monetary measure of the market value of all the final goods and services produced in a period of time, often annually. GDP per capita does not, however, reflect differences in the cost of living and the inflation rates of the countries; therefore using a basis of GDP per capita at purchasing power parity is arguably more useful when comparing differences in living standards between nations.

Exam Probability: **Low**

14. *Answer choices:*

(see index for correct answer)

- a. capital formation
- b. Fixed capital

- c. Gross domestic product

Guidance: level 1

:: ::

In financial markets, a share is a unit used as mutual funds, limited partnerships, and real estate investment trusts. The owner of _____ in the corporation/company is a shareholder of the corporation. A share is an indivisible unit of capital, expressing the ownership relationship between the company and the shareholder. The denominated value of a share is its face value, and the total of the face value of issued _____ represent the capital of a company, which may not reflect the market value of those _____.

Exam Probability: **Medium**

15. *Answer choices:*
(see index for correct answer)

- a. co-culture
- b. levels of analysis
- c. empathy
- d. Shares

Guidance: level 1

:: Industry ::

_____ describes various measures of the efficiency of production. Often, a _____ measure is expressed as the ratio of an aggregate output to a single input or an aggregate input used in a production process, i.e. output per unit of input. Most common example is the labour _____ measure, e.g., such as GDP per worker. There are many different definitions of _____ and the choice among them depends on the purpose of the _____ measurement and/or data availability. The key source of difference between various _____ measures is also usually related to how the outputs and the inputs are aggregated into scalars to obtain such a ratio-type measure of _____ .

Exam Probability: **Medium**

16. *Answer choices:*
(see index for correct answer)

- a. Industrialisation
- b. Productivity
- c. Cartoning machine
- d. Prefabrication

Guidance: level 1

:: Consumer theory ::

A _____ is a technical term in psychology, economics and philosophy usually used in relation to choosing between alternatives. For example, someone prefers A over B if they would rather choose A than B.

Exam Probability: **Low**

17. *Answer choices:*

(see index for correct answer)

- a. Elasticity of intertemporal substitution
- b. Preference
- c. Snob effect
- d. Demand

Guidance: level 1

:: Television commercials ::

_____ is a phenomenon whereby something new and somehow valuable is formed. The created item may be intangible or a physical object.

Exam Probability: **Low**

18. *Answer choices:*

(see index for correct answer)

- a. Blipvert
- b. Creativity
- c. Dreamer
- d. The Program Exchange

Guidance: level 1

:: Commerce ::

A _____ is a company or individual that purchases goods or services with the intention of selling them rather than consuming or using them. This is usually done for profit. One example can be found in the industry of telecommunications, where companies buy excess amounts of transmission capacity or call time from other carriers and resell it to smaller carriers.

Exam Probability: **Medium**

19. *Answer choices:*

(see index for correct answer)

- a. Receipt
- b. Statutory holdback
- c. Car boot sale
- d. Reseller

Guidance: level 1

:: Management ::

A _____ describes the rationale of how an organization creates, delivers, and captures value, in economic, social, cultural or other contexts. The process of _____ construction and modification is also called _____ innovation and forms a part of business strategy.

Exam Probability: **Low**

20. *Answer choices:*

(see index for correct answer)

- a. Radical transparency
- b. Business model
- c. Corporate transparency
- d. Success trap

Guidance: level 1

:: ::

_____ , or auditory perception, is the ability to perceive sounds by detecting vibrations, changes in the pressure of the surrounding medium through time, through an organ such as the ear. The academic field concerned with _____ is auditory science.

Exam Probability: **Low**

21. *Answer choices:*

(see index for correct answer)

- a. surface-level diversity
- b. Hearing
- c. Sarbanes-Oxley act of 2002
- d. levels of analysis

Guidance: level 1

:: Stochastic processes ::

_____ in its modern meaning is a "new idea, creative thoughts, new imaginations in form of device or method". _____ is often also viewed as the application of better solutions that meet new requirements, unarticulated needs, or existing market needs. Such _____ takes place through the provision of more-effective products, processes, services, technologies, or business models that are made available to markets, governments and society. An _____ is something original and more effective and, as a consequence, new, that "breaks into" the market or society. _____ is related to, but not the same as, invention, as _____ is more apt to involve the practical implementation of an invention to make a meaningful impact in the market or society, and not all _____ s require an invention. _____ often manifests itself via the engineering process, when the problem being solved is of a technical or scientific nature. The opposite of _____ is exnovation.

Exam Probability: **Medium**

22. *Answer choices:*

(see index for correct answer)

- a. Sample-continuous process
- b. Interacting particle system
- c. Innovation
- d. Extinction probability

Guidance: level 1

:: Project management ::

_____ is the right to exercise power, which can be formalized by a state and exercised by way of judges, appointed executives of government, or the ecclesiastical or priestly appointed representatives of a God or other deities.

Exam Probability: **Low**

23. *Answer choices:*

(see index for correct answer)

- a. Budgeted cost of work performed
- b. Small-scale project management
- c. Project management 2.0
- d. ISO 21500

Guidance: level 1

:: Contract law ::

A _____ is a legally-binding agreement which recognises and governs the rights and duties of the parties to the agreement. A _____ is legally enforceable because it meets the requirements and approval of the law. An agreement typically involves the exchange of goods, services, money, or promises of any of those. In the event of breach of _____ , the law awards the injured party access to legal remedies such as damages and cancellation.

Exam Probability: **High**

24. *Answer choices:*

(see index for correct answer)

- a. Contract
- b. The Death of Contract
- c. Parametric contract
- d. United States contract law

Guidance: level 1

:: ::

_____, in general use, is a devotion and faithfulness to a nation, cause, philosophy, country, group, or person. Philosophers disagree on what can be an object of _____, as some argue that _____ is strictly interpersonal and only another human being can be the object of _____. The definition of _____ in law and political science is the fidelity of an individual to a nation, either one's nation of birth, or one's declared home nation by oath.

Exam Probability: **Low**

25. *Answer choices:*

(see index for correct answer)

- a. personal values
- b. hierarchical perspective
- c. imperative
- d. Loyalty

Guidance: level 1

:: Marketing ::

_____ is research conducted for a problem that has not been studied more clearly, intended to establish priorities, develop operational definitions and improve the final research design. _____ helps determine the best research design, data-collection method and selection of subjects. It should draw definitive conclusions only with extreme caution. Given its fundamental nature, _____ often relies on techniques such as.

Exam Probability: **Medium**

26. *Answer choices:*

(see index for correct answer)

- a. Email production
- b. MWW
- c. Exploratory research
- d. Lead management

Guidance: level 1

:: Consumer behaviour ::

_____ refers to the ability of a company or product to retain its customers over some specified period. High _____ means customers of the product or business tend to return to, continue to buy or in some other way not defect to another product or business, or to non-use entirely. Selling organizations generally attempt to reduce customer defections. _____ starts with the first contact an organization has with a customer and continues throughout the entire lifetime of a relationship and successful retention efforts take this entire lifecycle into account. A company's ability to attract and retain new customers is related not only to its product or services, but also to the way it services its existing customers, the value the customers actually generate as a result of utilizing the solutions, and the reputation it creates within and across the marketplace.

Exam Probability: **Low**

27. *Answer choices:*

(see index for correct answer)

- a. Mobile anthropology
- b. Cocooning
- c. Snackwell effect
- d. Customer retention

Guidance: level 1

:: ::

Bloomberg Businessweek is an American weekly business magazine published since 2009 by Bloomberg L.P. Businessweek, founded in 1929, aimed to provide information and interpretation about events in the business world. The magazine is headquartered in New York City. Megan Murphy served as editor from November 2016; she stepped down from the role in January 2018 and Joel Weber was appointed in her place. The magazine is published 47 times a year.

Exam Probability: **Medium**

28. *Answer choices:*

(see index for correct answer)

- a. levels of analysis
- b. corporate values
- c. cultural
- d. information systems assessment

Guidance: level 1

:: Marketing ::

_____ is based on a marketing concept which can be adopted by an organization as a strategy for business expansion. Where implemented, a franchisor licenses its know-how, procedures, intellectual property, use of its business model, brand, and rights to sell its branded products and services to a franchisee. In return the franchisee pays certain fees and agrees to comply with certain obligations, typically set out in a Franchise Agreement.

Exam Probability: **Medium**

29. *Answer choices:*

(see index for correct answer)

- a. Packshot
- b. Franchising
- c. Customer insight
- d. Generic brand

Guidance: level 1

:: Survey methodology ::

A _____ is the procedure of systematically acquiring and recording information about the members of a given population. The term is used mostly in connection with national population and housing _____ es; other common _____ es include agriculture, business, and traffic _____ es. The United Nations defines the essential features of population and housing _____ es as "individual enumeration, universality within a defined territory, simultaneity and defined periodicity", and recommends that population _____ es be taken at least every 10 years. United Nations recommendations also cover _____ topics to be collected, official definitions, classifications and other useful information to co-ordinate international practice.

Exam Probability: **Medium**

30. *Answer choices:*

(see index for correct answer)

- a. Scale analysis
- b. Self-report study
- c. World Association for Public Opinion Research
- d. Sampling

Guidance: level 1

:: Advertising ::

_____ is the behavioral and cognitive process of selectively concentrating on a discrete aspect of information, whether deemed subjective or objective, while ignoring other perceivable information. It is a state of arousal. It is the taking possession by the mind in clear and vivid form of one out of what seem several simultaneous objects or trains of thought. Focalization, the concentration of consciousness, is of its essence. _____ has also been described as the allocation of limited cognitive processing resources.

Exam Probability: **Low**

31. *Answer choices:*
(see index for correct answer)

- a. Attention
- b. Advertising Standards Authority
- c. Patent medicine
- d. Accepted pairing

Guidance: level 1

:: Asset ::

In financial accounting, an _____ is any resource owned by the business. Anything tangible or intangible that can be owned or controlled to produce value and that is held by a company to produce positive economic value is an _____ . Simply stated, _____ s represent value of ownership that can be converted into cash . The balance sheet of a firm records the monetary value of the _____ s owned by that firm. It covers money and other valuables belonging to an individual or to a business.

Exam Probability: **Low**

32. *Answer choices:*
(see index for correct answer)

- a. Current asset
- b. Fixed asset

Guidance: level 1

:: Consumer behaviour ::

_____ is an activity in which a customer browses the available goods or services presented by one or more retailers with the potential intent to purchase a suitable selection of them. A typology of shopper types has been developed by scholars which identifies one group of shoppers as recreational shoppers, that is, those who enjoy _____ and view it as a leisure activity.

Exam Probability: **Low**

33. Answer choices:

(see index for correct answer)

- a. Cocooning
- b. Consumer behaviour
- c. Communal shopping
- d. Shopping

Guidance: level 1

:: ::

_____ is the process of gathering and measuring information on targeted variables in an established system, which then enables one to answer relevant questions and evaluate outcomes. _____ is a component of research in all fields of study including physical and social sciences, humanities, and business. While methods vary by discipline, the emphasis on ensuring accurate and honest collection remains the same. The goal for all _____ is to capture quality evidence that allows analysis to lead to the formulation of convincing and credible answers to the questions that have been posed.

Exam Probability: **Low**

34. Answer choices:

(see index for correct answer)

- a. Data collection
- b. functional perspective

- c. open system
- d. co-culture

Guidance: level 1

:: Data management ::

_____ is a form of intellectual property that grants the creator of an original creative work an exclusive legal right to determine whether and under what conditions this original work may be copied and used by others, usually for a limited term of years. The exclusive rights are not absolute but limited by limitations and exceptions to _____ law, including fair use. A major limitation on _____ on ideas is that _____ protects only the original expression of ideas, and not the underlying ideas themselves.

Exam Probability: **Low**

35. *Answer choices:*
(see index for correct answer)

- a. Copyright
- b. Operational system
- c. Database transaction
- d. Signed overpunch

Guidance: level 1

:: ::

_____ is a means of protection from financial loss. It is a form of risk management, primarily used to hedge against the risk of a contingent or uncertain loss

Exam Probability: **Medium**

36. *Answer choices:*

(see index for correct answer)

- a. empathy
- b. similarity-attraction theory
- c. corporate values
- d. process perspective

Guidance: level 1

:: Management occupations ::

_____ ship is the process of designing, launching and running a new business, which is often initially a small business. The people who create these businesses are called _____ s.

Exam Probability: **Low**

37. *Answer choices:*

(see index for correct answer)

- a. General partner
- b. Chief reputation officer
- c. Entrepreneur
- d. Business magnate

Guidance: level 1

:: Evaluation methods ::

In natural and social sciences, and sometimes in other fields, _____ is the systematic empirical investigation of observable phenomena via statistical, mathematical, or computational techniques. The objective of _____ is to develop and employ mathematical models, theories, and hypotheses pertaining to phenomena. The process of measurement is central to _____ because it provides the fundamental connection between empirical observation and mathematical expression of quantitative relationships.

Exam Probability: **Low**

38. *Answer choices:*

(see index for correct answer)

- a. Advanced Concept Technology Demonstration
- b. Rubric
- c. Economic impact analysis

- d. Moral statistics

Guidance: level 1

:: Product management ::

_____ or brand stretching is a marketing strategy in which a firm marketing a product with a well-developed image uses the same brand name in a different product category. The new product is called a spin-off. Organizations use this strategy to increase and leverage brand equity. An example of a _____ is Jello-gelatin creating Jello pudding pops. It increases awareness of the brand name and increases profitability from offerings in more than one product category.

Exam Probability: **Medium**

39. *Answer choices:*
(see index for correct answer)

- a. Pareto chart
- b. Visual brand language
- c. Technology acceptance model
- d. Brand extension

Guidance: level 1

:: ::

_____ or accountancy is the measurement, processing, and communication of financial information about economic entities such as businesses and corporations. The modern field was established by the Italian mathematician Luca Pacioli in 1494. _____ , which has been called the "language of business", measures the results of an organization's economic activities and conveys this information to a variety of users, including investors, creditors, management, and regulators. Practitioners of _____ are known as accountants. The terms " _____ " and "financial reporting" are often used as synonyms.

Exam Probability: **Medium**

40. *Answer choices:*

(see index for correct answer)

- a. Accounting
- b. Character
- c. interpersonal communication
- d. deep-level diversity

Guidance: level 1

:: Public relations ::

_____ is the public visibility or awareness for any product, service or company. It may also refer to the movement of information from its source to the general public, often but not always via the media. The subjects of _____ include people, goods and services, organizations, and works of art or entertainment.

Exam Probability: **High**

41. *Answer choices:*

(see index for correct answer)

- a. Ice block expedition of 1959
- b. Publicity
- c. Kompromat
- d. Information subsidy

Guidance: level 1

:: Marketing by medium ::

_____ or viral advertising is a business strategy that uses existing social networks to promote a product. Its name refers to how consumers spread information about a product with other people in their social networks, much in the same way that a virus spreads from one person to another. It can be delivered by word of mouth or enhanced by the network effects of the Internet and mobile networks.

Exam Probability: **High**

42. *Answer choices:*

(see index for correct answer)

- a. Digital marketing
- b. Viral marketing

- c. Social intelligence architect
- d. Social video marketing

Guidance: level 1

:: Business models ::

_____ es are privately owned corporations, partnerships, or sole proprietorships that have fewer employees and/or less annual revenue than a regular-sized business or corporation. Businesses are defined as "small" in terms of being able to apply for government support and qualify for preferential tax policy varies depending on the country and industry. _____ es range from fifteen employees under the Australian Fair Work Act 2009, fifty employees according to the definition used by the European Union, and fewer than five hundred employees to qualify for many U.S. _____ Administration programs. While _____ es can also be classified according to other methods, such as annual revenues, shipments, sales, assets, or by annual gross or net revenue or net profits, the number of employees is one of the most widely used measures.

Exam Probability: **Low**

43. *Answer choices:*

(see index for correct answer)

- a. Revenue model
- b. Professional open source
- c. Product-service system
- d. Data as a service

Guidance: level 1

:: Supply chain management terms ::

In business and finance, _____ is a system of organizations, people, activities, information, and resources involved in moving a product or service from supplier to customer. _____ activities involve the transformation of natural resources, raw materials, and components into a finished product that is delivered to the end customer. In sophisticated _____ systems, used products may re-enter the _____ at any point where residual value is recyclable. _____ s link value chains.

Exam Probability: **High**

44. *Answer choices:*
(see index for correct answer)

- a. Last mile
- b. Supply chain
- c. Stockout
- d. Overstock

Guidance: level 1

:: ::

_____ is the practice of deliberately managing the spread of information between an individual or an organization and the public. _____ may include an organization or individual gaining exposure to their audiences using topics of public interest and news items that do not require direct payment. This differentiates it from advertising as a form of marketing communications. _____ is the idea of creating coverage for clients for free, rather than marketing or advertising. But now, advertising is also a part of greater PR Activities. An example of good _____ would be generating an article featuring a client, rather than paying for the client to be advertised next to the article. The aim of _____ is to inform the public, prospective customers, investors, partners, employees, and other stakeholders and ultimately persuade them to maintain a positive or favorable view about the organization, its leadership, products, or political decisions. _____ professionals typically work for PR and marketing firms, businesses and companies, government, and public officials as PIOs and nongovernmental organizations, and nonprofit organizations. Jobs central to _____ include account coordinator, account executive, account supervisor, and media relations manager.

Exam Probability: **Low**

45. *Answer choices:*

(see index for correct answer)

- a. Sarbanes-Oxley act of 2002
- b. levels of analysis
- c. process perspective
- d. information systems assessment

Guidance: level 1

:: Brand management ::

_____ refers to the extent to which customers are able to recall or recognise a brand. _____ is a key consideration in consumer behavior, advertising management, brand management and strategy development. The consumer's ability to recognise or recall a brand is central to purchasing decision-making. Purchasing cannot proceed unless a consumer is first aware of a product category and a brand within that category. Awareness does not necessarily mean that the consumer must be able to recall a specific brand name, but he or she must be able to recall sufficient distinguishing features for purchasing to proceed. For instance, if a consumer asks her friend to buy her some gum in a "blue pack", the friend would be expected to know which gum to buy, even though neither friend can recall the precise brand name at the time.

Exam Probability: **Low**

46. *Answer choices:*

(see index for correct answer)

- a. Sustainability brand
- b. Principle Group
- c. Brand awareness
- d. Brand relationship

Guidance: level 1

:: Manufacturing ::

A _____ is a building for storing goods. _____ s are used by manufacturers, importers, exporters, wholesalers, transport businesses, customs, etc. They are usually large plain buildings in industrial parks on the outskirts of cities, towns or villages.

Exam Probability: **Low**

47. *Answer choices:*

(see index for correct answer)

- a. Can seamer
- b. Boutique manufacturing
- c. Advanced planning and scheduling
- d. Ppc cycle

Guidance: level 1

:: Income ::

_____ is a ratio between the net profit and cost of investment resulting from an investment of some resources. A high ROI means the investment's gains favorably to its cost. As a performance measure, ROI is used to evaluate the efficiency of an investment or to compare the efficiencies of several different investments. In purely economic terms, it is one way of relating profits to capital invested. _____ is a performance measure used by businesses to identify the efficiency of an investment or number of different investments.

Exam Probability: **Low**

48. *Answer choices:*

(see index for correct answer)

- a. Trinity study
- b. Income earner
- c. Return on investment
- d. Passive income

Guidance: level 1

:: Investment ::

In finance, the benefit from an _____ is called a return. The return may consist of a gain realised from the sale of property or an _____, unrealised capital appreciation, or _____ income such as dividends, interest, rental income etc., or a combination of capital gain and income. The return may also include currency gains or losses due to changes in foreign currency exchange rates.

Exam Probability: **Low**

49. *Answer choices:*

(see index for correct answer)

- a. Greater fool theory
- b. Umbrella fund

- c. Investment
- d. Special settlement

Guidance: level 1

:: Retailing ::

_____ is the process of selling consumer goods or services to customers through multiple channels of distribution to earn a profit. _____ ers satisfy demand identified through a supply chain. The term "_____ er" is typically applied where a service provider fills the small orders of a large number of individuals, who are end-users, rather than large orders of a small number of wholesale, corporate or government clientele. Shopping generally refers to the act of buying products. Sometimes this is done to obtain final goods, including necessities such as food and clothing; sometimes it takes place as a recreational activity. Recreational shopping often involves window shopping and browsing: it does not always result in a purchase.

Exam Probability: **Low**

50. *Answer choices:*

(see index for correct answer)

- a. Motorized shopping cart
- b. Shopping channel
- c. Omni-channel Retailing
- d. Shopping mall

Guidance: level 1

:: Data management ::

In computing, a _____ , also known as an enterprise _____ , is a system used for reporting and data analysis, and is considered a core component of business intelligence. DWs are central repositories of integrated data from one or more disparate sources. They store current and historical data in one single place that are used for creating analytical reports for workers throughout the enterprise.

Exam Probability: **High**

51. *Answer choices:*

(see index for correct answer)

- a. Approximate inference
- b. Nonlinear medium
- c. Data warehouse
- d. Control break

Guidance: level 1

:: ::

_____ is the production of products for use or sale using labour and machines, tools, chemical and biological processing, or formulation. The term may refer to a range of human activity, from handicraft to high tech, but is most commonly applied to industrial design, in which raw materials are transformed into finished goods on a large scale. Such finished goods may be sold to other manufacturers for the production of other, more complex products, such as aircraft, household appliances, furniture, sports equipment or automobiles, or sold to wholesalers, who in turn sell them to retailers, who then sell them to end users and consumers.

Exam Probability: **High**

52. *Answer choices:*

(see index for correct answer)

- a. interpersonal communication
- b. hierarchical perspective
- c. corporate values
- d. Manufacturing

Guidance: level 1

:: Pricing ::

_____ is unwanted sound judged to be unpleasant, loud or disruptive to hearing. From a physics standpoint, _____ is indistinguishable from sound, as both are vibrations through a medium, such as air or water. The difference arises when the brain receives and perceives a sound.

Exam Probability: **Low**

53. *Answer choices:*

(see index for correct answer)

- a. Cost-plus contract
- b. The price of milk
- c. Peak-load pricing
- d. Electricity pricing

Guidance: level 1

:: Production and manufacturing ::

_____ consists of organization-wide efforts to "install and make permanent climate where employees continuously improve their ability to provide on demand products and services that customers will find of particular value." "Total" emphasizes that departments in addition to production are obligated to improve their operations; "management" emphasizes that executives are obligated to actively manage quality through funding, training, staffing, and goal setting. While there is no widely agreed-upon approach, TQM efforts typically draw heavily on the previously developed tools and techniques of quality control. TQM enjoyed widespread attention during the late 1980s and early 1990s before being overshadowed by ISO 9000, Lean manufacturing, and Six Sigma.

Exam Probability: **Medium**

54. *Answer choices:*

(see index for correct answer)

- a. Job shop
- b. Total Quality Management
- c. PA512
- d. Transfer line

Guidance: level 1

:: Advertising ::

A _____ is a large outdoor advertising structure, typically found in high-traffic areas such as alongside busy roads. _____ s present large advertisements to passing pedestrians and drivers. Typically showing witty slogans and distinctive visuals, _____ s are highly visible in the top designated market areas.

Exam Probability: **Low**

55. *Answer choices:*
(see index for correct answer)

- a. Targeted advertising
- b. Advertising elasticity of demand
- c. Media context studies
- d. Reply marketing

Guidance: level 1

:: Marketing ::

_____ is the process of using surveys to evaluate consumer acceptance of a new product idea prior to the introduction of a product to the market. It is important not to confuse _____ with advertising testing, brand testing and packaging testing; as is sometimes done. _____ focuses on the basic product idea, without the embellishments and puffery inherent in advertising.

Exam Probability: **Low**

56. *Answer choices:*

(see index for correct answer)

- a. Concept testing
- b. Drug coupon
- c. Ayelet Gneezy
- d. Product lining

Guidance: level 1

:: Marketing ::

_____ is a marketing practice of individuals or organizations. It allows them to sell products or services to other companies or organizations that resell them, use them in their products or services or use them to support their works.

Exam Probability: **High**

57. *Answer choices:*

(see index for correct answer)

- a. Business marketing
- b. Content Curation Marketing
- c. Golden sample
- d. Franchising

Guidance: level 1

:: ::

In law, a _____ is a coming together of parties to a dispute, to present information in a tribunal, a formal setting with the authority to adjudicate claims or disputes. One form of tribunal is a court. The tribunal, which may occur before a judge, jury, or other designated trier of fact, aims to achieve a resolution to their dispute.

Exam Probability: **High**

58. *Answer choices:*

(see index for correct answer)

- a. Trial
- b. interpersonal communication

- c. information systems assessment
- d. personal values

Guidance: level 1

:: Product development ::

_____ is the understanding of the dynamics of the product in order to showcase the best qualities and maximum features of the product. Marketers spend a lot of time and research in order to target their attended audience. Marketers will look into a _____ before marketing a product towards their customers.

Exam Probability: **Low**

59. Answer choices:

(see index for correct answer)

- a. Engineering design management
- b. Virtual product development
- c. Design brief
- d. Product concept

Guidance: level 1

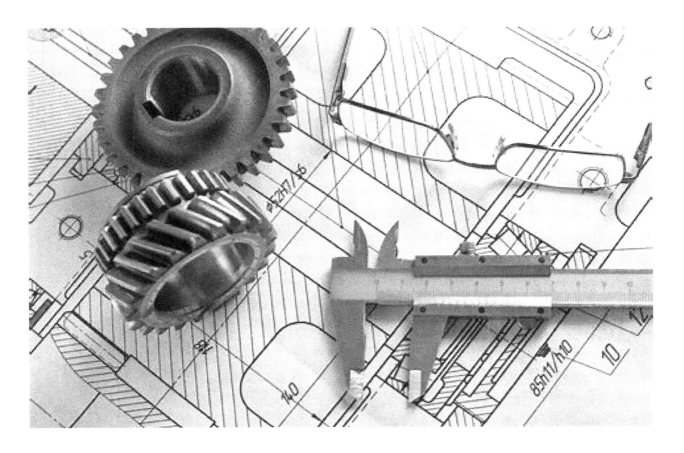

Manufacturing

Manufacturing is the production of merchandise for use or sale using labor and machines, tools, chemical and biological processing, or formulation. The term may refer to a range of human activity, from handicraft to high tech, but is most commonly applied to industrial design , in which raw materials are transformed into finished goods on a large scale. Such finished goods may be sold to other manufacturers for the production of other, more complex products, such as aircraft, household appliances, furniture, sports equipment or automobiles, or sold to wholesalers, who in turn sell them to retailers, who then sell them to end users and consumers.

⠒ ⠒

_____ refers to the confirmation of certain characteristics of an object, person, or organization. This confirmation is often, but not always, provided by some form of external review, education, assessment, or audit. Accreditation is a specific organization's process of _____ . According to the National Council on Measurement in Education, a _____ test is a credentialing test used to determine whether individuals are knowledgeable enough in a given occupational area to be labeled "competent to practice" in that area.

Exam Probability: **Low**

1. *Answer choices:*

(see index for correct answer)

- a. hierarchical
- b. Certification
- c. similarity-attraction theory
- d. Sarbanes-Oxley act of 2002

Guidance: level 1

:: ::

In sales, commerce and economics, a _____ is the recipient of a good, service, product or an idea - obtained from a seller, vendor, or supplier via a financial transaction or exchange for money or some other valuable consideration.

Exam Probability: **Medium**

2. *Answer choices:*

(see index for correct answer)

- a. surface-level diversity
- b. Customer
- c. empathy
- d. levels of analysis

Guidance: level 1

:: Promotion and marketing communications ::

The _____ of American Manufacturers, now ThomasNet, is an online platform for supplier discovery and product sourcing in the US and Canada. It was once known as the "big green books" and "Thomas Registry", and was a multi-volume directory of industrial product information covering 650,000 distributors, manufacturers and service companies within 67,000-plus industrial categories that is now published on ThomasNet.

Exam Probability: **Low**

3. *Answer choices:*

(see index for correct answer)

- a. Secret ingredient
- b. Thomas Register

- c. Worthy Book
- d. CollarCard

Guidance: level 1

:: Production and manufacturing ::

_____ consists of organization-wide efforts to "install and make permanent climate where employees continuously improve their ability to provide on demand products and services that customers will find of particular value." "Total" emphasizes that departments in addition to production are obligated to improve their operations; "management" emphasizes that executives are obligated to actively manage quality through funding, training, staffing, and goal setting. While there is no widely agreed-upon approach, TQM efforts typically draw heavily on the previously developed tools and techniques of quality control. TQM enjoyed widespread attention during the late 1980s and early 1990s before being overshadowed by ISO 9000, Lean manufacturing, and Six Sigma.

Exam Probability: **Low**

4. *Answer choices:*

(see index for correct answer)

- a. Original design manufacturer
- b. Workmanship
- c. Total quality management
- d. Follow-the-sun

Guidance: level 1

:: ::

A _____ consists of an orchestrated and repeatable pattern of business activity enabled by the systematic organization of resources into processes that transform materials, provide services, or process information. It can be depicted as a sequence of operations, the work of a person or group, the work of an organization of staff, or one or more simple or complex mechanisms.

Exam Probability: **Low**

5. *Answer choices:*

(see index for correct answer)

- a. hierarchical perspective
- b. similarity-attraction theory
- c. information systems assessment
- d. corporate values

Guidance: level 1

:: Risk analysis ::

Supply-chain risk management is "the implementation of strategies to manage both everyday and exceptional risks along the supply chain based on continuous risk assessment with the objective of reducing vulnerability and ensuring continuity".

Exam Probability: **Low**

6. *Answer choices:*

(see index for correct answer)

- a. Collateral consequence
- b. Marine accident investigation
- c. Supply chain risk management
- d. Litigation risk analysis

Guidance: level 1

:: Data management ::

_____ is an object-oriented program and library developed by CERN. It was originally designed for particle physics data analysis and contains several features specific to this field, but it is also used in other applications such as astronomy and data mining. The latest release is 6.16.00, as of 2018-11-14.

Exam Probability: **High**

7. *Answer choices:*

(see index for correct answer)

- a. ROOT
- b. Data management
- c. Rescentris

- d. Data integration

Guidance: level 1

:: Project management ::

A _____ is a source or supply from which a benefit is produced and it has some utility. _____ s can broadly be classified upon their availability—they are classified into renewable and non-renewable _____ s.Examples of non renewable _____ s are coal ,crude oil natural gas nuclear energy etc. Examples of renewable _____ s are air,water,wind,solar energy etc. They can also be classified as actual and potential on the basis of level of development and use, on the basis of origin they can be classified as biotic and abiotic, and on the basis of their distribution, as ubiquitous and localized . An item becomes a _____ with time and developing technology. Typically, _____ s are materials, energy, services, staff, knowledge, or other assets that are transformed to produce benefit and in the process may be consumed or made unavailable. Benefits of _____ utilization may include increased wealth, proper functioning of a system, or enhanced well-being. From a human perspective a natural _____ is anything obtained from the environment to satisfy human needs and wants. From a broader biological or ecological perspective a _____ satisfies the needs of a living organism .

Exam Probability: **Medium**

8. *Answer choices:*

(see index for correct answer)

- a. RationalPlan
- b. LibrePlan
- c. Resource

- d. project triangle

Guidance: level 1

:: Management ::

In organizational studies, _____ is the efficient and effective development of an organization's resources when they are needed. Such resources may include financial resources, inventory, human skills, production resources, or information technology and natural resources.

Exam Probability: **Medium**

9. *Answer choices:*

(see index for correct answer)

- a. Toxic leader
- b. Empowerment
- c. Dynamic enterprise modeling
- d. Resource management

Guidance: level 1

:: ::

_____ is a kind of action that occur as two or more objects have an effect upon one another. The idea of a two-way effect is essential in the concept of _____ , as opposed to a one-way causal effect. A closely related term is interconnectivity, which deals with the _____ s of _____ s within systems: combinations of many simple _____ s can lead to surprising emergent phenomena. _____ has different tailored meanings in various sciences. Changes can also involve _____ .

Exam Probability: **High**

10. *Answer choices:*

(see index for correct answer)

- a. Interaction
- b. personal values
- c. deep-level diversity
- d. hierarchical perspective

Guidance: level 1

:: Semiconductor companies ::

_____ Corporation is a Japanese multinational conglomerate corporation headquartered in Konan, Minato, Tokyo. Its diversified business includes consumer and professional electronics, gaming, entertainment and financial services. The company owns the largest music entertainment business in the world, the largest video game console business and one of the largest video game publishing businesses, and is one of the leading manufacturers of electronic products for the consumer and professional markets, and a leading player in the film and television entertainment industry. _____ was ranked 97th on the 2018 Fortune Global 500 list.

Exam Probability: **High**

11. *Answer choices:*

(see index for correct answer)

- a. Nuvoton
- b. Kodenshi AUK Group
- c. Conemtech
- d. Intersil

Guidance: level 1

:: Production economics ::

_____ is the creation of a whole that is greater than the simple sum of its parts. The term _____ comes from the Attic Greek word sea synergia from synergos, , meaning "working together".

Exam Probability: **High**

12. *Answer choices:*

(see index for correct answer)

- a. Synergy
- b. Product pipeline
- c. Limiting factor
- d. Marginal cost of capital schedule

Guidance: level 1

:: Goods ::

In most contexts, the concept of _____ denotes the conduct that should be preferred when posed with a choice between possible actions. _____ is generally considered to be the opposite of evil, and is of interest in the study of morality, ethics, religion and philosophy. The specific meaning and etymology of the term and its associated translations among ancient and contemporary languages show substantial variation in its inflection and meaning depending on circumstances of place, history, religious, or philosophical context.

Exam Probability: **High**

13. *Answer choices:*

(see index for correct answer)

- a. Information good
- b. Substitute good
- c. Positional good
- d. Good

Guidance: level 1

:: Project management ::

_____ s can take many forms depending on the type of project being implemented and the nature of the organization. The _____ details the project deliverables and describes the major objectives. The objectives should include measurable success criteria for the project.

Exam Probability: **High**

14. *Answer choices:*

(see index for correct answer)

- a. Project portfolio management
- b. PRINCE2
- c. Scope statement
- d. ISO 10006

Guidance: level 1

:: Help desk ::

Data center management is the collection of tasks performed by those responsible for managing ongoing operation of a data center This includes Business service management and planning for the future.

Exam Probability: **Medium**

15. *Answer choices:*

(see index for correct answer)

- a. HEAT
- b. Help desk
- c. Technical support
- d. SysAid Technologies

Guidance: level 1

:: Industrial processes ::

A _____ is a device used for high-temperature heating. The name derives from Latin word fornax, which means oven. The heat energy to fuel a _____ may be supplied directly by fuel combustion, by electricity such as the electric arc _____ , or through induction heating in induction _____ s.

Exam Probability: **Medium**

16. *Answer choices:*

(see index for correct answer)

- a. Cryogenic nitrogen plant
- b. Lead chamber process
- c. Air separation
- d. Supercritical drying

Guidance: level 1

:: Production and manufacturing ::

In industry, _____ is a system of maintaining and improving the integrity of production and quality systems through the machines, equipment, processes, and employees that add business value to an organization.

Exam Probability: **Low**

17. *Answer choices:*

(see index for correct answer)

- a. Highly accelerated stress audit
- b. First pass yield
- c. Total productive maintenance
- d. Economic region of production

Guidance: level 1

:: Costs ::

In microeconomic theory, the _____, or alternative cost, of making a particular choice is the value of the most valuable choice out of those that were not taken. In other words, opportunity that will require sacrifices.

Exam Probability: **High**

18. *Answer choices:*

(see index for correct answer)

- a. Search cost
- b. Opportunity cost
- c. Sliding scale
- d. Total cost of acquisition

Guidance: level 1

:: Management ::

_____ is a category of business activity made possible by software tools that aim to provide customers with both independence from vendors and better means for engaging with vendors. These same tools can also apply to individuals' relations with other institutions and organizations.

Exam Probability: **Low**

19. *Answer choices:*

(see index for correct answer)

- a. Technology scouting
- b. Strategic management
- c. Libertarian management
- d. Action item

Guidance: level 1

:: Outsourcing ::

_____ is the practice of sourcing from the global market for goods and services across geopolitical boundaries. _____ often aims to exploit global efficiencies in the delivery of a product or service. These efficiencies include low cost skilled labor, low cost raw material and other economic factors like tax breaks and low trade tariffs. A large number of Information Technology projects and Services, including IS Applications and Mobile Apps and database services are outsourced globally to countries like Pakistan and India for more economical pricing.

Exam Probability: **Low**

20. *Answer choices:*

(see index for correct answer)

- a. Global sourcing
- b. Extengineering
- c. Transition methodology
- d. Talentica Software

Guidance: level 1

:: Retailing ::

_____ is the process of selling consumer goods or services to customers through multiple channels of distribution to earn a profit. _____ ers satisfy demand identified through a supply chain. The term " _____ er" is typically applied where a service provider fills the small orders of a large number of individuals, who are end-users, rather than large orders of a small number of wholesale, corporate or government clientele. Shopping generally refers to the act of buying products. Sometimes this is done to obtain final goods, including necessities such as food and clothing; sometimes it takes place as a recreational activity. Recreational shopping often involves window shopping and browsing: it does not always result in a purchase.

Exam Probability: **High**

21. *Answer choices:*

(see index for correct answer)

- a. Retail
- b. Dry goods
- c. Endcap
- d. Street date

Guidance: level 1

:: Materials ::

A _____ , also known as a feedstock, unprocessed material, or primary commodity, is a basic material that is used to produce goods, finished products, energy, or intermediate materials which are feedstock for future finished products. As feedstock, the term connotes these materials are bottleneck assets and are highly important with regard to producing other products. An example of this is crude oil, which is a _____ and a feedstock used in the production of industrial chemicals, fuels, plastics, and pharmaceutical goods; lumber is a _____ used to produce a variety of products including all types of furniture. The term "_____" denotes materials in minimally processed or unprocessed in states; e.g., raw latex, crude oil, cotton, coal, raw biomass, iron ore, air, logs, or water i.e. "...any product of agriculture, forestry, fishing and any other mineral that is in its natural form or which has undergone the transformation required to prepare it for internationally marketing in substantial volumes."

Exam Probability: **High**

22. *Answer choices:*
(see index for correct answer)

- a. Ice substitute
- b. Exotic material
- c. Raw material
- d. Nanophase material

Guidance: level 1

:: Manufacturing ::

A _____ is an object used to extend the ability of an individual to modify features of the surrounding environment. Although many animals use simple _____ s, only human beings, whose use of stone _____ s dates back hundreds of millennia, use _____ s to make other _____ s. The set of _____ s needed to perform different tasks that are part of the same activity is called gear or equipment.

Exam Probability: **Medium**

23. *Answer choices:*
(see index for correct answer)

- a. Process manufacturing
- b. Fixture
- c. Tool
- d. Ashery

Guidance: level 1

:: Chemical reactions ::

A _____ is a process that leads to the chemical transformation of one set of chemical substances to another. Classically, _____ s encompass changes that only involve the positions of electrons in the forming and breaking of chemical bonds between atoms, with no change to the nuclei , and can often be described by a chemical equation. Nuclear chemistry is a sub-discipline of chemistry that involves the _____ s of unstable and radioactive elements where both electronic and nuclear changes can occur.

Exam Probability: **Medium**

24. *Answer choices:*

(see index for correct answer)

- a. Adduct
- b. Retarder
- c. Homolysis
- d. Alkaline hydrolysis

Guidance: level 1

:: Industrial engineering ::

The _____ is the design of any task that aims to describe or explain the variation of information under conditions that are hypothesized to reflect the variation. The term is generally associated with experiments in which the design introduces conditions that directly affect the variation, but may also refer to the design of quasi-experiments, in which natural conditions that influence the variation are selected for observation.

Exam Probability: **Medium**

25. *Answer choices:*

(see index for correct answer)

- a. Work Measurement
- b. Activity relationship chart
- c. Therblig
- d. Design of experiments

Guidance: level 1

:: Building materials ::

_____ is an alloy of iron and carbon, and sometimes other elements. Because of its high tensile strength and low cost, it is a major component used in buildings, infrastructure, tools, ships, automobiles, machines, appliances, and weapons.

Exam Probability: **High**

26. *Answer choices:*

(see index for correct answer)

- a. Innowood
- b. Biorock
- c. Pavement

- d. Vinyl composition tile

Guidance: level 1

:: Outsourcing ::

A _____ is a document that solicits proposal, often made through a bidding process, by an agency or company interested in procurement of a commodity, service, or valuable asset, to potential suppliers to submit business proposals. It is submitted early in the procurement cycle, either at the preliminary study, or procurement stage.

Exam Probability: **High**

27. *Answer choices:*

(see index for correct answer)

- a. Sourcing agent
- b. Service-level agreement
- c. Request for proposal
- d. PFSweb

Guidance: level 1

:: Metal forming ::

_____ is a type of motion that combines rotation and translation of that object with respect to a surface, such that, if ideal conditions exist, the two are in contact with each other without sliding.

Exam Probability: **Low**

28. *Answer choices:*

(see index for correct answer)

- a. Metal spinning
- b. Rotary piercing
- c. Cold sizing
- d. Rolling

Guidance: level 1

:: Production economics ::

_____ is the joint use of a resource or space. It is also the process of dividing and distributing. In its narrow sense, it refers to joint or alternating use of inherently finite goods, such as a common pasture or a shared residence. Still more loosely, "_____" can actually mean giving something as an outright gift: for example, to "share" one's food really means to give some of it as a gift. _____ is a basic component of human interaction, and is responsible for strengthening social ties and ensuring a person's well-being.

Exam Probability: **High**

29. *Answer choices:*

(see index for correct answer)

- a. Productive capacity
- b. Choice of techniques
- c. Production theory
- d. Sharing

Guidance: level 1

:: ::

A _____ is a covering that is applied to the surface of an object, usually referred to as the substrate. The purpose of applying the _____ may be decorative, functional, or both. The _____ itself may be an all-over _____ , completely covering the substrate, or it may only cover parts of the substrate. An example of all of these types of _____ is a product label on many drinks bottles- one side has an all-over functional _____ and the other side has one or more decorative _____ s in an appropriate pattern to form the words and images.

Exam Probability: **High**

30. *Answer choices:*

(see index for correct answer)

- a. similarity-attraction theory
- b. information systems assessment

- c. hierarchical
- d. Coating

Guidance: level 1

:: Quality assurance ::

Organizations that issue credentials or certify third parties against official standards are themselves formally accredited by _____ bodies ; hence they are sometimes known as "accredited certification bodies". The _____ process ensures that their certification practices are acceptable, typically meaning that they are competent to test and certify third parties, behave ethically and employ suitable quality assurance.

Exam Probability: **Medium**

31. *Answer choices:*
(see index for correct answer)

- a. Commission on Accreditation of Rehabilitation Facilities
- b. Hospital accreditation
- c. Accreditation
- d. Certificate of Conformity to Technical Regulation

Guidance: level 1

:: Unit operations ::

_____ is a discipline of thermal engineering that concerns the generation, use, conversion, and exchange of thermal energy between physical systems. _____ is classified into various mechanisms, such as thermal conduction, thermal convection, thermal radiation, and transfer of energy by phase changes. Engineers also consider the transfer of mass of differing chemical species, either cold or hot, to achieve _____ . While these mechanisms have distinct characteristics, they often occur simultaneously in the same system.

Exam Probability: **Medium**

32. *Answer choices:*

(see index for correct answer)

- a. Distillation
- b. Heat transfer
- c. Unit Operations of Chemical Engineering
- d. Settling

Guidance: level 1

:: Business planning ::

_____ is an organization's process of defining its strategy, or direction, and making decisions on allocating its resources to pursue this strategy. It may also extend to control mechanisms for guiding the implementation of the strategy. _____ became prominent in corporations during the 1960s and remains an important aspect of strategic management. It is executed by strategic planners or strategists, who involve many parties and research sources in their analysis of the organization and its relationship to the environment in which it competes.

Exam Probability: **Low**

33. *Answer choices:*

(see index for correct answer)

- a. Exit planning
- b. Strategic planning
- c. Community Futures
- d. Business war games

Guidance: level 1

:: Costs ::

In economics, _____ is the total economic cost of production and is made up of variable cost, which varies according to the quantity of a good produced and includes inputs such as labour and raw materials, plus fixed cost, which is independent of the quantity of a good produced and includes inputs that cannot be varied in the short term: fixed costs such as buildings and machinery, including sunk costs if any. Since cost is measured per unit of time, it is a flow variable.

Exam Probability: **Low**

34. *Answer choices:*

(see index for correct answer)

- a. Total cost
- b. Social cost
- c. Total cost of acquisition
- d. Sliding scale

Guidance: level 1

:: Sampling (statistics) ::

_____ uses statistical sampling to determine whether to accept or reject a production lot of material. It has been a common quality control technique used in industry. It is usually done as products leaves the factory, or in some cases even within the factory. Most often a producer supplies a consumer a number of items and a decision to accept or reject the items is made by determining the number of defective items in a sample from the lot. The lot is accepted if the number of defects falls below where the acceptance number or otherwise the lot is rejected.

Exam Probability: **Medium**

35. *Answer choices:*

(see index for correct answer)

- a. Time use survey
- b. Response bias
- c. Sampling error
- d. Deep sampling

Guidance: level 1

:: Project management ::

_____ is the right to exercise power, which can be formalized by a state and exercised by way of judges, appointed executives of government, or the ecclesiastical or priestly appointed representatives of a God or other deities.

Exam Probability: **Low**

36. *Answer choices:*

(see index for correct answer)

- a. project triangle
- b. Cost estimate
- c. Value of work done
- d. Project workforce management

Guidance: level 1

:: Project management ::

A _____ is the approximation of the cost of a program, project, or operation. The _____ is the product of the cost estimating process. The _____ has a single total value and may have identifiable component values. A problem with a cost overrun can be avoided with a credible, reliable, and accurate _____ . A cost estimator is the professional who prepares _____ s. There are different types of cost estimators, whose title may be preceded by a modifier, such as building estimator, or electrical estimator, or chief estimator. Other professionals such as quantity surveyors and cost engineers may also prepare _____ s or contribute to _____ s. In the US, according to the Bureau of Labor Statistics, there were 185,400 cost estimators in 2010. There are around 75,000 professional quantity surveyors working in the UK.

Exam Probability: **High**

37. Answer choices:

(see index for correct answer)

- a. Case competition
- b. Project Management Institute
- c. Australian Institute of Project Management
- d. Integrated product team

Guidance: level 1

:: Production and manufacturing ::

_____ is a comprehensive and rigorous industrial process by which a previously sold, leased, used, worn or non-functional product or part is returned to a 'like-new' or 'better-than-new' condition, from both a quality and performance perspective, through a controlled, reproducible and sustainable process.

Exam Probability: **High**

38. Answer choices:

(see index for correct answer)

- a. Fab lab
- b. Direct numerical control
- c. SynqNet
- d. Remanufacturing

Guidance: level 1

:: Costs ::

_____ is the process used by companies to reduce their costs and increase their profits. Depending on a company's services or product, the strategies can vary. Every decision in the product development process affects cost.

Exam Probability: **High**

39. *Answer choices:*

(see index for correct answer)

- a. Cost overrun
- b. Repugnancy costs
- c. Cost per paper
- d. Cost reduction

Guidance: level 1

:: Decision theory ::

_____ is a method developed in Japan beginning in 1966 to help transform the voice of the customer into engineering characteristics for a product. Yoji Akao, the original developer, described QFD as a "method to transform qualitative user demands into quantitative parameters, to deploy the functions forming quality, and to deploy methods for achieving the design quality into subsystems and component parts, and ultimately to specific elements of the manufacturing process." The author combined his work in quality assurance and quality control points with function deployment used in value engineering.

Exam Probability: **High**

40. *Answer choices:*

(see index for correct answer)

- a. Quality function deployment
- b. Policy
- c. Minimax
- d. Option grid

Guidance: level 1

:: Information technology management ::

_____ is a collective term for all approaches to prepare, support and help individuals, teams, and organizations in making organizational change. The most common change drivers include: technological evolution, process reviews, crisis, and consumer habit changes; pressure from new business entrants, acquisitions, mergers, and organizational restructuring. It includes methods that redirect or redefine the use of resources, business process, budget allocations, or other modes of operation that significantly change a company or organization. Organizational _____ considers the full organization and what needs to change, while _____ may be used solely to refer to how people and teams are affected by such organizational transition. It deals with many different disciplines, from behavioral and social sciences to information technology and business solutions.

Exam Probability: **Medium**

41. *Answer choices:*

(see index for correct answer)

- a. Change management
- b. Information model
- c. One-to-one marketing
- d. Accelops

Guidance: level 1

:: Project management ::

_____ is a marketing activity that does an aggregate plan for the production process, in advance of 6 to 18 months, to give an idea to management as to what quantity of materials and other resources are to be procured and when, so that the total cost of operations of the organization is kept to the minimum over that period.

Exam Probability: **Low**

42. *Answer choices:*
(see index for correct answer)

- a. Effort management
- b. Advanced Integrated Practice
- c. The Chicken and the Pig
- d. Scrumedge

Guidance: level 1

:: Management ::

_____ is a formal technique useful where many possible courses of action are competing for attention. In essence, the problem-solver estimates the benefit delivered by each action, then selects a number of the most effective actions that deliver a total benefit reasonably close to the maximal possible one.

Exam Probability: **High**

43. Answer choices:

(see index for correct answer)

- a. Target culture
- b. Enterprise planning system
- c. Supply network
- d. Pareto analysis

Guidance: level 1

:: Information technology management ::

_____ within quality management systems and information technology systems is a process—either formal or informal—used to ensure that changes to a product or system are introduced in a controlled and coordinated manner. It reduces the possibility that unnecessary changes will be introduced to a system without forethought, introducing faults into the system or undoing changes made by other users of software. The goals of a _____ procedure usually include minimal disruption to services, reduction in back-out activities, and cost-effective utilization of resources involved in implementing change.

Exam Probability: **Low**

44. Answer choices:

(see index for correct answer)

- a. Digital continuity
- b. Change control

- c. Information technology consulting
- d. Storage virtualization

Guidance: level 1

:: Project management ::

A _____ is a team whose members usually belong to different groups, functions and are assigned to activities for the same project. A team can be divided into sub-teams according to need. Usually _____ s are only used for a defined period of time. They are disbanded after the project is deemed complete. Due to the nature of the specific formation and disbandment, _____ s are usually in organizations.

Exam Probability: **High**

45. *Answer choices:*

(see index for correct answer)

- a. Life-cycle cost analysis
- b. Project management 2.0
- c. Project team
- d. Master of Science in Project Management

Guidance: level 1

:: Information technology management ::

_____ is the discipline of engineering concerned with the principles and practice of product and service quality assurance and control. In the software development, it is the management, development, operation and maintenance of IT systems and enterprise architectures with a high quality standard.

Exam Probability: **Medium**

46. *Answer choices:*

(see index for correct answer)

- a. Ekatva
- b. Information repository
- c. Quality Engineering
- d. IT Interaction Model

Guidance: level 1

:: Industries ::

The _____ comprises the companies that produce industrial chemicals. Central to the modern world economy, it converts raw materials into more than 70,000 different products. The plastics industry contains some overlap, as most chemical companies produce plastic as well as other chemicals.

Exam Probability: **Medium**

47. Answer choices:

(see index for correct answer)

- a. Motorsport industry
- b. Chemical industry
- c. Naval stores industry
- d. Alcohol industry

Guidance: level 1

:: Industrial equipment ::

_____ s are heat exchangers typically used to provide heat to the bottom of industrial distillation columns. They boil the liquid from the bottom of a distillation column to generate vapors which are returned to the column to drive the distillation separation. The heat supplied to the column by the _____ at the bottom of the column is removed by the condenser at the top of the column.

Exam Probability: **Medium**

48. Answer choices:

(see index for correct answer)

- a. Vacuum truck
- b. Single-ended recuperative burner
- c. Reboiler
- d. Coiled tubing

Guidance: level 1

:: Supply chain management terms ::

In business and finance, _____ is a system of organizations, people, activities, information, and resources involved in moving a product or service from supplier to customer. _____ activities involve the transformation of natural resources, raw materials, and components into a finished product that is delivered to the end customer. In sophisticated _____ systems, used products may re-enter the _____ at any point where residual value is recyclable. _____ s link value chains.

Exam Probability: **Medium**

49. *Answer choices:*
(see index for correct answer)

- a. Direct shipment
- b. Supply chain
- c. Consumable
- d. Last mile

Guidance: level 1

:: Business process ::

A committee is a body of one or more persons that is subordinate to a deliberative assembly. Usually, the assembly sends matters into a committee as a way to explore them more fully than would be possible if the assembly itself were considering them. Committees may have different functions and their type of work differ depending on the type of the organization and its needs.

Exam Probability: **Low**

50. *Answer choices:*

(see index for correct answer)

- a. Steering committee
- b. IBM Blueworks Live
- c. Bonita BPM
- d. Outsourced document processing

Guidance: level 1

:: Consortia ::

A _____ is an association of two or more individuals, companies, organizations or governments with the objective of participating in a common activity or pooling their resources for achieving a common goal.

Exam Probability: **High**

51. *Answer choices:*

(see index for correct answer)

- a. Serial Port Memory Technology
- b. PICMG
- c. Ericsson Hewlett Packard Telecom
- d. Consortium

Guidance: level 1

:: Quality management ::

_____ ensures that an organization, product or service is consistent. It has four main components: quality planning, quality assurance, quality control and quality improvement. _____ is focused not only on product and service quality, but also on the means to achieve it. _____ , therefore, uses quality assurance and control of processes as well as products to achieve more consistent quality. What a customer wants and is willing to pay for it determines quality. It is written or unwritten commitment to a known or unknown consumer in the market . Thus, quality can be defined as fitness for intended use or, in other words, how well the product performs its intended function

Exam Probability: **Medium**

52. *Answer choices:*

(see index for correct answer)

- a. EFQM
- b. Quality management
- c. External quality assessment

- d. Regulatory translation

Guidance: level 1

:: ::

_____ refers to a business or organization attempting to acquire goods or services to accomplish its goals. Although there are several organizations that attempt to set standards in the _____ process, processes can vary greatly between organizations. Typically the word " _____ " is not used interchangeably with the word "procurement", since procurement typically includes expediting, supplier quality, and transportation and logistics in addition to _____ .

Exam Probability: **Medium**

53. *Answer choices:*

(see index for correct answer)

- a. open system
- b. personal values
- c. empathy
- d. Purchasing

Guidance: level 1

:: Asset ::

In financial accounting, an _____ is any resource owned by the business. Anything tangible or intangible that can be owned or controlled to produce value and that is held by a company to produce positive economic value is an _____ . Simply stated, _____ s represent value of ownership that can be converted into cash . The balance sheet of a firm records the monetary value of the _____ s owned by that firm. It covers money and other valuables belonging to an individual or to a business.

Exam Probability: **Low**

54. *Answer choices:*
(see index for correct answer)

- a. Asset
- b. Current asset

Guidance: level 1

:: ::

Catalysis is the process of increasing the rate of a chemical reaction by adding a substance known as a _____ , which is not consumed in the catalyzed reaction and can continue to act repeatedly. Because of this, only very small amounts of _____ are required to alter the reaction rate in principle.

Exam Probability: **Medium**

55. Answer choices:

(see index for correct answer)

- a. empathy
- b. Catalyst
- c. levels of analysis
- d. cultural

Guidance: level 1

:: Production and manufacturing ::

_____ was a management-led program to eliminate defects in industrial production that enjoyed brief popularity in American industry from 1964 to the early 1970s. Quality expert Philip Crosby later incorporated it into his "Absolutes of Quality Management" and it enjoyed a renaissance in the American automobile industry—as a performance goal more than as a program—in the 1990s. Although applicable to any type of enterprise, it has been primarily adopted within supply chains wherever large volumes of components are being purchased.

Exam Probability: **Low**

56. Answer choices:

(see index for correct answer)

- a. Simatic S5 PLC
- b. Cellular manufacturing
- c. Detailed division of labor

- d. Performance supervision system

Guidance: level 1

:: Finance ::

_____ is a financial estimate intended to help buyers and owners determine the direct and indirect costs of a product or system. It is a management accounting concept that can be used in full cost accounting or even ecological economics where it includes social costs.

Exam Probability: **Medium**

57. *Answer choices:*
(see index for correct answer)

- a. Trail commission
- b. Leximetrics
- c. Total cost of ownership
- d. Receivership

Guidance: level 1

:: Management ::

In inventory management, _____ is the order quantity that minimizes the total holding costs and ordering costs. It is one of the oldest classical production scheduling models. The model was developed by Ford W. Harris in 1913, but R. H. Wilson, a consultant who applied it extensively, and K. Andler are given credit for their in-depth analysis.

Exam Probability: **Medium**

58. *Answer choices:*
(see index for correct answer)

- a. Best practice
- b. Project cost management
- c. Association management company
- d. Economic order quantity

Guidance: level 1

:: ::

An _____ is a company that produces parts and equipment that may be marketed by another manufacturer. For example, Foxconn, a Taiwanese electronics contract manufacturing company, which produces a variety of parts and equipment for companies such as Apple Inc., Dell, Google, Huawei, Nintendo, etc., is the largest OEM company in the world by both scale and revenue.

Exam Probability: **High**

59. *Answer choices:*

(see index for correct answer)

- a. interpersonal communication
- b. empathy
- c. hierarchical
- d. Character

Guidance: level 1

Commerce

Commerce relates to "the exchange of goods and services, especially on a large scale." It includes legal, economic, political, social, cultural and technological systems that operate in any country or internationally.

:: Management ::

The term _____ refers to measures designed to increase the degree of autonomy and self-determination in people and in communities in order to enable them to represent their interests in a responsible and self-determined way, acting on their own authority. It is the process of becoming stronger and more confident, especially in controlling one's life and claiming one's rights. _____ as action refers both to the process of self- _____ and to professional support of people, which enables them to overcome their sense of powerlessness and lack of influence, and to recognize and use their resources. To do work with power.

Exam Probability: **Medium**

1. *Answer choices:*

(see index for correct answer)

- a. Unified interoperability
- b. Advisory board
- c. Target operating model
- d. Empowerment

Guidance: level 1

:: Supply chain management ::

A _____ is a type of auction in which the traditional roles of buyer and seller are reversed. Thus, there is one buyer and many potential sellers. In an ordinary auction, buyers compete to obtain goods or services by offering increasingly higher prices. In contrast, in a _____ , the sellers compete to obtain business from the buyer and prices will typically decrease as the sellers underbid each other.

Exam Probability: **Medium**

2. *Answer choices:*

(see index for correct answer)

- a. Supply chain cyber security
- b. Spend analysis
- c. Customs-Trade Partnership Against Terrorism
- d. Reverse auction

Guidance: level 1

:: Commercial item transport and distribution ::

A _____ in common law countries is a person or company that transports goods or people for any person or company and that is responsible for any possible loss of the goods during transport. A _____ offers its services to the general public under license or authority provided by a regulatory body. The regulatory body has usually been granted "ministerial authority" by the legislation that created it. The regulatory body may create, interpret, and enforce its regulations upon the _____ with independence and finality, as long as it acts within the bounds of the enabling legislation.

Exam Probability: **Medium**

3. *Answer choices:*

(see index for correct answer)

- a. Common carrier
- b. Unit load
- c. Sea protest
- d. DCT Industrial Trust

Guidance: level 1

:: Business models ::

A _____ is "an autonomous association of persons united voluntarily to meet their common economic, social, and cultural needs and aspirations through a jointly-owned and democratically-controlled enterprise". _____ s may include.

Exam Probability: **Low**

4. *Answer choices:*

(see index for correct answer)

- a. Consumer cooperative
- b. Trade printing
- c. Cooperative

- d. Lemonade stand

Guidance: level 1

:: Scientific method ::

In the social sciences and life sciences, a _____ is a research method involving an up-close, in-depth, and detailed examination of a subject of study, as well as its related contextual conditions.

Exam Probability: **Medium**

5. *Answer choices:*

(see index for correct answer)

- a. explanatory research
- b. pilot project
- c. Preference test
- d. Case study

Guidance: level 1

:: E-commerce ::

_____, cybersecurity or information technology security is the protection of computer systems from theft or damage to their hardware, software or electronic data, as well as from disruption or misdirection of the services they provide.

Exam Probability: **Medium**

6. *Answer choices:*

(see index for correct answer)

- a. Primecoin
- b. Playism
- c. Lyoness
- d. Computer security

Guidance: level 1

:: ::

_____ is the collection of techniques, skills, methods, and processes used in the production of goods or services or in the accomplishment of objectives, such as scientific investigation. _____ can be the knowledge of techniques, processes, and the like, or it can be embedded in machines to allow for operation without detailed knowledge of their workings. Systems applying _____ by taking an input, changing it according to the system's use, and then producing an outcome are referred to as _____ systems or technological systems.

Exam Probability: **Medium**

7. *Answer choices:*

(see index for correct answer)

- a. deep-level diversity
- b. hierarchical
- c. information systems assessment
- d. levels of analysis

Guidance: level 1

:: Management ::

A _____ is an idea of the future or desired result that a person or a group of people envisions, plans and commits to achieve. People endeavor to reach _____ s within a finite time by setting deadlines.

Exam Probability: **Medium**

8. *Answer choices:*

(see index for correct answer)

- a. Kata
- b. Goal
- c. Balanced scorecard
- d. Success trap

Guidance: level 1

:: ::

_____ is the collaborative effort of a team to achieve a common goal or to complete a task in the most effective and efficient way. This concept is seen within the greater framework of a team, which is a group of interdependent individuals who work together towards a common goal. Basic requirements for effective _____ are an adequate team size, available resources for the team to make use of, and clearly defined roles within the team in order for everyone to have a clear purpose. _____ is present in any context where a group of people are working together to achieve a common goal. These contexts include an industrial organization, athletics, a school, and the healthcare system. In each of these settings, the level of _____ and interdependence can vary from low, to intermediate, to high, depending on the amount of communication, interaction, and collaboration present between team members.

Exam Probability: **High**

9. *Answer choices:*

(see index for correct answer)

- a. imperative
- b. co-culture
- c. functional perspective
- d. hierarchical perspective

Guidance: level 1

:: Goods ::

In most contexts, the concept of _____ denotes the conduct that should be preferred when posed with a choice between possible actions. _____ is generally considered to be the opposite of evil, and is of interest in the study of morality, ethics, religion and philosophy. The specific meaning and etymology of the term and its associated translations among ancient and contemporary languages show substantial variation in its inflection and meaning depending on circumstances of place, history, religious, or philosophical context.

Exam Probability: **Low**

10. *Answer choices:*
(see index for correct answer)

- a. Intermediate good
- b. Credence good
- c. Experience good
- d. Normal good

Guidance: level 1

:: ::

_____ is both a research area and a practical skill encompassing the ability of an individual or organization to "lead" or guide other individuals, teams, or entire organizations. Specialist literature debates various viewpoints, contrasting Eastern and Western approaches to _____ , and also United States versus European approaches. U.S. academic environments define _____ as "a process of social influence in which a person can enlist the aid and support of others in the accomplishment of a common task".

Exam Probability: **Low**

11. *Answer choices:*

(see index for correct answer)

- a. Leadership
- b. similarity-attraction theory
- c. hierarchical
- d. information systems assessment

Guidance: level 1

:: ::

_____ Corporation is an American multinational technology company with headquarters in Redmond, Washington. It develops, manufactures, licenses, supports and sells computer software, consumer electronics, personal computers, and related services. Its best known software products are the _____ Windows line of operating systems, the _____ Office suite, and the Internet Explorer and Edge Web browsers. Its flagship hardware products are the Xbox video game consoles and the _____ Surface lineup of touchscreen personal computers. As of 2016, it is the world's largest software maker by revenue, and one of the world's most valuable companies. The word "_____" is a portmanteau of "microcomputer" and "software". _____ is ranked No. 30 in the 2018 Fortune 500 rankings of the largest United States corporations by total revenue.

Exam Probability: **Low**

12. *Answer choices:*

(see index for correct answer)

- a. surface-level diversity
- b. Sarbanes-Oxley act of 2002
- c. imperative
- d. Microsoft

Guidance: level 1

:: Economics terminology ::

_____ is the total receipts a seller can obtain from selling goods or services to buyers. It can be written as P × Q, which is the price of the goods multiplied by the quantity of the sold goods.

Exam Probability: **Low**

13. *Answer choices:*

(see index for correct answer)

- a. Total revenue
- b. fungible
- c. payee
- d. Bond issue

Guidance: level 1

:: Management accounting ::

In economics, _____ s, indirect costs or overheads are business expenses that are not dependent on the level of goods or services produced by the business. They tend to be time-related, such as interest or rents being paid per month, and are often referred to as overhead costs. This is in contrast to variable costs, which are volume-related and unknown at the beginning of the accounting year. For a simple example, such as a bakery, the monthly rent for the baking facilities, and the monthly payments for the security system and basic phone line are _____ s, as they do not change according to how much bread the bakery produces and sells. On the other hand, the wage costs of the bakery are variable, as the bakery will have to hire more workers if the production of bread increases. Economists reckon _____ as a entry barrier for new entrepreneurs.

Exam Probability: **Medium**

14. *Answer choices:*

(see index for correct answer)

- a. Certified Management Accountant
- b. Throughput accounting
- c. Fixed cost
- d. Pre-determined overhead rate

Guidance: level 1

:: ::

_____ characterises the behaviour of a system or model whose components interact in multiple ways and follow local rules, meaning there is no reasonable higher instruction to define the various possible interactions.

Exam Probability: **High**

15. *Answer choices:*

(see index for correct answer)

- a. interpersonal communication
- b. functional perspective
- c. information systems assessment
- d. open system

Guidance: level 1

:: Globalization-related theories ::

_____ is the process in which a nation is being improved in the sector of the economic, political, and social well-being of its people. The term has been used frequently by economists, politicians, and others in the 20th and 21st centuries. The concept, however, has been in existence in the West for centuries. "Modernization, "westernization", and especially "industrialization" are other terms often used while discussing _____ . _____ has a direct relationship with the environment and environmental issues. _____ is very often confused with industrial development, even in some academic sources.

Exam Probability: **High**

16. *Answer choices:*

(see index for correct answer)

- a. post-industrial
- b. postmodernism
- c. Capitalism

Guidance: level 1

:: ::

Competition law is a law that promotes or seeks to maintain market competition by regulating anti-competitive conduct by companies. Competition law is implemented through public and private enforcement. Competition law is known as "_____ law" in the United States for historical reasons, and as "anti-monopoly law" in China and Russia. In previous years it has been known as trade practices law in the United Kingdom and Australia. In the European Union, it is referred to as both _____ and competition law.

Exam Probability: **Low**

17. *Answer choices:*

(see index for correct answer)

- a. levels of analysis
- b. surface-level diversity

- c. interpersonal communication
- d. Antitrust

Guidance: level 1

:: Income ::

In business and accounting, net income is an entity's income minus cost of goods sold, expenses and taxes for an accounting period. It is computed as the residual of all revenues and gains over all expenses and losses for the period, and has also been defined as the net increase in shareholders' equity that results from a company's operations. In the context of the presentation of financial statements, the IFRS Foundation defines net income as synonymous with profit and loss. The difference between revenue and the cost of making a product or providing a service, before deducting overheads, payroll, taxation, and interest payments. This is different from operating income .

Exam Probability: **Medium**

18. *Answer choices:*

(see index for correct answer)

- a. Bottom line
- b. Net national income
- c. Real estate investing
- d. Passive income

Guidance: level 1

:: Marketing techniques ::

_____ is the activity of dividing a broad consumer or business market, normally consisting of existing and potential customers, into sub-groups of consumers based on some type of shared characteristics. In dividing or segmenting markets, researchers typically look for common characteristics such as shared needs, common interests, similar lifestyles or even similar demographic profiles. The overall aim of segmentation is to identify high yield segments – that is, those segments that are likely to be the most profitable or that have growth potential – so that these can be selected for special attention .

Exam Probability: **High**

19. *Answer choices:*

(see index for correct answer)

- a. Virtual event
- b. unique selling point
- c. Product demonstration
- d. Market segmentation

Guidance: level 1

:: Debt ::

_____ , in finance and economics, is payment from a borrower or deposit-taking financial institution to a lender or depositor of an amount above repayment of the principal sum , at a particular rate. It is distinct from a fee which the borrower may pay the lender or some third party. It is also distinct from dividend which is paid by a company to its shareholders from its profit or reserve, but not at a particular rate decided beforehand, rather on a pro rata basis as a share in the reward gained by risk taking entrepreneurs when the revenue earned exceeds the total costs.

Exam Probability: **Low**

20. *Answer choices:*

(see index for correct answer)

- a. Crown debt
- b. Interest
- c. Debt-lag
- d. External debt

Guidance: level 1

:: ::

An _____ is an area of the production, distribution, or trade, and consumption of goods and services by different agents. Understood in its broadest sense, 'The _____ is defined as a social domain that emphasize the practices, discourses, and material expressions associated with the production, use, and management of resources'. Economic agents can be individuals, businesses, organizations, or governments. Economic transactions occur when two parties agree to the value or price of the transacted good or service, commonly expressed in a certain currency. However, monetary transactions only account for a small part of the economic domain.

Exam Probability: **High**

21. *Answer choices:*

(see index for correct answer)

- a. Economy
- b. hierarchical
- c. similarity-attraction theory
- d. surface-level diversity

Guidance: level 1

:: E-commerce ::

_____ is a United States-based payment gateway service provider allowing merchants to accept credit card and electronic check payments through their website and over an Internet Protocol connection. Founded in 1996, _____ is now a subsidiary of Visa Inc. Its service permits customers to enter credit card and shipping information directly onto a web page, in contrast to some alternatives that require the customer to sign up for a payment service before performing a transaction.

Exam Probability: **High**

22. *Answer choices:*

(see index for correct answer)

- a. Self-certifying key
- b. Pay at the pump
- c. AsiaPay
- d. Authorize.Net

Guidance: level 1

:: E-commerce ::

IBM _____ also known as WCS is a software platform framework for e-commerce, including marketing, sales, customer and order processing functionality in a tailorable, integrated package. It is a single, unified platform which offers the ability to do business directly with consumers, with businesses, indirectly through channel partners, or all of these simultaneously. _____ is a customizable, scalable and high availability solution built on the Java - Java EE platform using open standards, such as XML, and Web services.

Exam Probability: **Low**

23. *Answer choices:*

(see index for correct answer)

- a. ISO 8583
- b. WebSphere Commerce
- c. Digital credential
- d. Playism

Guidance: level 1

:: ::

A _____ is a graphic mark, emblem, or symbol used to aid and promote public identification and recognition. It may be of an abstract or figurative design or include the text of the name it represents as in a wordmark.

Exam Probability: **High**

24. Answer choices:

(see index for correct answer)

- a. Character
- b. deep-level diversity
- c. open system
- d. levels of analysis

Guidance: level 1

:: Business law ::

A _____ is a group of people who jointly supervise the activities of an organization, which can be either a for-profit business, nonprofit organization, or a government agency. Such a board's powers, duties, and responsibilities are determined by government regulations and the organization's own constitution and bylaws. These authorities may specify the number of members of the board, how they are to be chosen, and how often they are to meet.

Exam Probability: **Low**

25. Answer choices:

(see index for correct answer)

- a. Bulk sale
- b. License
- c. Duty of fair representation

- d. Board of directors

Guidance: level 1

:: Marketing ::

_____ is the percentage of a market accounted for by a specific entity. In a survey of nearly 200 senior marketing managers, 67% responded that they found the revenue- "dollar _____" metric very useful, while 61% found "unit _____" very useful.

Exam Probability: **Low**

26. *Answer choices:*

(see index for correct answer)

- a. Gimmick
- b. Digital native
- c. Market share
- d. Cannibalization

Guidance: level 1

:: Production economics ::

In microeconomics, _____ are the cost advantages that enterprises obtain due to their scale of operation, with cost per unit of output decreasing with increasing scale.

Exam Probability: **Low**

27. *Answer choices:*

(see index for correct answer)

- a. Economies of scale
- b. Split-off point
- c. Post-Fordism
- d. Synergy

Guidance: level 1

:: Production economics ::

In economics and related disciplines, a _____ is a cost in making any economic trade when participating in a market.

Exam Probability: **Medium**

28. *Answer choices:*

(see index for correct answer)

- a. Transaction cost
- b. Capitalist mode of production
- c. Marginal product
- d. Specialization

Guidance: level 1

:: ::

A _____ is a person who trades in commodities produced by other people. Historically, a _____ is anyone who is involved in business or trade. _____ s have operated for as long as industry, commerce, and trade have existed. During the 16th-century, in Europe, two different terms for _____ s emerged: One term, meerseniers, described local traders such as bakers, grocers, etc.; while a new term, koopman (Dutch: koopman, described _____ s who operated on a global stage, importing and exporting goods over vast distances, and offering added-value services such as credit and finance.

Exam Probability: **Medium**

29. *Answer choices:*
(see index for correct answer)

- a. personal values
- b. functional perspective
- c. similarity-attraction theory
- d. Merchant

Guidance: level 1

:: Commerce ::

A _____ is an employee within a company, business or other organization who is responsible at some level for buying or approving the acquisition of goods and services needed by the company. Responsible for buying the best quality products, goods and services for their company at the most competitive prices, _____ s work in a wide range of sectors for many different organizations. The position responsibilities may be the same as that of a buyer or purchasing agent, or may include wider supervisory or managerial responsibilities. A _____ may oversee the acquisition of materials needed for production, general supplies for offices and facilities, equipment, or construction contracts. A _____ often supervises purchasing agents and buyers, but in small companies the _____ may also be the purchasing agent or buyer. The _____ position may also carry the title "Procurement Manager" or in the public sector, "Procurement Officer". He or she can come from both an Engineering or Economics background.

Exam Probability: **Low**

30. *Answer choices:*
(see index for correct answer)

- a. Too cheap to meter
- b. Economic entity
- c. Purchasing manager
- d. Treasure voyages

Guidance: level 1

:: Statutory law ::

_____ or statute law is written law set down by a body of legislature or by a singular legislator . This is as opposed to oral or customary law; or regulatory law promulgated by the executive or common law of the judiciary. Statutes may originate with national, state legislatures or local municipalities.

Exam Probability: **Medium**

31. *Answer choices:*

(see index for correct answer)

- a. ratification
- b. statute law
- c. Statute of repose
- d. incorporation by reference

Guidance: level 1

:: Budgets ::

A _____ is a financial plan for a defined period, often one year. It may also include planned sales volumes and revenues, resource quantities, costs and expenses, assets, liabilities and cash flows. Companies, governments, families and other organizations use it to express strategic plans of activities or events in measurable terms.

Exam Probability: **Medium**

32. *Answer choices:*

(see index for correct answer)

- a. Marginal budgeting for bottlenecks
- b. Budget
- c. Budget set
- d. Personal budget

Guidance: level 1

:: Workplace ::

_____ is asystematic determination of a subject's merit, worth and significance, using criteria governed by a set of standards. It can assist an organization, program, design, project or any other intervention or initiative to assess any aim, realisable concept/proposal, or any alternative, to help in decision-making; or to ascertain the degree of achievement or value in regard to the aim and objectives and results of any such action that has been completed. The primary purpose of _____ , in addition to gaining insight into prior or existing initiatives, is to enable reflection and assist in the identification of future change.

Exam Probability: **High**

33. *Answer choices:*

(see index for correct answer)

- a. Workplace spirituality
- b. Evaluation
- c. Workplace listening
- d. Workplace revenge

Guidance: level 1

:: Materials ::

A _____ , also known as a feedstock, unprocessed material, or primary commodity, is a basic material that is used to produce goods, finished products, energy, or intermediate materials which are feedstock for future finished products. As feedstock, the term connotes these materials are bottleneck assets and are highly important with regard to producing other products. An example of this is crude oil, which is a _____ and a feedstock used in the production of industrial chemicals, fuels, plastics, and pharmaceutical goods; lumber is a _____ used to produce a variety of products including all types of furniture. The term " _____ " denotes materials in minimally processed or unprocessed in states; e.g., raw latex, crude oil, cotton, coal, raw biomass, iron ore, air, logs, or water i.e. "...any product of agriculture, forestry, fishing and any other mineral that is in its natural form or which has undergone the transformation required to prepare it for internationally marketing in substantial volumes."

Exam Probability: **Medium**

34. *Answer choices:*

(see index for correct answer)

- a. Printing and writing paper
- b. Agamassan
- c. Raw material
- d. Sealant

Guidance: level 1

:: International trade ::

_____ involves the transfer of goods or services from one person or entity to another, often in exchange for money. A system or network that allows _____ is called a market.

Exam Probability: **Medium**

35. *Answer choices:*

(see index for correct answer)

- a. Trade Act of 1974
- b. Technical barriers to trade
- c. International Standards of Accounting and Reporting
- d. Oriental Development Company

Guidance: level 1

:: Warrants issued in Hong Kong Stock Exchange ::

_____ is a chemical element with symbol Ag and atomic number 47. A soft, white, lustrous transition metal, it exhibits the highest electrical conductivity, thermal conductivity, and reflectivity of any metal. The metal is found in the Earth's crust in the pure, free elemental form , as an alloy with gold and other metals, and in minerals such as argentite and chlorargyrite. Most _____ is produced as a byproduct of copper, gold, lead, and zinc refining.

Exam Probability: **High**

36. *Answer choices:*

(see index for correct answer)

- a. Silver
- b. Dongfang Electric
- c. Sino Land
- d. Beijing Capital International Airport Company Limited

Guidance: level 1

:: Marketing by medium ::

_____, also called online marketing or Internet advertising or web advertising, is a form of marketing and advertising which uses the Internet to deliver promotional marketing messages to consumers. Many consumers find _____ disruptive and have increasingly turned to ad blocking for a variety of reasons. When software is used to do the purchasing, it is known as programmatic advertising.

Exam Probability: **High**

37. *Answer choices:*

(see index for correct answer)

- a. New media marketing
- b. Direct Text Marketing
- c. Online advertising
- d. Brand infiltration

Guidance: level 1

:: ::

A trade fair is an exhibition organized so that companies in a specific industry can showcase and demonstrate their latest products and services, meet with industry partners and customers, study activities of rivals, and examine recent market trends and opportunities. In contrast to consumer fairs, only some trade fairs are open to the public, while others can only be attended by company representatives and members of the press, therefore _____ s are classified as either "public" or "trade only". A few fairs are hybrids of the two; one example is the Frankfurt Book Fair, which is trade only for its first three days and open to the general public on its final two days. They are held on a continuing basis in virtually all markets and normally attract companies from around the globe. For example, in the U.S., there are currently over 10,000 _____ s held every year, and several online directories have been established to help organizers, attendees, and marketers identify appropriate events.

Exam Probability: **High**

38. *Answer choices:*

(see index for correct answer)

- a. hierarchical
- b. Trade show
- c. Sarbanes-Oxley act of 2002
- d. information systems assessment

Guidance: level 1

:: Minimum wage ::

A _____ is the lowest remuneration that employers can legally pay their workers—the price floor below which workers may not sell their labor. Most countries had introduced _____ legislation by the end of the 20th century.

Exam Probability: **Low**

39. *Answer choices:*
(see index for correct answer)

- a. Minimum Wage Fairness Act
- b. Working poor
- c. Minimum wage
- d. National Anti-Sweating League

Guidance: level 1

:: ::

_____ is an American restaurant chain and international franchise which was founded in 1958 by Dan and Frank Carney. The company is known for its Italian-American cuisine menu, including pizza and pasta, as well as side dishes and desserts. _____ has 18,431 restaurants worldwide as of December 31, 2018, making it the world's largest pizza chain in terms of locations. It is a subsidiary of Yum! Brands, Inc., one of the world's largest restaurant companies.

Exam Probability: **Low**

40. Answer choices:

(see index for correct answer)

- a. hierarchical perspective
- b. functional perspective
- c. co-culture
- d. Sarbanes-Oxley act of 2002

Guidance: level 1

:: Stock market ::

The _____ of a corporation is all of the shares into which ownership of the corporation is divided. In American English, the shares are commonly known as " _____ s". A single share of the _____ represents fractional ownership of the corporation in proportion to the total number of shares. This typically entitles the _____ holder to that fraction of the company's earnings, proceeds from liquidation of assets , or voting power, often dividing these up in proportion to the amount of money each _____ holder has invested. Not all _____ is necessarily equal, as certain classes of _____ may be issued for example without voting rights, with enhanced voting rights, or with a certain priority to receive profits or liquidation proceeds before or after other classes of shareholders.

Exam Probability: **Low**

41. Answer choices:

(see index for correct answer)

- a. Trading turret
- b. End of day
- c. Prime Standard
- d. Chi-X Global

Guidance: level 1

:: Mereology ::

_____ , in the abstract, is what belongs to or with something, whether as an attribute or as a component of said thing. In the context of this article, it is one or more components , whether physical or incorporeal, of a person's estate; or so belonging to, as in being owned by, a person or jointly a group of people or a legal entity like a corporation or even a society. Depending on the nature of the _____ , an owner of _____ has the right to consume, alter, share, redefine, rent, mortgage, pawn, sell, exchange, transfer, give away or destroy it, or to exclude others from doing these things, as well as to perhaps abandon it; whereas regardless of the nature of the _____ , the owner thereof has the right to properly use it , or at the very least exclusively keep it.

Exam Probability: **High**

42. *Answer choices:*

(see index for correct answer)

- a. Mereological nihilism
- b. Simple
- c. Property

- d. Mereotopology

Guidance: level 1

:: Dot-com bubble ::

_____ was an online grocery business that filed bankruptcy in 2001 after 3 years of operation and was later folded into Amazon.com. It was headquartered in Foster City, California, United States. It delivered products to customers' homes within a 30-minute window of their choosing. At its peak, it offered service in ten US markets: the San Francisco Bay Area; Dallas; Sacramento; San Diego; Los Angeles; Orange County, California; Chicago; Seattle; Portland, Oregon; and Atlanta, Georgia. The company had hoped to expand to 26 cities by 2001.

Exam Probability: **High**

43. *Answer choices:*

(see index for correct answer)

- a. @Home Network
- b. DrinkExchange
- c. Webvan
- d. Pay to surf

Guidance: level 1

:: Payment systems ::

_____ s are part of a payment system issued by financial institutions, such as a bank, to a customer that enables its owner to access the funds in the customer's designated bank accounts, or through a credit account and make payments by electronic funds transfer and access automated teller machines. Such cards are known by a variety of names including bank cards, ATM cards, MAC , client cards, key cards or cash cards.

Exam Probability: **Medium**

44. *Answer choices:*

(see index for correct answer)

- a. K-CASH
- b. Substitute check
- c. Sistema de Pagamentos em Moeda Local
- d. Payment card

Guidance: level 1

:: Business law ::

The _____ , first published in 1952, is one of a number of Uniform Acts that have been established as law with the goal of harmonizing the laws of sales and other commercial transactions across the United States of America through UCC adoption by all 50 states, the District of Columbia, and the Territories of the United States.

Exam Probability: **Low**

45. *Answer choices:*

(see index for correct answer)

- a. Complex structured finance transactions
- b. Chattel mortgage
- c. Official Assignee
- d. Uniform Commercial Code

Guidance: level 1

:: ::

In the broadest sense, _____ is any practice which contributes to the sale of products to a retail consumer. At a retail in-store level, _____ refers to the variety of products available for sale and the display of those products in such a way that it stimulates interest and entices customers to make a purchase.

Exam Probability: **High**

46. *Answer choices:*

(see index for correct answer)

- a. hierarchical
- b. cultural

- c. hierarchical perspective
- d. Merchandising

Guidance: level 1

:: ::

_____ is the extraction of valuable minerals or other geological materials from the earth, usually from an ore body, lode, vein, seam, reef or placer deposit. These deposits form a mineralized package that is of economic interest to the miner.

Exam Probability: **Medium**

47. *Answer choices:*

(see index for correct answer)

- a. Character
- b. process perspective
- c. Mining
- d. co-culture

Guidance: level 1

:: E-commerce ::

Customer to customer markets provide an innovative way to allow customers to interact with each other. Traditional markets require business to customer relationships, in which a customer goes to the business in order to purchase a product or service. In customer to customer markets, the business facilitates an environment where customers can sell goods or services to each other. Other types of markets include business to business and business to customer.

Exam Probability: **High**

48. *Answer choices:*

(see index for correct answer)

- a. Demandware
- b. Wanelo
- c. Foodie.fm
- d. Consumer-to-consumer

Guidance: level 1

:: Human resource management ::

_____ are the people who make up the workforce of an organization, business sector, or economy. "Human capital" is sometimes used synonymously with "_____", although human capital typically refers to a narrower effect. Likewise, other terms sometimes used include manpower, talent, labor, personnel, or simply people.

Exam Probability: **Medium**

49. Answer choices:

(see index for correct answer)

- a. Talent supply chain management
- b. Adaptive performance
- c. Human resources
- d. Selection ratio

Guidance: level 1

:: ::

_____ Holdings, Inc. is an American company operating a worldwide online payments system that supports online money transfers and serves as an electronic alternative to traditional paper methods like checks and money orders. The company operates as a payment processor for online vendors, auction sites, and many other commercial users, for which it charges a fee in exchange for benefits such as one-click transactions and password memory. _____ 's payment system, also called _____ , is considered a type of payment rail.

Exam Probability: **Medium**

50. Answer choices:

(see index for correct answer)

- a. corporate values
- b. Sarbanes-Oxley act of 2002
- c. empathy

- d. hierarchical perspective

Guidance: level 1

:: Industry ::

_____ , also known as flow production or continuous production, is the production of large amounts of standardized products, including and especially on assembly lines. Together with job production and batch production, it is one of the three main production methods.

Exam Probability: **High**

51. *Answer choices:*

(see index for correct answer)

- a. Maintenance engineering
- b. Industrial society
- c. Mass production
- d. Industrialisation

Guidance: level 1

:: ::

In marketing jargon, product lining is offering several related products for sale individually. Unlike product bundling, where several products are combined into one group, which is then offered for sale as a units, product lining involves offering the products for sale separately. A line can comprise related products of various sizes, types, colors, qualities, or prices. Line depth refers to the number of subcategories a category has. Line consistency refers to how closely related the products that make up the line are. Line vulnerability refers to the percentage of sales or profits that are derived from only a few products in the line.

Exam Probability: **Medium**

52. *Answer choices:*

(see index for correct answer)

- a. Product line
- b. functional perspective
- c. levels of analysis
- d. Sarbanes-Oxley act of 2002

Guidance: level 1

:: ::

_____ is a term frequently used in marketing. It is a measure of how products and services supplied by a company meet or surpass customer expectation. _____ is defined as "the number of customers, or percentage of total customers, whose reported experience with a firm, its products, or its services exceeds specified satisfaction goals."

Exam Probability: **Low**

53. *Answer choices:*

(see index for correct answer)

- a. deep-level diversity
- b. empathy
- c. open system
- d. Customer satisfaction

Guidance: level 1

:: Information technology management ::

_____ s or pop-ups are forms of online advertising on the World Wide Web. A pop-up is a graphical user interface display area, usually a small window, that suddenly appears in the foreground of the visual interface. The pop-up window containing an advertisement is usually generated by JavaScript that uses cross-site scripting, sometimes with a secondary payload that uses Adobe Flash. They can also be generated by other vulnerabilities/security holes in browser security.

Exam Probability: **Low**

54. *Answer choices:*

(see index for correct answer)

- a. SFIAPlus

- b. Library Review
- c. Business Information Services Library
- d. Pop-up ad

Guidance: level 1

:: ::

_____ is a qualitative measure used to relate the quality of motor vehicle traffic service. LOS is used to analyze roadways and intersections by categorizing traffic flow and assigning quality levels of traffic based on performance measure like vehicle speed, density, congestion, etc.

Exam Probability: **High**

55. *Answer choices:*

(see index for correct answer)

- a. similarity-attraction theory
- b. hierarchical
- c. Level of service
- d. empathy

Guidance: level 1

:: Economic globalization ::

_____ is an agreement in which one company hires another company to be responsible for a planned or existing activity that is or could be done internally, and sometimes involves transferring employees and assets from one firm to another.

Exam Probability: **Medium**

56. *Answer choices:*

(see index for correct answer)

- a. Outsourcing
- b. global financial

Guidance: level 1

:: Organizational structure ::

An _____ defines how activities such as task allocation, coordination, and supervision are directed toward the achievement of organizational aims.

Exam Probability: **Medium**

57. *Answer choices:*

(see index for correct answer)

- a. Organization of the New York City Police Department

- b. Blessed Unrest
- c. Followership
- d. Organizational structure

Guidance: level 1

:: Income ::

_____ is a ratio between the net profit and cost of investment resulting from an investment of some resources. A high ROI means the investment's gains favorably to its cost. As a performance measure, ROI is used to evaluate the efficiency of an investment or to compare the efficiencies of several different investments. In purely economic terms, it is one way of relating profits to capital invested. _____ is a performance measure used by businesses to identify the efficiency of an investment or number of different investments.

Exam Probability: **Medium**

58. *Answer choices:*
(see index for correct answer)

- a. Return on investment
- b. Aggregate income
- c. Stipend
- d. Private income

Guidance: level 1

The Walt _____ Company, commonly known as Walt _____ or simply _____ , is an American diversified multinational mass media and entertainment conglomerate headquartered at the Walt _____ Studios in Burbank, California.

Exam Probability: **High**

59. *Answer choices:*

(see index for correct answer)

- a. empathy
- b. Disney
- c. Sarbanes-Oxley act of 2002
- d. hierarchical

Guidance: level 1

Business ethics

Business ethics (also known as corporate ethics) is a form of applied ethics or professional ethics, that examines ethical principles and moral or ethical problems that can arise in a business environment. It applies to all aspects of business conduct and is relevant to the conduct of individuals and entire organizations. These ethics originate from individuals, organizational statements or from the legal system. These norms, values, ethical, and unethical practices are what is used to guide business. They help those businesses maintain a better connection with their stakeholders.

_____ Ltd. is the world's 2nd largest offshore drilling contractor and is based in Vernier, Switzerland. The company has offices in 20 countries, including Switzerland, Canada, United States, Norway, Scotland, India, Brazil, Singapore, Indonesia and Malaysia.

Exam Probability: **Low**

1. *Answer choices:*

(see index for correct answer)

- a. Transocean
- b. similarity-attraction theory
- c. interpersonal communication
- d. empathy

Guidance: level 1

:: Electronic waste ::

_____ or e-waste describes discarded electrical or electronic devices. Used electronics which are destined for refurbishment, reuse, resale, salvage, recycling through material recovery, or disposal are also considered e-waste. Informal processing of e-waste in developing countries can lead to adverse human health effects and environmental pollution.

Exam Probability: **High**

2. Answer choices:

(see index for correct answer)

- a. Solving the E-waste Problem
- b. Computer liquidator
- c. Electronic waste
- d. ReGlobe

Guidance: level 1

:: ::

A _____ service is an online platform which people use to build social networks or social relationship with other people who share similar personal or career interests, activities, backgrounds or real-life connections.

Exam Probability: **High**

3. Answer choices:

(see index for correct answer)

- a. surface-level diversity
- b. co-culture
- c. Character
- d. Social networking

Guidance: level 1

:: Anti-competitive behaviour ::

_____ is a secret cooperation or deceitful agreement in order to deceive others, although not necessarily illegal, as a conspiracy. A secret agreement between two or more parties to limit open competition by deceiving, misleading, or defrauding others of their legal rights, or to obtain an objective forbidden by law typically by defrauding or gaining an unfair market advantage is an example of _____ . It is an agreement among firms or individuals to divide a market, set prices, limit production or limit opportunities. It can involve "unions, wage fixing, kickbacks, or misrepresenting the independence of the relationship between the colluding parties". In legal terms, all acts effected by _____ are considered void.

Exam Probability: **Low**

4. *Answer choices:*

(see index for correct answer)

- a. Collusion
- b. Transports Schiocchet Excursions
- c. Group boycott
- d. Ringfencing

Guidance: level 1

:: Progressive Era in the United States ::

The Clayton Antitrust Act of 1914, was a part of United States antitrust law with the goal of adding further substance to the U.S. antitrust law regime; the _____ sought to prevent anticompetitive practices in their incipiency. That regime started with the Sherman Antitrust Act of 1890, the first Federal law outlawing practices considered harmful to consumers. The _____ specified particular prohibited conduct, the three-level enforcement scheme, the exemptions, and the remedial measures.

Exam Probability: **Low**

5. *Answer choices:*

(see index for correct answer)

- a. pragmatism
- b. Clayton Antitrust Act
- c. Mann Act

Guidance: level 1

:: Social responsibility ::

The United Nations Global Compact is a non-binding United Nations pact to encourage businesses worldwide to adopt sustainable and socially responsible policies, and to report on their implementation. The _____ is a principle-based framework for businesses, stating ten principles in the areas of human rights, labor, the environment and anti-corruption. Under the Global Compact, companies are brought together with UN agencies, labor groups and civil society. Cities can join the Global Compact through the Cities Programme.

Exam Probability: **Medium**

6. *Answer choices:*

(see index for correct answer)

- a. Stakeholder engagement
- b. Socially responsible business
- c. UN Global Compact
- d. Socially responsible marketing

Guidance: level 1

:: ::

A _____ is an organization, usually a group of people or a company, authorized to act as a single entity and recognized as such in law. Early incorporated entities were established by charter. Most jurisdictions now allow the creation of new _____ s through registration.

Exam Probability: **High**

7. *Answer choices:*

(see index for correct answer)

- a. Corporation
- b. process perspective
- c. corporate values

- d. personal values

Guidance: level 1

:: Waste ::

_____ is any unwanted material in all forms that can cause harm. Many of today's household products such as televisions, computers and phones contain toxic chemicals that can pollute the air and contaminate soil and water. Disposing of such waste is a major public health issue.

Exam Probability: **High**

8. *Answer choices:*
(see index for correct answer)

- a. Green waste
- b. Demolition waste
- c. Inert waste
- d. Universal waste

Guidance: level 1

:: ::

The _____ is an agency of the United States Department of Labor. Congress established the agency under the Occupational Safety and Health Act, which President Richard M. Nixon signed into law on December 29, 1970. OSHA's mission is to "assure safe and healthy working conditions for working men and women by setting and enforcing standards and by providing training, outreach, education and assistance". The agency is also charged with enforcing a variety of whistleblower statutes and regulations. OSHA is currently headed by Acting Assistant Secretary of Labor Loren Sweatt. OSHA's workplace safety inspections have been shown to reduce injury rates and injury costs without adverse effects to employment, sales, credit ratings, or firm survival.

Exam Probability: **Low**

9. *Answer choices:*

(see index for correct answer)

- a. Occupational Safety and Health Administration
- b. similarity-attraction theory
- c. Sarbanes-Oxley act of 2002
- d. interpersonal communication

Guidance: level 1

:: Offshoring ::

A _____ is the temporary suspension or permanent termination of employment of an employee or, more commonly, a group of employees for business reasons, such as personnel management or downsizing an organization. Originally, _____ referred exclusively to a temporary interruption in work, or employment but this has evolved to a permanent elimination of a position in both British and US English, requiring the addition of "temporary" to specify the original meaning of the word. A _____ is not to be confused with wrongful termination. Laid off workers or displaced workers are workers who have lost or left their jobs because their employer has closed or moved, there was insufficient work for them to do, or their position or shift was abolished . Downsizing in a company is defined to involve the reduction of employees in a workforce. Downsizing in companies became a popular practice in the 1980s and early 1990s as it was seen as a way to deliver better shareholder value as it helps to reduce the costs of employers . Indeed, recent research on downsizing in the U.S., UK, and Japan suggests that downsizing is being regarded by management as one of the preferred routes to help declining organizations, cutting unnecessary costs, and improve organizational performance. Usually a _____ occurs as a cost cutting measure.

Exam Probability: **High**

10. *Answer choices:*

(see index for correct answer)

- a. Nearshoring
- b. Offshore outsourcing
- c. Layoff
- d. Sourcing advisory

Guidance: level 1

:: ::

_____ or accountancy is the measurement, processing, and communication of financial information about economic entities such as businesses and corporations. The modern field was established by the Italian mathematician Luca Pacioli in 1494. _____, which has been called the "language of business", measures the results of an organization's economic activities and conveys this information to a variety of users, including investors, creditors, management, and regulators. Practitioners of _____ are known as accountants. The terms "_____" and "financial reporting" are often used as synonyms.

Exam Probability: **Low**

11. *Answer choices:*

(see index for correct answer)

- a. Character
- b. Accounting
- c. hierarchical perspective
- d. open system

Guidance: level 1

:: Water law ::

The _____ is the primary federal law in the United States governing water pollution. Its objective is to restore and maintain the chemical, physical, and biological integrity of the nation's waters; recognizing the responsibilities of the states in addressing pollution and providing assistance to states to do so, including funding for publicly owned treatment works for the improvement of wastewater treatment; and maintaining the integrity of wetlands. It is one of the United States' first and most influential modern environmental laws. As with many other major U.S. federal environmental statutes, it is administered by the U.S. Environmental Protection Agency , in coordination with state governments. Its implementing regulations are codified at 40 C.F.R. Subchapters D, N, and O .

Exam Probability: **High**

12. *Answer choices:*

(see index for correct answer)

- a. Permanent water rights
- b. Water law
- c. Clean Water Act
- d. The Helsinki Rules on the Uses of the Waters of International Rivers

Guidance: level 1

:: Cultural appropriation ::

_____ is a social and economic order that encourages the acquisition of goods and services in ever-increasing amounts. With the industrial revolution, but particularly in the 20th century, mass production led to an economic crisis: there was overproduction—the supply of goods would grow beyond consumer demand, and so manufacturers turned to planned obsolescence and advertising to manipulate consumer spending. In 1899, a book on _____ published by Thorstein Veblen, called The Theory of the Leisure Class, examined the widespread values and economic institutions emerging along with the widespread "leisure time" in the beginning of the 20th century. In it Veblen "views the activities and spending habits of this leisure class in terms of conspicuous and vicarious consumption and waste. Both are related to the display of status and not to functionality or usefulness."

Exam Probability: **Low**

13. *Answer choices:*

(see index for correct answer)

- a. Consumerism
- b. Wigger
- c. Global village
- d. Representation of African Americans in media

Guidance: level 1

:: Labor rights ::

The _____ is the concept that people have a human _____, or engage in productive employment, and may not be prevented from doing so. The _____ is enshrined in the Universal Declaration of Human Rights and recognized in international human rights law through its inclusion in the International Covenant on Economic, Social and Cultural Rights, where the _____ emphasizes economic, social and cultural development.

Exam Probability: **Medium**

14. *Answer choices:*

(see index for correct answer)

- a. Labor rights
- b. China Labour Bulletin
- c. Kate Mullany House
- d. Right to work

Guidance: level 1

:: Production and manufacturing ::

_____ is a set of techniques and tools for process improvement. Though as a shortened form it may be found written as 6S, it should not be confused with the methodology known as 6S.

Exam Probability: **Medium**

15. *Answer choices:*

(see index for correct answer)

- a. Food processing
- b. CTQ tree
- c. SafetyBUS p
- d. MAPICS

Guidance: level 1

:: Coal ::

_____ is a combustible black or brownish-black sedimentary rock, formed as rock strata called _____ seams. _____ is mostly carbon with variable amounts of other elements; chiefly hydrogen, sulfur, oxygen, and nitrogen. _____ is formed if dead plant matter decays into peat and over millions of years the heat and pressure of deep burial converts the peat into _____ . Vast deposits of _____ originates in former wetlands—called _____ forests—that covered much of the Earth's tropical land areas during the late Carboniferous and Permian times.

Exam Probability: **Medium**

16. *Answer choices:*

(see index for correct answer)

- a. Coal
- b. Liptinite

- c. Maceral
- d. Black coal equivalent

Guidance: level 1

:: Corporate scandals ::

The _____ was a privately held international group of financial services companies controlled by Allen Stanford, until it was seized by United States authorities in early 2009. Headquartered in the Galleria Tower II in Uptown Houston, Texas, it had 50 offices in several countries, mainly in the Americas, included the Stanford International Bank, and said it managed US$8.5 billion of assets for more than 30,000 clients in 136 countries on six continents. On February 17, 2009, U.S. Federal agents placed the company into receivership due to charges of fraud. Ten days later, the U.S. Securities and Exchange Commission amended its complaint to accuse Stanford of turning the company into a "massive Ponzi scheme".

Exam Probability: **Medium**

17. *Answer choices:*
(see index for correct answer)

- a. Xybernaut
- b. AOL search data leak
- c. S-Chips Scandals
- d. Guinness share-trading fraud

Guidance: level 1

:: False advertising law ::

The Lanham Act is the primary federal trademark statute of law in the United States. The Act prohibits a number of activities, including trademark infringement, trademark dilution, and false advertising.

Exam Probability: **High**

18. *Answer choices:*

(see index for correct answer)

- a. POM Wonderful LLC v. Coca-Cola Co.
- b. Lanham Act

Guidance: level 1

:: Carbon finance ::

The _____ is an international treaty which extends the 1992 United Nations Framework Convention on Climate Change that commits state parties to reduce greenhouse gas emissions, based on the scientific consensus that global warming is occurring and it is extremely likely that human-made CO_2 emissions have predominantly caused it. The _____ was adopted in Kyoto, Japan on 11 December 1997 and entered into force on 16 February 2005. There are currently 192 parties to the Protocol.

Exam Probability: **Low**

19. *Answer choices:*

(see index for correct answer)

- a. Element Markets
- b. Carbon Trust
- c. Tianjin Climate Exchange
- d. Kyoto Protocol

Guidance: level 1

:: Business ethics ::

_____ is a persistent pattern of mistreatment from others in the workplace that causes either physical or emotional harm. It can include such tactics as verbal, nonverbal, psychological, physical abuse and humiliation. This type of workplace aggression is particularly difficult because, unlike the typical school bully, workplace bullies often operate within the established rules and policies of their organization and their society. In the majority of cases, bullying in the workplace is reported as having been by someone who has authority over their victim. However, bullies can also be peers, and occasionally subordinates. Research has also investigated the impact of the larger organizational context on bullying as well as the group-level processes that impact on the incidence and maintenance of bullying behaviour. Bullying can be covert or overt. It may be missed by superiors; it may be known by many throughout the organization. Negative effects are not limited to the targeted individuals, and may lead to a decline in employee morale and a change in organizational culture. It can also take place as overbearing supervision, constant criticism, and blocking promotions.

Exam Probability: **Medium**

20. *Answer choices:*

(see index for correct answer)

- a. Surface Transportation Assistance Act
- b. Institute for Business and Professional Ethics
- c. Workplace bullying
- d. Proceedings of the International Association for Business and Society

Guidance: level 1

:: Workplace ::

In business management, _____ is a management style whereby a manager closely observes and/or controls the work of his/her subordinates or employees.

Exam Probability: **High**

21. *Answer choices:*

(see index for correct answer)

- a. Workplace strategy
- b. Workplace relationships
- c. Micromanagement
- d. Workplace incivility

Guidance: level 1

:: Fraud ::

In the United States, _____ is the claiming of Medicare health care reimbursement to which the claimant is not entitled. There are many different types of _____ , all of which have the same goal: to collect money from the Medicare program illegitimately.

Exam Probability: **Medium**

22. *Answer choices:*

(see index for correct answer)

- a. Lip-synching in music
- b. Lip sync
- c. misleading advertising
- d. Medicare fraud

Guidance: level 1

:: ::

The Catholic Church, also known as the Roman Catholic Church, is the largest Christian church, with approximately 1.3 billion baptised Catholics worldwide as of 2017. As the world's oldest continuously functioning international institution, it has played a prominent role in the history and development of Western civilisation. The church is headed by the Bishop of Rome, known as the pope. Its central administration, the Holy See, is in the Vatican City, an enclave within the city of Rome in Italy.

Exam Probability: **High**

23. *Answer choices:*

(see index for correct answer)

- a. process perspective
- b. information systems assessment
- c. empathy
- d. Catholicism

Guidance: level 1

:: United Kingdom labour law ::

The _____ was a series of programs, public work projects, financial reforms, and regulations enacted by President Franklin D. Roosevelt in the United States between 1933 and 1936. It responded to needs for relief, reform, and recovery from the Great Depression. Major federal programs included the Civilian Conservation Corps , the Civil Works Administration , the Farm Security Administration , the National Industrial Recovery Act of 1933 and the Social Security Administration . They provided support for farmers, the unemployed, youth and the elderly. The _____ included new constraints and safeguards on the banking industry and efforts to re-inflate the economy after prices had fallen sharply. _____ programs included both laws passed by Congress as well as presidential executive orders during the first term of the presidency of Franklin D. Roosevelt.

Exam Probability: **Low**

24. *Answer choices:*

(see index for correct answer)

- a. Mutual trust and confidence
- b. New Deal
- c. Collective Redundancies Directive
- d. Transnational Works Council Directive

Guidance: level 1

:: Private equity ::

In finance, a high-yield bond is a bond that is rated below investment grade. These bonds have a higher risk of default or other adverse credit events, but typically pay higher yields than better quality bonds in order to make them attractive to investors.

Exam Probability: **Medium**

25. *Answer choices:*

(see index for correct answer)

- a. Private Equity Growth Capital Council
- b. Junk bond
- c. LBO valuation model
- d. SVOX

Guidance: level 1

:: ::

The _____ to Fight AIDS, Tuberculosis and Malaria is an international financing organization that aims to "attract, leverage and invest additional resources to end the epidemics of HIV/AIDS, tuberculosis and malaria to support attainment of the Sustainable Development Goals established by the United Nations." A public-private partnership, the organization maintains its secretariat in Geneva, Switzerland. The organization began operations in January 2002. Microsoft founder Bill Gates was one of the first private foundations among many bilateral donors to provide seed money for the partnership.

Exam Probability: **High**

26. *Answer choices:*

(see index for correct answer)

- a. functional perspective
- b. process perspective
- c. Global Fund
- d. hierarchical perspective

Guidance: level 1

:: Patent law ::

A _____ is generally any statement intended to specify or delimit the scope of rights and obligations that may be exercised and enforced by parties in a legally recognized relationship. In contrast to other terms for legally operative language, the term _____ usually implies situations that involve some level of uncertainty, waiver, or risk.

Exam Probability: **Medium**

27. *Answer choices:*

(see index for correct answer)

- a. Opposition proceeding
- b. Patent prosecution

- c. Patent ambush
- d. Disclaimer

Guidance: level 1

:: ::

_____ Corporation was an American energy, commodities, and services company based in Houston, Texas. It was founded in 1985 as a merger between Houston Natural Gas and InterNorth, both relatively small regional companies. Before its bankruptcy on December 3, 2001, _____ employed approximately 29,000 staff and was a major electricity, natural gas, communications and pulp and paper company, with claimed revenues of nearly $101 billion during 2000. Fortune named _____ "America's Most Innovative Company" for six consecutive years.

Exam Probability: **Medium**

28. *Answer choices:*

(see index for correct answer)

- a. functional perspective
- b. similarity-attraction theory
- c. hierarchical perspective
- d. process perspective

Guidance: level 1

:: United States federal defense and national security legislation ::

The USA _____ is an Act of the U.S. Congress that was signed into law by President George W. Bush on October 26, 2001. The title of the Act is a contrived three letter initialism preceding a seven letter acronym, which in combination stand for Uniting and Strengthening America by Providing Appropriate Tools Required to Intercept and Obstruct Terrorism Act of 2001. The acronym was created by a 23 year old Congressional staffer, Chris Kyle.

Exam Probability: **High**

29. *Answer choices:*
(see index for correct answer)

- a. Export Administration Act
- b. Patriot Act

Guidance: level 1

:: ::

_____ is a region of India consisting of the Indian states of Bihar, Jharkhand, West Bengal, Odisha and also the union territory Andaman and Nicobar Islands. West Bengal's capital Kolkata is the largest city of this region. The Kolkata Metropolitan Area is the country's third largest.

Exam Probability: **High**

30. *Answer choices:*

(see index for correct answer)

- a. deep-level diversity
- b. hierarchical
- c. East India
- d. Character

Guidance: level 1

:: Utilitarianism ::

_____ is a family of consequentialist ethical theories that promotes actions that maximize happiness and well-being for the majority of a population. Although different varieties of _____ admit different characterizations, the basic idea behind all of them is to in some sense maximize utility, which is often defined in terms of well-being or related concepts. For instance, Jeremy Bentham, the founder of _____ , described utility as

Exam Probability: **Low**

31. *Answer choices:*

(see index for correct answer)

- a. Mohism
- b. The Collected Works of Jeremy Bentham
- c. Felicific calculus

- d. Utilitarianism

Guidance: level 1

:: Social philosophy ::

The _____ describes the unintended social benefits of an individual's self-interested actions. Adam Smith first introduced the concept in The Theory of Moral Sentiments, written in 1759, invoking it in reference to income distribution. In this work, however, the idea of the market is not discussed, and the word "capitalism" is never used.

Exam Probability: **Low**

32. *Answer choices:*
(see index for correct answer)

- a. vacancy chain
- b. Societal attitudes towards abortion
- c. Freedom to contract
- d. Veil of Ignorance

Guidance: level 1

:: Industrial ecology ::

_____ is a strategy for reducing the amount of waste created and released into the environment, particularly by industrial facilities, agriculture, or consumers. Many large corporations view P2 as a method of improving the efficiency and profitability of production processes by technology advancements. Legislative bodies have enacted P2 measures, such as the _____ Act of 1990 and the Clean Air Act Amendments of 1990 by the United States Congress.

Exam Probability: **Low**

33. *Answer choices:*

(see index for correct answer)

- a. Life Cycle Engineering
- b. Anthropogenic metabolism
- c. Waste hierarchy
- d. Pollution Prevention

Guidance: level 1

:: Business ethics ::

A _____ is a person who exposes any kind of information or activity that is deemed illegal, unethical, or not correct within an organization that is either private or public. The information of alleged wrongdoing can be classified in many ways: violation of company policy/rules, law, regulation, or threat to public interest/national security, as well as fraud, and corruption. Those who become _____ s can choose to bring information or allegations to surface either internally or externally. Internally, a _____ can bring his/her accusations to the attention of other people within the accused organization such as an immediate supervisor. Externally, a _____ can bring allegations to light by contacting a third party outside of an accused organization such as the media, government, law enforcement, or those who are concerned. _____ s, however, take the risk of facing stiff reprisal and retaliation from those who are accused or alleged of wrongdoing.

Exam Probability: **Medium**

34. *Answer choices:*

(see index for correct answer)

- a. Institute for Business and Professional Ethics
- b. Whistleblower
- c. Corporate crime
- d. Sweatshop

Guidance: level 1

:: Market-based policy instruments ::

Cause marketing is defined as a type of corporate social responsibility, in which a company's promotional campaign has the dual purpose of increasing profitability while bettering society.

Exam Probability: **High**

35. *Answer choices:*

(see index for correct answer)

- a. Cause-related marketing
- b. Fiscal localism
- c. Tax choice
- d. Regional Clean Air Incentives Market

Guidance: level 1

:: Business ethics ::

_____ is a type of harassment technique that relates to a sexual nature and the unwelcome or inappropriate promise of rewards in exchange for sexual favors. _____ includes a range of actions from mild transgressions to sexual abuse or assault. Harassment can occur in many different social settings such as the workplace, the home, school, churches, etc. Harassers or victims may be of any gender.

Exam Probability: **High**

36. Answer choices:

(see index for correct answer)

- a. Burson-Marsteller
- b. Ethical corporate social responsibility
- c. Sexual harassment
- d. Destructionism

Guidance: level 1

:: Renewable energy ::

A _____ is a fuel that is produced through contemporary biological processes, such as agriculture and anaerobic digestion, rather than a fuel produced by geological processes such as those involved in the formation of fossil fuels, such as coal and petroleum, from prehistoric biological matter. If the source biomatter can regrow quickly, the resulting fuel is said to be a form of renewable energy.

Exam Probability: **High**

37. Answer choices:

(see index for correct answer)

- a. Biofuel
- b. Solar water heating
- c. Biomass Energy Centre
- d. Cogeneration

Guidance: level 1

:: ::

The _____ of 1973 serves as the enacting legislation to carry out the provisions outlined in The Convention on International Trade in Endangered Species of Wild Fauna and Flora . Designed to protect critically imperiled species from extinction as a "consequence of economic growth and development untempered by adequate concern and conservation", the ESA was signed into law by President Richard Nixon on December 28, 1973. The law requires federal agencies to consult with the Fish and Wildlife Service &/or the NOAA Fisheries Service to ensure their actions are not likely to jeopardize the continued existence of any listed species or result in the destruction or adverse modification of designated critical habitat of such species. The U.S. Supreme Court found that "the plain intent of Congress in enacting" the ESA "was to halt and reverse the trend toward species extinction, whatever the cost." The Act is administered by two federal agencies, the United States Fish and Wildlife Service and the National Marine Fisheries Service .

Exam Probability: **Medium**

38. *Answer choices:*

(see index for correct answer)

- a. Sarbanes-Oxley act of 2002
- b. imperative
- c. functional perspective
- d. Endangered Species Act

Guidance: level 1

:: ::

Bernard Lawrence _____ is an American former market maker, investment advisor, financier, fraudster, and convicted felon, who is currently serving a federal prison sentence for offenses related to a massive Ponzi scheme. He is the former non-executive chairman of the NASDAQ stock market, the confessed operator of the largest Ponzi scheme in world history, and the largest financial fraud in U.S. history. Prosecutors estimated the fraud to be worth $64.8 billion based on the amounts in the accounts of _____ 's 4,800 clients as of November 30, 2008.

Exam Probability: **High**

39. *Answer choices:*

(see index for correct answer)

- a. similarity-attraction theory
- b. Character
- c. imperative
- d. levels of analysis

Guidance: level 1

:: Industry ::

_____ is the manner in which a given entity has decided to address issues of energy development including energy production, distribution and consumption. The attributes of _____ may include legislation, international treaties, incentives to investment, guidelines for energy conservation, taxation and other public policy techniques. Energy is a core component of modern economies. A functioning economy requires not only labor and capital but also energy, for manufacturing processes, transportation, communication, agriculture, and more.

Exam Probability: **High**

40. *Answer choices:*

(see index for correct answer)

- a. Permissible exposure limit
- b. Energy policy
- c. Unexpected events
- d. The Year in Industry

Guidance: level 1

:: ::

A _____ is the ability to carry out a task with determined results often within a given amount of time, energy, or both. _____s can often be divided into domain-general and domain-specific _____s. For example, in the domain of work, some general _____s would include time management, teamwork and leadership, self-motivation and others, whereas domain-specific _____s would be used only for a certain job. _____ usually requires certain environmental stimuli and situations to assess the level of _____ being shown and used.

Exam Probability: **Low**

41. *Answer choices:*
(see index for correct answer)

- a. surface-level diversity
- b. Skill
- c. interpersonal communication
- d. corporate values

Guidance: level 1

The Ethics & Compliance Initiative was formed in 2015 and consists of three nonprofit organizations: the Ethics Research Center, the Ethics & Compliance Association, and the Ethics & Compliance Certification Institute. Based in Arlington, Virginia, United States, ECI is devoted to the advancement of high ethical standards and practices in public and private institutions, and provides research about ethical standards, workplace integrity, and compliance practices and processes.

Exam Probability: **Medium**

42. *Answer choices:*

(see index for correct answer)

- a. Ethics Resource Center
- b. corporate values
- c. Sarbanes-Oxley act of 2002
- d. imperative

Guidance: level 1

:: Cognitive biases ::

In personality psychology, _____ is the degree to which people believe that they have control over the outcome of events in their lives, as opposed to external forces beyond their control. Understanding of the concept was developed by Julian B. Rotter in 1954, and has since become an aspect of personality studies. A person's "locus" is conceptualized as internal or external .

Exam Probability: **Medium**

43. *Answer choices:*

(see index for correct answer)

- a. Forer effect
- b. Picture superiority effect
- c. Attribution bias
- d. Barnum effect

Guidance: level 1

:: Decentralization ::

_____ or sub _____ mainly refers to the unrestricted growth in many urban areas of housing, commercial development, and roads over large expanses of land, with little concern for urban planning. In addition to describing a particular form of urbanization, the term also relates to the social and environmental consequences associated with this development. In Continental Europe the term "peri-urbanisation" is often used to denote similar dynamics and phenomena, although the term _____ is currently being used by the European Environment Agency. There is widespread disagreement about what constitutes sprawl and how to quantify it. For example, some commentators measure sprawl only with the average number of residential units per acre in a given area. But others associate it with decentralization , discontinuity , segregation of uses, and so forth.

Exam Probability: **High**

44. *Answer choices:*

(see index for correct answer)

- a. Urban sprawl
- b. Regions of Morocco
- c. Water supply and sanitation in Yemen
- d. District Rural Development Agencies

Guidance: level 1

:: Criminal law ::

_____ is the body of law that relates to crime. It proscribes conduct perceived as threatening, harmful, or otherwise endangering to the property, health, safety, and moral welfare of people inclusive of one's self. Most _____ is established by statute, which is to say that the laws are enacted by a legislature. _____ includes the punishment and rehabilitation of people who violate such laws. _____ varies according to jurisdiction, and differs from civil law, where emphasis is more on dispute resolution and victim compensation, rather than on punishment or rehabilitation. Criminal procedure is a formalized official activity that authenticates the fact of commission of a crime and authorizes punitive or rehabilitative treatment of the offender.

Exam Probability: **Low**

45. *Answer choices:*

(see index for correct answer)

- a. mitigating factor

- b. Self-incrimination
- c. Criminal law
- d. Mala in se

Guidance: level 1

:: Labour law ::

An _____ is special or specified circumstances that partially or fully exempt a person or organization from performance of a legal obligation so as to avoid an unreasonable or disproportionate burden or obstacle.

Exam Probability: **Low**

46. *Answer choices:*

(see index for correct answer)

- a. Non-compete clause
- b. Michele Tiraboschi
- c. Works council
- d. Undue hardship

Guidance: level 1

:: ::

The _____ is an institution of the European Union, responsible for proposing legislation, implementing decisions, upholding the EU treaties and managing the day-to-day business of the EU. Commissioners swear an oath at the European Court of Justice in Luxembourg City, pledging to respect the treaties and to be completely independent in carrying out their duties during their mandate. Unlike in the Council of the European Union, where members are directly and indirectly elected, and the European Parliament, where members are directly elected, the Commissioners are proposed by the Council of the European Union, on the basis of suggestions made by the national governments, and then appointed by the European Council after the approval of the European Parliament.

Exam Probability: **Low**

47. *Answer choices:*

(see index for correct answer)

- a. levels of analysis
- b. European Commission
- c. information systems assessment
- d. similarity-attraction theory

Guidance: level 1

:: United States federal labor legislation ::

The _____ of 1988 is a United States federal law that generally prevents employers from using polygraph tests, either for pre-employment screening or during the course of employment, with certain exemptions.

Exam Probability: **High**

48. Answer choices:

(see index for correct answer)

- a. Alien Contract Labor Law
- b. Age Discrimination in Employment Act
- c. Employee Polygraph Protection Act
- d. Employment Act of 1946

Guidance: level 1

:: Business law ::

A _____ is an arrangement where parties, known as partners, agree to cooperate to advance their mutual interests. The partners in a _____ may be individuals, businesses, interest-based organizations, schools, governments or combinations. Organizations may partner to increase the likelihood of each achieving their mission and to amplify their reach. A _____ may result in issuing and holding equity or may be only governed by a contract.

Exam Probability: **High**

49. Answer choices:

(see index for correct answer)

- a. Lessor
- b. Companies law

- c. Unfair Commercial Practices Directive
- d. Ladenschlussgesetz

Guidance: level 1

:: ::

The _____ of 1906 was the first of a series of significant consumer protection laws which was enacted by Congress in the 20th century and led to the creation of the Food and Drug Administration. Its main purpose was to ban foreign and interstate traffic in adulterated or mislabeled food and drug products, and it directed the U.S. Bureau of Chemistry to inspect products and refer offenders to prosecutors. It required that active ingredients be placed on the label of a drug's packaging and that drugs could not fall below purity levels established by the United States Pharmacopeia or the National Formulary. The Jungle by Upton Sinclair with its graphic and revolting descriptions of unsanitary conditions and unscrupulous practices rampant in the meatpacking industry, was an inspirational piece that kept the public's attention on the important issue of unhygienic meat processing plants that later led to food inspection legislation. Sinclair quipped, "I aimed at the public's heart and by accident I hit it in the stomach," as outraged readers demanded and got the pure food law.

Exam Probability: **Low**

50. *Answer choices:*

(see index for correct answer)

- a. co-culture
- b. information systems assessment

- c. Pure Food and Drug Act
- d. process perspective

Guidance: level 1

:: Environmental economics ::

_____ is an institutional arrangement designed to help producers in developing countries achieve better trading conditions. Members of the _____ movement advocate the payment of higher prices to exporters, as well as improved social and environmental standards. The movement focuses in particular on commodities, or products which are typically exported from developing countries to developed countries, but also consumed in domestic markets most notably handicrafts, coffee, cocoa, wine, sugar, fresh fruit, chocolate, flowers and gold. The movement seeks to promote greater equity in international trading partnerships through dialogue, transparency, and respect. It promotes sustainable development by offering better trading conditions to, and securing the rights of, marginalized producers and workers in developing countries. _____ is grounded in three core beliefs; first, producers have the power to express unity with consumers. Secondly, the world trade practices that currently exist promote the unequal distribution of wealth between nations. Lastly, buying products from producers in developing countries at a fair price is a more efficient way of promoting sustainable development than traditional charity and aid.

Exam Probability: **High**

51. *Answer choices:*

(see index for correct answer)

- a. The Green Economist

- b. Energy descent
- c. Fair trade
- d. Green New Deal

Guidance: level 1

:: ::

The _____ was a severe worldwide economic depression that took place mostly during the 1930s, beginning in the United States. The timing of the _____ varied across nations; in most countries it started in 1929 and lasted until the late-1930s. It was the longest, deepest, and most widespread depression of the 20th century. In the 21st century, the _____ is commonly used as an example of how intensely the world's economy can decline.

Exam Probability: **Medium**

52. *Answer choices:*

(see index for correct answer)

- a. open system
- b. interpersonal communication
- c. Great Depression
- d. surface-level diversity

Guidance: level 1

:: Organizational structure ::

An _____ defines how activities such as task allocation, coordination, and supervision are directed toward the achievement of organizational aims.

Exam Probability: **Low**

53. *Answer choices:*
(see index for correct answer)

- a. Organization of the New York City Police Department
- b. Automated Bureaucracy
- c. The Starfish and the Spider
- d. Followership

Guidance: level 1

:: Globalization-related theories ::

_____ is an economic system based on the private ownership of the means of production and their operation for profit. Characteristics central to _____ include private property, capital accumulation, wage labor, voluntary exchange, a price system, and competitive markets. In a capitalist market economy, decision-making and investment are determined by every owner of wealth, property or production ability in financial and capital markets, whereas prices and the distribution of goods and services are mainly determined by competition in goods and services markets.

Exam Probability: **Medium**

54. *Answer choices:*

(see index for correct answer)

- a. Capitalism
- b. postmodernism
- c. post-industrial

Guidance: level 1

:: Price fixing convictions ::

_____ AG is a German multinational conglomerate company headquartered in Berlin and Munich and the largest industrial manufacturing company in Europe with branch offices abroad.

Exam Probability: **High**

55. *Answer choices:*

(see index for correct answer)

- a. Asahi Glass Co.
- b. Siemens
- c. Archer Daniels Midland
- d. Anheuser-Busch InBev

Guidance: level 1

:: Corporate crime ::

_____ LLP, based in Chicago, was an American holding company. Formerly one of the "Big Five" accounting firms, the firm had provided auditing, tax, and consulting services to large corporations. By 2001, it had become one of the world's largest multinational companies.

Exam Probability: **Low**

56. *Answer choices:*

(see index for correct answer)

- a. Walter Forbes
- b. Arthur Andersen
- c. Tip and Trade
- d. General Development Corporation

Guidance: level 1

:: Auditing ::

_____ , as defined by accounting and auditing, is a process for assuring of an organization's objectives in operational effectiveness and efficiency, reliable financial reporting, and compliance with laws, regulations and policies. A broad concept, _____ involves everything that controls risks to an organization.

Exam Probability: **Medium**

57. *Answer choices:*

(see index for correct answer)

- a. Sales tax audit
- b. Audit management
- c. Certified Quality Auditor
- d. Joint audit

Guidance: level 1

Oriental Nicety, formerly _____ , Exxon Mediterranean, SeaRiver Mediterranean, S/R Mediterranean, Mediterranean, and Dong Fang Ocean, was an oil tanker that gained notoriety after running aground in Prince William Sound spilling hundreds of thousands of barrels of crude oil in Alaska. On March 24, 1989, while owned by the former Exxon Shipping Company, and captained by Joseph Hazelwood and First Mate James Kunkel bound for Long Beach, California, the vessel ran aground on the Bligh Reef resulting in the second largest oil spill in United States history. The size of the spill is estimated to have been 40,900 to 120,000 m3 , or 257,000 to 750,000 barrels. In 1989, the _____ oil spill was listed as the 54th largest spill in history.

Exam Probability: **Medium**

58. *Answer choices:*

(see index for correct answer)

- a. cultural
- b. open system
- c. surface-level diversity
- d. Exxon Valdez

Guidance: level 1

:: Confidence tricks ::

A _____ is a form of fraud that lures investors and pays profits to earlier investors with funds from more recent investors. The scheme leads victims to believe that profits are coming from product sales or other means, and they remain unaware that other investors are the source of funds. A _____ can maintain the illusion of a sustainable business as long as new investors contribute new funds, and as long as most of the investors do not demand full repayment and still believe in the non-existent assets they are purported to own.

Exam Probability: **Medium**

59. *Answer choices:*

(see index for correct answer)

- a. Reloading scam
- b. Drop swindle
- c. Cold reading
- d. Ponzi scheme

Guidance: level 1

Accounting

Accounting or accountancy is the measurement, processing, and communication of financial information about economic entities such as businesses and corporations. The modern field was established by the Italian mathematician Luca Pacioli in 1494. Accounting, which has been called the "language of business", measures the results of an organization's economic activities and conveys this information to a variety of users, including investors, creditors, management, and regulators.

:: Accounting terminology ::

Accounts are typically defined by an identifier and a caption or header and are coded by account type. In computerized accounting systems with computable quantity accounting, the accounts can have a quantity measure definition.

Exam Probability: **High**

1. *Answer choices:*

(see index for correct answer)

- a. Enterprise liquidity
- b. Accounting equation
- c. Record to report
- d. General ledger

Guidance: level 1

:: Marketing ::

_____ or stock is the goods and materials that a business holds for the ultimate goal of resale.

Exam Probability: **Medium**

2. *Answer choices:*

(see index for correct answer)

- a. Marketing warfare strategies
- b. Azerbaijan Marketing Society
- c. Price war
- d. Inventory

Guidance: level 1

:: ::

From an accounting perspective, _____ is crucial because _____ and _____ taxes considerably affect the net income of most companies and because they are subject to laws and regulations.

Exam Probability: **Medium**

3. *Answer choices:*
(see index for correct answer)

- a. Payroll
- b. open system
- c. process perspective
- d. Sarbanes-Oxley act of 2002

Guidance: level 1

:: Taxation ::

A _____ is a person or organization subject to pay a tax. _____ s have an Identification Number, a reference number issued by a government to its citizens.

Exam Probability: **Medium**

4. *Answer choices:*

(see index for correct answer)

- a. Tax Freedom Day
- b. Privatized tax collection
- c. Taxpayer
- d. Tax cut

Guidance: level 1

:: Loans ::

In corporate finance, a _____ is a medium- to long-term debt instrument used by large companies to borrow money, at a fixed rate of interest. The legal term "_____" originally referred to a document that either creates a debt or acknowledges it, but in some countries the term is now used interchangeably with bond, loan stock or note. A _____ is thus like a certificate of loan or a loan bond evidencing the fact that the company is liable to pay a specified amount with interest and although the money raised by the _____ s becomes a part of the company's capital structure, it does not become share capital. Senior _____ s get paid before subordinate _____ s, and there are varying rates of risk and payoff for these categories.

Exam Probability: **Medium**

5. *Answer choices:*

(see index for correct answer)

- a. Hard money loan
- b. Federal Perkins Loan
- c. Debenture
- d. Student loan

Guidance: level 1

:: Management accounting ::

_____ is a professional certification credential in the management accounting and financial management fields. The certification signifies that the person possesses knowledge in the areas of financial planning, analysis, control, decision support, and professional ethics. The CMA is a U.S.-based, globally recognized certification offered by the Institute of Management Accountants.

Exam Probability: **Low**

6. *Answer choices:*

(see index for correct answer)

- a. Backflush accounting
- b. RCA open-source application

- c. Managerial risk accounting
- d. Certified Management Accountant

Guidance: level 1

:: Free accounting software ::

A _____ is the principal book or computer file for recording and totaling economic transactions measured in terms of a monetary unit of account by account type, with debits and credits in separate columns and a beginning monetary balance and ending monetary balance for each account.

Exam Probability: **Low**

7. *Answer choices:*
(see index for correct answer)

- a. HomeBank
- b. TurboCASH
- c. LedgerSMB
- d. JFin

Guidance: level 1

:: Accounting software ::

_____ is any item or verifiable record that is generally accepted as payment for goods and services and repayment of debts, such as taxes, in a particular country or socio-economic context. The main functions of _____ are distinguished as: a medium of exchange, a unit of account, a store of value and sometimes, a standard of deferred payment. Any item or verifiable record that fulfils these functions can be considered as _____ .

Exam Probability: **Low**

8. *Answer choices:*

(see index for correct answer)

- a. PyBookie
- b. Money
- c. Microsoft Office Accounting
- d. ProSama 2010

Guidance: level 1

:: Generally Accepted Accounting Principles ::

The _____ principle is a cornerstone of accrual accounting together with the matching principle. They both determine the accounting period in which revenues and expenses are recognized. According to the principle, revenues are recognized when they are realized or realizable, and are earned , no matter when cash is received. In cash accounting – in contrast – revenues are recognized when cash is received no matter when goods or services are sold.

Exam Probability: **Medium**

9. *Answer choices:*

(see index for correct answer)

- a. Chinese accounting standards
- b. Gross income
- c. Pro forma
- d. Financial position of the United States

Guidance: level 1

:: Management ::

The _____ is a strategy performance management tool – a semi-standard structured report, that can be used by managers to keep track of the execution of activities by the staff within their control and to monitor the consequences arising from these actions.

Exam Probability: **Low**

10. *Answer choices:*

(see index for correct answer)

- a. Innovation management
- b. Balanced scorecard
- c. Allegiance

- d. SimulTrain

Guidance: level 1

:: Corporations law ::

_____ , also referred to as the certificate of incorporation or the corporate charter, are a document or charter that establishes the existence of a corporation in the United States and Canada. They generally are filed with the Secretary of State or other company registrar.

Exam Probability: **Medium**

11. *Answer choices:*
(see index for correct answer)

- a. Non-stock corporation
- b. Corporate lawyer
- c. Articles of incorporation
- d. Director primacy

Guidance: level 1

:: Tax avoidance ::

_____ s are any method of reducing taxable income resulting in a reduction of the payments to tax collecting entities, including state and federal governments. The methodology can vary depending on local and international tax laws.

Exam Probability: **Medium**

12. *Answer choices:*

(see index for correct answer)

- a. Disposable ship
- b. Tax shelter
- c. Son of Boss
- d. Estate planning

Guidance: level 1

:: Taxation ::

In a tax system, the _____ is the ratio at which a business or person is taxed. There are several methods used to present a _____ : statutory, average, marginal, and effective. These rates can also be presented using different definitions applied to a tax base: inclusive and exclusive.

Exam Probability: **Low**

13. *Answer choices:*

(see index for correct answer)

- a. Tax rate
- b. African Tax Administration Forum
- c. Fixed tax
- d. Virtual tax

Guidance: level 1

:: Valuation (finance) ::

The _____ is one of three major groups of methodologies, called valuation approaches, used by appraisers. It is particularly common in commercial real estate appraisal and in business appraisal. The fundamental math is similar to the methods used for financial valuation, securities analysis, or bond pricing. However, there are some significant and important modifications when used in real estate or business valuation.

Exam Probability: **Low**

14. *Answer choices:*

(see index for correct answer)

- a. Income approach
- b. Channel check
- c. Residual income valuation
- d. Diminution in value

Guidance: level 1

:: Finance ::

A _____ , publicly-traded company, publicly-held company, publicly-listed company, or public limited company is a corporation whose ownership is dispersed among the general public in many shares of stock which are freely traded on a stock exchange or in over-the-counter markets. In some jurisdictions, public companies over a certain size must be listed on an exchange. A _____ can be listed or unlisted .

Exam Probability: **Low**

15. *Answer choices:*

(see index for correct answer)

- a. Momentum investing
- b. Public company
- c. Tangible common equity
- d. Electronic communication network

Guidance: level 1

:: Income taxes ::

An _____ is a tax imposed on individuals or entities that varies with respective income or profits. _____ generally is computed as the product of a tax rate times taxable income. Taxation rates may vary by type or characteristics of the taxpayer.

Exam Probability: **High**

16. *Answer choices:*

(see index for correct answer)

- a. Income tax
- b. Illinois Fair Tax
- c. State income tax
- d. Depreciation recapture

Guidance: level 1

:: Investment ::

In economics, _____ is spending which increases the availability of fixed capital goods or means of production and goods inventories. It is the total spending on newly produced physical capital and on inventories —that is, gross investment—minus replacement investment, which simply replaces depreciated capital goods. It is productive capital formation plus net additions to the stock of housing and the stock of inventories.

Exam Probability: **Medium**

17. Answer choices:

(see index for correct answer)

- a. Net investment
- b. Stabilization clause
- c. Manager of managers fund
- d. Media for equity

Guidance: level 1

:: Generally Accepted Accounting Principles ::

In accounting, an economic item's _____ is the original nominal monetary value of that item. _____ accounting involves reporting assets and liabilities at their _____ s, which are not updated for changes in the items' values. Consequently, the amounts reported for these balance sheet items often differ from their current economic or market values.

Exam Probability: **Medium**

18. Answer choices:

(see index for correct answer)

- a. French generally accepted accounting principles
- b. Historical cost
- c. Operating income before depreciation and amortization
- d. AICPA Statements of Position

Guidance: level 1

:: Management ::

Business _____ is a discipline in operations management in which people use various methods to discover, model, analyze, measure, improve, optimize, and automate business processes. BPM focuses on improving corporate performance by managing business processes. Any combination of methods used to manage a company's business processes is BPM. Processes can be structured and repeatable or unstructured and variable. Though not required, enabling technologies are often used with BPM.

Exam Probability: **High**

19. *Answer choices:*
(see index for correct answer)

- a. Participative decision-making
- b. Process Management
- c. SimulTrain
- d. Systems analysis

Guidance: level 1

:: Real property law ::

A _____ or millage rate is an ad valorem tax on the value of a property, usually levied on real estate. The tax is levied by the governing authority of the jurisdiction in which the property is located. This can be a national government, a federated state, a county or geographical region or a municipality. Multiple jurisdictions may tax the same property. This tax can be contrasted to a rent tax which is based on rental income or imputed rent, and a land value tax, which is a levy on the value of land, excluding the value of buildings and other improvements.

Exam Probability: **High**

20. *Answer choices:*

(see index for correct answer)

- a. Charter
- b. Infectious invalidity
- c. Property tax
- d. Open mines doctrine

Guidance: level 1

:: Generally Accepted Accounting Principles ::

_____ is a small amount of discretionary funds in the form of cash used for expenditures where it is not sensible to make any disbursement by cheque, because of the inconvenience and costs of writing, signing, and then cashing the cheque.

Exam Probability: **Low**

21. *Answer choices:*

(see index for correct answer)

- a. Generally accepted accounting principles
- b. Petty cash
- c. deferred revenue
- d. Insurance asset management

Guidance: level 1

:: Organizational theory ::

Decentralisation is the process by which the activities of an organization, particularly those regarding planning and decision making, are distributed or delegated away from a central, authoritative location or group. Concepts of _____ have been applied to group dynamics and management science in private businesses and organizations, political science, law and public administration, economics, money and technology.

Exam Probability: **High**

22. *Answer choices:*

(see index for correct answer)

- a. Decentralization
- b. Solid line reporting

- c. Stages of growth model
- d. Organigraph

Guidance: level 1

:: Accounting terminology ::

In accounting/accountancy, _____ are journal entries usually made at the end of an accounting period to allocate income and expenditure to the period in which they actually occurred. The revenue recognition principle is the basis of making _____ that pertain to unearned and accrued revenues under accrual-basis accounting. They are sometimes called Balance Day adjustments because they are made on balance day.

Exam Probability: **High**

23. *Answer choices:*

(see index for correct answer)

- a. Accrued liabilities
- b. Checkoff
- c. Adjusting entries
- d. Account

Guidance: level 1

:: Corporate taxation in the United States ::

A _____, under United States federal income tax law, refers to any corporation that is taxed separately from its owners. A _____ is distinguished from an S corporation, which generally is not taxed separately. Most major companies are treated as _____ s for U.S. federal income tax purposes. _____ s and S corporations both enjoy limited liability, but only _____ s are subject to corporate income taxation.

Exam Probability: **High**

24. *Answer choices:*

(see index for correct answer)

- a. Franchise tax
- b. C corporation
- c. Undistributed profits tax
- d. Entity classification election

Guidance: level 1

:: Business models ::

A _____, _____ company or daughter company is a company that is owned or controlled by another company, which is called the parent company, parent, or holding company. The _____ can be a company, corporation, or limited liability company. In some cases it is a government or state-owned enterprise. In some cases, particularly in the music and book publishing industries, subsidiaries are referred to as imprints.

Exam Probability: **Medium**

25. *Answer choices:*

(see index for correct answer)

- a. Subscription business model
- b. Subsidiary
- c. Technology push
- d. Utility computing

Guidance: level 1

:: Basic financial concepts ::

In finance, maturity or _____ refers to the final payment date of a loan or other financial instrument, at which point the principal is due to be paid.

Exam Probability: **High**

26. *Answer choices:*

(see index for correct answer)

- a. Present value of benefits
- b. Forward guidance
- c. Maturity date
- d. Short interest

Guidance: level 1

:: Bank regulation ::

_____ is a measure implemented in many countries to protect bank depositors, in full or in part, from losses caused by a bank's inability to pay its debts when due. _____ systems are one component of a financial system safety net that promotes financial stability.

Exam Probability: **Low**

27. *Answer choices:*

(see index for correct answer)

- a. Bank regulation
- b. Deposit insurance
- c. Capitis deminutio
- d. Basel Committee on Banking Supervision

Guidance: level 1

:: Financial ratios ::

_____ is a financial ratio that indicates the percentage of a company's assets that are provided via debt. It is the ratio of total debt and total assets.

Exam Probability: **Medium**

28. *Answer choices:*

(see index for correct answer)

- a. price-to-cash flow ratio
- b. Days in inventory
- c. Statutory liquidity ratio
- d. Debt ratio

Guidance: level 1

:: ::

The _____ is a private, non-profit organization standard-setting body whose primary purpose is to establish and improve Generally Accepted Accounting Principles within the United States in the public's interest. The Securities and Exchange Commission designated the FASB as the organization responsible for setting accounting standards for public companies in the US. The FASB replaced the American Institute of Certified Public Accountants' Accounting Principles Board on July 1, 1973.

Exam Probability: **Medium**

29. Answer choices:

(see index for correct answer)

- a. similarity-attraction theory
- b. deep-level diversity
- c. levels of analysis
- d. Financial Accounting Standards Board

Guidance: level 1

:: Taxation ::

_____ refers to the base upon which an income tax system imposes tax. Generally, it includes some or all items of income and is reduced by expenses and other deductions. The amounts included as income, expenses, and other deductions vary by country or system. Many systems provide that some types of income are not taxable and some expenditures not deductible in computing _____ . Some systems base tax on _____ of the current period, and some on prior periods. _____ may refer to the income of any taxpayer, including individuals and corporations, as well as entities that themselves do not pay tax, such as partnerships, in which case it may be called "net profit".

Exam Probability: **Medium**

30. Answer choices:

(see index for correct answer)

- a. Direct tax
- b. Fiscal memory devices

- c. Honorarium
- d. Taxable income

Guidance: level 1

:: United States Generally Accepted Accounting Principles ::

In the United States, the _____, Subpart F of the OMB Uniform Guidance, is a rigorous, organization-wide audit or examination of an entity that expends $750,000 or more of federal assistance received for its operations. Usually performed annually, the _____ 's objective is to provide assurance to the US federal government as to the management and use of such funds by recipients such as states, cities, universities, non-profit organizations, and Indian Tribes. The audit is typically performed by an independent certified public accountant and encompasses both financial and compliance components. The _____ s must be submitted to the Federal Audit Clearinghouse along with a data collection form, Form SF-SAC.

Exam Probability: **High**

31. *Answer choices:*
(see index for correct answer)

- a. Permanent fund
- b. Impaired asset
- c. Single Audit
- d. Working Group on Financial Markets

Guidance: level 1

:: Asset ::

_____ s, also known as tangible assets or property, plant and equipment, is a term used in accounting for assets and property that cannot easily be converted into cash. This can be compared with current assets such as cash or bank accounts, described as liquid assets. In most cases, only tangible assets are referred to as fixed. IAS 16 defines _____ s as assets whose future economic benefit is probable to flow into the entity, whose cost can be measured reliably. _____ s belong to one of 2 types:"Freehold Assets" – assets which are purchased with legal right of ownership and used,and "Leasehold Assets" – assets used by owner without legal right for a particular period of time.

Exam Probability: **Low**

32. *Answer choices:*
(see index for correct answer)

- a. Current asset
- b. Asset

Guidance: level 1

:: International Financial Reporting Standards ::

_____ , usually called IFRS, are standards issued by the IFRS Foundation and the International Accounting Standards Board to provide a common global language for business affairs so that company accounts are understandable and comparable across international boundaries. They are a consequence of growing international shareholding and trade and are particularly important for companies that have dealings in several countries. They are progressively replacing the many different national accounting standards. They are the rules to be followed by accountants to maintain books of accounts which are comparable, understandable, reliable and relevant as per the users internal or external. IFRS, with the exception of IAS 29 Financial Reporting in Hyperinflationary Economies and IFRIC 7 Applying the Restatement Approach under IAS 29, are authorized in terms of the historical cost paradigm. IAS 29 and IFRIC 7 are authorized in terms of the units of constant purchasing power paradigm.IAS 2 is related to inventories in this standard we talk about the stock its production process etcIFRS began as an attempt to harmonize accounting across the European Union but the value of harmonization quickly made the concept attractive around the world. However, it has been debated whether or not de facto harmonization has occurred. Standards that were issued by IASC are still within use today and go by the name International Accounting Standards , while standards issued by IASB are called IFRS. IAS were issued between 1973 and 2001 by the Board of the International Accounting Standards Committee . On 1 April 2001, the new International Accounting Standards Board took over from the IASC the responsibility for setting International Accounting Standards. During its first meeting the new Board adopted existing IAS and Standing Interpretations Committee standards . The IASB has continued to develop standards calling the new standards " _____ ".

Exam Probability: **Medium**

33. *Answer choices:*

(see index for correct answer)

- a. IAS 16
- b. IAS 7
- c. International Financial Reporting Standards

- d. IFRS Foundation

Guidance: level 1

:: Generally Accepted Accounting Principles ::

Paid-in capital is capital that is contributed to a corporation by investors by purchase of stock from the corporation, the primary market, not by purchase of stock in the open market from other stockholders. It includes share capital as well as additional paid-in capital.

Exam Probability: **High**

34. *Answer choices:*

(see index for correct answer)

- a. Contributed capital
- b. Shares outstanding
- c. Matching principle
- d. Net profit

Guidance: level 1

:: Real estate ::

Amortisation is paying off an amount owed over time by making planned, incremental payments of principal and interest. To amortise a loan means "to kill it off". In accounting, amortisation refers to charging or writing off an intangible asset's cost as an operational expense over its estimated useful life to reduce a company's taxable income.

Exam Probability: **Medium**

35. *Answer choices:*

(see index for correct answer)

- a. Perch
- b. Land agent
- c. AMP Technologies
- d. Amortization

Guidance: level 1

:: Finance ::

In accounting, _____ is the portion of a subsidiary corporation's stock that is not owned by the parent corporation. The magnitude of the _____ in the subsidiary company is generally less than 50% of outstanding shares, or the corporation would generally cease to be a subsidiary of the parent.

Exam Probability: **Medium**

36. *Answer choices:*

(see index for correct answer)

- a. Minority interest
- b. Spot date
- c. Subordinated debt
- d. Monetary system

Guidance: level 1

:: Inventory ::

_____ is the maximum amount of goods, or inventory, that a company can possibly sell during this fiscal year. It has the formula.

Exam Probability: **Low**

37. *Answer choices:*

(see index for correct answer)

- a. Cost of goods available for sale
- b. Spare part
- c. Safety stock
- d. Phantom inventory

Guidance: level 1

:: Accounting terminology ::

A _____ contains all the accounts for recording transactions relating to a company's assets, liabilities, owners' equity, revenue, and expenses. In modern accounting software or ERP, the _____ works as a central repository for accounting data transferred from all subledgers or modules like accounts payable, accounts receivable, cash management, fixed assets, purchasing and projects. The _____ is the backbone of any accounting system which holds financial and non-financial data for an organization. The collection of all accounts is known as the _____ . Each account is known as a ledger account. In a manual or non-computerized system this may be a large book. The statement of financial position and the statement of income and comprehensive income are both derived from the _____ . Each account in the _____ consists of one or more pages. The _____ is where posting to the accounts occurs. Posting is the process of recording amounts as credits , and amounts as debits , in the pages of the _____ . Additional columns to the right hold a running activity total .

Exam Probability: **Low**

38. *Answer choices:*

(see index for correct answer)

- a. General ledger
- b. Checkoff
- c. Accrual
- d. managerial accounting

Guidance: level 1

:: Quality control tools ::

A _____ is a type of diagram that represents an algorithm, workflow or process. _____ can also be defined as a diagramatic representation of an algorithm .

Exam Probability: **Low**

39. *Answer choices:*

(see index for correct answer)

- a. Scatter diagram
- b. Fishbone diagram
- c. EVOP
- d. Run chart

Guidance: level 1

:: Accounting in the United States ::

The _____ is located in Norwalk, Connecticut, United States. It was organized in 1972 as a non-stock, Delaware Corporation. It is an independent organization in the private sector, operating with the goal of ensuring objectivity and integrity in financial reporting standards.

Exam Probability: **Low**

40. *Answer choices:*

(see index for correct answer)

- a. Positive assurance
- b. Accounting Today
- c. Revolving fund
- d. Legal liability of certified public accountants

Guidance: level 1

:: ::

An _____, for United States federal income tax, is a closely held corporation that makes a valid election to be taxed under Subchapter S of Chapter 1 of the Internal Revenue Code. In general, _____ s do not pay any income taxes. Instead, the corporation's income or losses are divided among and passed through to its shareholders. The shareholders must then report the income or loss on their own individual income tax returns.

Exam Probability: **High**

41. *Answer choices:*

(see index for correct answer)

- a. S corporation
- b. imperative
- c. cultural
- d. surface-level diversity

Guidance: level 1

:: ::

A _____ is a fund into which a sum of money is added during an employee's employment years, and from which payments are drawn to support the person's retirement from work in the form of periodic payments. A _____ may be a "defined benefit plan" where a fixed sum is paid regularly to a person, or a "defined contribution plan" under which a fixed sum is invested and then becomes available at retirement age. _____ s should not be confused with severance pay; the former is usually paid in regular installments for life after retirement, while the latter is typically paid as a fixed amount after involuntary termination of employment prior to retirement.

Exam Probability: **Medium**

42. *Answer choices:*

(see index for correct answer)

- a. open system
- b. interpersonal communication
- c. Character
- d. Pension

Guidance: level 1

:: ::

A _____ is an individual or institution that legally owns one or more shares of stock in a public or private corporation. _____ s may be referred to as members of a corporation. Legally, a person is not a _____ in a corporation until their name and other details are entered in the corporation's register of _____ s or members.

Exam Probability: **Low**

43. *Answer choices:*

(see index for correct answer)

- a. hierarchical perspective
- b. functional perspective
- c. Sarbanes-Oxley act of 2002
- d. Shareholder

Guidance: level 1

:: Income ::

_____ is a ratio between the net profit and cost of investment resulting from an investment of some resources. A high ROI means the investment's gains favorably to its cost. As a performance measure, ROI is used to evaluate the efficiency of an investment or to compare the efficiencies of several different investments. In purely economic terms, it is one way of relating profits to capital invested. _____ is a performance measure used by businesses to identify the efficiency of an investment or number of different investments.

Exam Probability: **Low**

44. *Answer choices:*

(see index for correct answer)

- a. National average salary
- b. Property investment calculator
- c. Return on investment
- d. Creative real estate investing

Guidance: level 1

:: Payment systems ::

An _____ is an electronic telecommunications device that enables customers of financial institutions to perform financial transactions, such as cash withdrawals, deposits, transfer funds, or obtaining account information, at any time and without the need for direct interaction with bank staff.

Exam Probability: **Medium**

45. *Answer choices:*

(see index for correct answer)

- a. Automated teller machine
- b. Fedwire
- c. Wire transfer

- d. Invoicera

Guidance: level 1

:: Business ::

The seller, or the provider of the goods or services, completes a sale in response to an acquisition, appropriation, requisition or a direct interaction with the buyer at the point of sale. There is a passing of title of the item, and the settlement of a price, in which agreement is reached on a price for which transfer of ownership of the item will occur. The seller, not the purchaser typically executes the sale and it may be completed prior to the obligation of payment. In the case of indirect interaction, a person who sells goods or service on behalf of the owner is known as a _____ man or _____ woman or _____ person, but this often refers to someone selling goods in a store/shop, in which case other terms are also common, including _____ clerk, shop assistant, and retail clerk.

Exam Probability: **Medium**

46. *Answer choices:*
(see index for correct answer)

- a. Operating subsidiary
- b. Price-based selling
- c. Gray ceiling
- d. First party leads

Guidance: level 1

:: Financial markets ::

_____ s are monetary contracts between parties. They can be created, traded, modified and settled. They can be cash, evidence of an ownership interest in an entity, or a contractual right to receive or deliver cash.

Exam Probability: **Medium**

47. *Answer choices:*
(see index for correct answer)

- a. Reset
- b. Price limit
- c. Exchange of futures for physicals
- d. Price-weighted index

Guidance: level 1

:: Business law ::

The expression " _____ " is somewhat confusing as it has a different meaning based on the context that is under consideration. From a product characteristic stand point, this type of a lease, as distinguished from a finance lease, is one where the lessor takes residual risk. As such, the lease is non full payout. From an accounting stand point, this type of lease results in off balance sheet financing.

Exam Probability: **Medium**

48. *Answer choices:*

(see index for correct answer)

- a. Operating lease
- b. Retroactive overtime
- c. Business license
- d. General assignment

Guidance: level 1

:: Information systems ::

An accounting as an information system is a system of collecting, storing and processing financial and accounting data that are used by decision makers. An _____ is generally a computer-based method for tracking accounting activity in conjunction with information technology resources. The resulting financial reports can be used internally by management or externally by other interested parties including investors, creditors and tax authorities. _____ s are designed to support all accounting functions and activities including auditing, financial accounting & reporting, managerial/ management accounting and tax. The most widely adopted accounting information systems are auditing and financial reporting modules.

Exam Probability: **Low**

49. *Answer choices:*

(see index for correct answer)

- a. Accounting information system
- b. Credit bureau
- c. Heritage Operations Processing System
- d. Management information system

Guidance: level 1

:: Generally Accepted Accounting Principles ::

_____ is a measure of a fixed or current asset's worth when held in inventory, in the field of accounting. NRV is part of the Generally Accepted Accounting Principles and International Financial Reporting Standards that apply to valuing inventory, so as to not overstate or understate the value of inventory goods. _____ is generally equal to the selling price of the inventory goods less the selling costs. Therefore, it is expected sales price less selling costs. NRV prevents overstating or understating of an assets value. NRV is the price cap when using the Lower of Cost or Market Rule.

Exam Probability: **Low**

50. *Answer choices:*

(see index for correct answer)

- a. Generally Accepted Accounting Practice
- b. Net realizable value
- c. Net profit
- d. Deprival value

Guidance: level 1

:: Commerce ::

Continuation of an entity as a _____ is presumed as the basis for financial reporting unless and until the entity's liquidation becomes imminent. Preparation of financial statements under this presumption is commonly referred to as the _____ basis of accounting. If and when an entity's liquidation becomes imminent, financial statements are prepared under the liquidation basis of accounting.

Exam Probability: **Medium**

51. *Answer choices:*
(see index for correct answer)

- a. Shipping list
- b. Retail loss prevention
- c. Going concern
- d. DataCash

Guidance: level 1

:: Business models ::

A _____ is a company that owns enough voting stock in another firm to control management and operation by influencing or electing its board of directors. The company is deemed a subsidiary of the _____.

Exam Probability: **Medium**

52. *Answer choices:*

(see index for correct answer)

- a. Parent company
- b. Brainsworking
- c. Technology push
- d. Dependent growth business model

Guidance: level 1

:: E-commerce ::

A _____ is a plastic payment card that can be used instead of cash when making purchases. It is similar to a credit card, but unlike a credit card, the money is immediately transferred directly from the cardholder's bank account when performing a transaction.

Exam Probability: **Low**

53. *Answer choices:*

(see index for correct answer)

- a. Beamdog
- b. Digital currency
- c. Debit card
- d. Mobile banking

Guidance: level 1

:: Stock market ::

_____ is a form of corporate equity ownership, a type of security. The terms voting share and ordinary share are also used frequently in other parts of the world; " _____ " being primarily used in the United States. They are known as Equity shares or Ordinary shares in the UK and other Commonwealth realms. This type of share gives the stockholder the right to share in the profits of the company, and to vote on matters of corporate policy and the composition of the members of the board of directors.

Exam Probability: **High**

54. *Answer choices:*

(see index for correct answer)

- a. Common stock
- b. Size premium
- c. Depositary receipt
- d. H share

Guidance: level 1

:: Generally Accepted Accounting Principles ::

In accounting, _____ is the income that a business have from its normal business activities, usually from the sale of goods and services to customers. _____ is also referred to as sales or turnover. Some companies receive _____ from interest, royalties, or other fees. _____ may refer to business income in general, or it may refer to the amount, in a monetary unit, earned during a period of time, as in "Last year, Company X had _____ of $42 million". Profits or net income generally imply total _____ minus total expenses in a given period. In accounting, in the balance statement it is a subsection of the Equity section and _____ increases equity, it is often referred to as the "top line" due to its position on the income statement at the very top. This is to be contrasted with the "bottom line" which denotes net income .

Exam Probability: **Low**

55. *Answer choices:*
(see index for correct answer)

- a. Engagement letter
- b. Deprival value
- c. Revenue
- d. Profit

Guidance: level 1

:: Management accounting ::

An _____ is a classification used for business units within an enterprise. The essential element of an _____ is that it is treated as a unit which is measured against its use of capital, as opposed to a cost or profit center, which are measured against raw costs or profits.

Exam Probability: **Low**

56. *Answer choices:*

(see index for correct answer)

- a. Grenzplankostenrechnung
- b. Backflush accounting
- c. Activity-based management
- d. Standard cost

Guidance: level 1

:: Accounting terminology ::

_____ is an independent, objective assurance and consulting activity designed to add value to and improve an organization's operations. It helps an organization accomplish its objectives by bringing a systematic, disciplined approach to evaluate and improve the effectiveness of risk management, control and governance processes. _____ achieves this by providing insight and recommendations based on analyses and assessments of data and business processes. With commitment to integrity and accountability, _____ provides value to governing bodies and senior management as an objective source of independent advice. Professionals called internal auditors are employed by organizations to perform the _____ activity.

Exam Probability: **Medium**

57. *Answer choices:*
(see index for correct answer)

- a. Impairment cost
- b. Accounts receivable
- c. outstanding balance
- d. profit and loss statement

Guidance: level 1

:: Accounting software ::

_____ is a freely available and global framework for exchanging business information. _____ allows the expression of semantic meaning commonly required in business reporting. The language is XML-based and uses the XML syntax and related XML technologies such as XML Schema, XLink, XPath, and Namespaces. One use of _____ is to define and exchange financial information, such as a financial statement. The _____ Specification is developed and published by _____ International, Inc. .

Exam Probability: **Medium**

58. *Answer choices:*

(see index for correct answer)

- a. Time tracking software
- b. 2Clix Software
- c. Amortization calculator
- d. Comparison of accounting software

Guidance: level 1

:: Management accounting ::

_____ is the profit the firm makes from serving a customer or customer group over a specified period of time, specifically the difference between the revenues earned from and the costs associated with the customer relationship in a specified period. According to Philip Kotler,"a profitable customer is a person, household or a company that overtime, yields a revenue stream that exceeds by an acceptable amount the company`s cost stream of attracting, selling and servicing the customer."

Exam Probability: **Medium**

59. *Answer choices:*

(see index for correct answer)

- a. Customer profitability
- b. Notional profit
- c. Target income sales
- d. Operating profit margin

Guidance: level 1

INDEX: Correct Answers

Foundations of Business

1. : Resource

2. c: Building

3. d: Competition

4. a: Globalization

5. b: Diagram

6. b: Career

7. : Schedule

8. c: Resource management

9. c: SWOT analysis

10. b: ASEAN

11. : Explanation

12. d: Project management

13. a: Crisis

14. c: Description

15. b: Balance sheet

16. c: Reputation

17. d: Image

18. c: Sexual harassment

19. : Present value

20. a: Stock

21. d: Planning

22. : Policy

23. c: Variable cost

24. b: Return on investment

25. d: Goal

26. : Solution

27. : Partnership

28. d: Mission statement

29. c: Bankruptcy

30. : Internal Revenue Service

31. : Corporation

32. c: Selling

33. b: Common stock

34. c: Perception

35. a: Risk management

36. a: Training

37. c: Case study

38. c: Interest rate

39. a: Loan

40. d: Dimension

41. : Corporate governance

42. d: ITeM

43. d: Ownership

44. c: Market value

45. c: Trade

46. d: Credit card

47. c: Opportunity cost

48. d: Organizational structure

49. c: Error

50. d: Economic growth

51. c: Frequency

52. : Regulation

53. a: Efficiency

54. : Arthur Andersen

55. : Inventory

56. d: Recession

57. : Expense

58. b: Preference

59. c: Retail

Management

1. d: Profit sharing

2. b: Delegation

3. d: Schedule

4. a: Training

5. : Shareholder

6. : Frequency

7. a: Project team

8. d: Checklist

9. c: Organization chart

10. c: 360-degree feedback

11. : Motivation

12. d: Halo effect

13. : Productivity

14. : Coaching

15. c: Problem

16. : Leadership development

17. c: Socialization

18. : Emotional intelligence

19. d: Grievance

20. d: Firm

21. b: Bias

22. b: Autonomy

23. a: Time management

24. b: Chief executive officer

25. c: Self-assessment

26. d: E-commerce

27. c: Resource management

28. b: Distance

29. c: Forecasting

30. : Governance

31. : Sharing

32. a: American Express

33. c: Product life cycle

34. : Vendor

35. b: Merger

36. b: Inventory control

37. c: Recruitment

38. b: International trade

39. c: Fixed cost

40. d: Ratio

41. c: Authority

42. d: Theory X

43. d: Reason

44. d: Vertical integration

45. b: Ownership

46. d: Intellectual property

47. d: Explanation

48. d: Research and development

49. : Integrity

50. a: Ambiguity

51. d: Discipline

52. : Customs

53. b: Overtime

54. : Proactive

55. : Interdependence

56. c: Pension

57. b: Threat

58. d: Total cost

59. : Strategy

Business law

1. : Categorical imperative

2. b: Directed verdict

3. : Sherman Act

4. a: Trial

5. b: Scienter

6. b: Policy

7. a: Financial privacy

8. : Tort

9. d: Ratification

10. d: Voidable

11. b: Wage

12. b: Apparent authority

13. b: Prohibition

14. b: Commercial Paper

15. a: False imprisonment

16. a: Securities and Exchange Commission

17. b: Comparative negligence

18. d: Reasonable person

19. a: Security interest

20. c: Void contract

21. c: Hearing

22. d: Manufacturing

23. b: Insurable interest

24. a: Welfare

25. a: Utilitarianism

26. c: Brand

27. a: Joint venture

28. c: Petition

29. b: Property

30. a: Marketing

31. a: Uniform Commercial Code

32. c: Federal government

33. d: Restraint of trade

34. d: Insider trading

35. c: Board of directors

36. b: Option contract

37. b: Jurisdiction

38. b: Constitution

39. : Tangible

40. a: Unconscionability

41. c: Promissory note

42. a: Sole proprietorship

43. c: Sexual harassment

44. d: Liquidation

45. c: Fiduciary

46. d: Consumer Good

47. c: Dividend

48. : Accounting

49. b: Res ipsa

50. : Eminent domain

51. c: Jury Trial

52. a: Charter

53. a: Lease

54. d: Verdict

55. a: Commerce Clause

56. b: Substantive law

57. b: Money laundering

58. d: Arbitration

59. : Complaint

Finance

1. b: Book value

2. a: Contribution margin

3. b: Property

4. : Cost of capital

5. d: Yield curve

6. c: Restructuring

7. c: Good

8. b: Inventory turnover

9. d: Interest rate risk

10. a: Operating lease

11. d: Capital asset pricing model

12. a: Capital lease

13. d: Preferred stock

14. d: Variable cost

15. d: Demand

16. : Financial Accounting Standards Board

17. b: Taxation

18. d: Presentation

19. a: Buyer

20. b: Variable Costing

21. b: Cost object

22. b: Going concern

23. b: Financial management

24. : Yield to maturity

25. : Cash flow

26. b: Contract

27. : Capital budgeting

28. c: Asset

29. b: Pension fund

30. d: Utility

31. d: Consideration

32. d: Incentive

33. d: Selling

34. : Stock market

35. c: Cost

36. : Accrual

37. a: Callable bond

38. a: Relevance

39. c: Currency

40. a: Primary market

41. b: Debt ratio

42. : Cost of goods sold

43. c: Intangible asset

44. : Pricing

45. a: Compound interest

46. d: Journal entry

47. a: Bank statement

48. c: Saving

49. : Certified Public Accountant

50. : Interest

51. d: Discounting

52. : Aging

53. a: Commercial paper

54. : Coupon

55. c: Limited liability

56. c: Accountant

57. : Maturity date

58. c: Capital asset

59. d: Audit

Human resource management

1. b: Cafeteria plan

2. d: Employee engagement

3. d: Employment

4. a: Ingratiation

5. a: Criterion validity

6. d: Workforce planning

7. : Delayering

8. : Authoritarianism

9. d: Peter Principle

10. a: Partnership

11. b: Job sharing

12. c: Cost leadership

13. a: Restructuring

14. a: Organizational socialization

15. a: Knowledge worker

16. c: Glass ceiling

17. a: Psychological contract

18. d: Age Discrimination in Employment Act

19. b: Merit pay

20. : Strategic planning

21. d: Empowerment

22. a: Needs analysis

23. d: Six Sigma

24. a: Overlearning

25. : Kaizen

26. a: Management

27. : Sick leave

28. d: Census

29. d: Social contract

30. d: Business game

31. a: Hostile work environment

32. a: E-learning

33. c: Decentralization

34. : Concurrent validity

35. b: Culture shock

36. d: Online assessment

37. : Collaboration

38. a: Cross-functional team

39. b: Coaching

40. b: Fair Labor Standards Act

41. b: Management by objectives

42. : Bureau of Labor Statistics

43. b: Works council

44. : Workplace bullying

45. d: Succession planning

46. d: Schedule

47. d: Individualism

48. a: Union shop

49. : Retraining

50. : Survey research

51. a: Telecommuting

52. b: Best practice

53. c: Content validity

54. c: Theory Z

55. b: Talent management

56. : Open shop

57. c: Action learning

58. c: Performance measurement

59. a: Cover letter

Information systems

1. a: Network management

2. b: Groupware

3. : Click fraud

4. c: Credit card

5. a: Google Docs

6. : Strategic information system

7. a: Outsourcing

8. c: Top-level domain

9. b: Star

10. b: Google

11. c: Information overload

12. : Virtual reality

13. : Trojan horse

14. d: Intranet

15. : Content management system

16. b: Data analysis

17. : Encryption

18. c: Privacy policy

19. c: Open source

20. d: Privacy

21. c: Business process

22. : Peer production

23. : Subscription

24. c: Identity theft

25. c: Microprocessor

26. : Online transaction processing

27. : Service level agreement

28. : Magnetic tape

29. d: Data mart

30. b: Text mining

31. : Business analytics

32. : Edge computing

33. d: Big data

34. c: Business process reengineering

35. c: World Wide Web

36. a: Joint application design

37. d: Downtime

38. : Query by Example

39. : Common Criteria

40. a: Password

41. d: Interactivity

42. : Help desk

43. d: Transport Layer Security

44. : E-commerce

45. d: Consumerization

46. a: Domain name

47. d: Computer fraud

48. d: Information

49. b: Availability

50. : ICANN

51. a: Information systems

52. d: Pop-up ad

53. a: Data governance

54. c: Zynga

55. c: Fault tolerance

56. : Craigslist

57. a: Random access

58. d: Dashboard

59. : Internet

Marketing

1. : General Motors

2. c: Sales management

3. : Consumer Protection

4. a: Database

5. : Information technology

6. : INDEX

7. a: Brand loyalty

8. b: Cooperative

9. d: Good

10. c: Disintermediation

11. c: Social marketing

12. a: Commerce

13. c: Personnel

14. c: Gross domestic product

15. d: Shares

16. b: Productivity

17. b: Preference

18. b: Creativity

19. d: Reseller

20. b: Business model

21. b: Hearing

22. c: Innovation

23. : Authority

24. a: Contract

25. d: Loyalty

26. c: Exploratory research

27. d: Customer retention

28. : Business Week

29. b: Franchising

30. : Census

31. a: Attention

32. c: Asset

33. d: Shopping

34. a: Data collection

35. a: Copyright

36. : Insurance

37. c: Entrepreneur

38. : Quantitative research

39. d: Brand extension

40. a: Accounting

41. b: Publicity

42. b: Viral marketing

43. : Small business

44. b: Supply chain

45. : Public relations

46. c: Brand awareness

47. : Warehouse

48. c: Return on investment

49. c: Investment

50. : Retail

51. c: Data warehouse

52. d: Manufacturing

53. : Noise

54. b: Total Quality Management

55. : Billboard

56. a: Concept testing

57. a: Business marketing

58. a: Trial

59. d: Product concept

Manufacturing

1. b: Certification

2. b: Customer

3. b: Thomas Register

4. c: Total quality management

5. : Workflow

6. c: Supply chain risk management

7. a: ROOT

8. c: Resource

9. d: Resource management

10. a: Interaction

11. : Sony

12. a: Synergy

13. d: Good

14. c: Scope statement

15. c: Technical support

16. : Furnace

17. c: Total productive maintenance

18. b: Opportunity cost

19. : Vendor relationship management

20. a: Global sourcing

21. a: Retail

22. c: Raw material

23. c: Tool

24. : Chemical reaction

25. d: Design of experiments

26. : Steel

27. c: Request for proposal

28. d: Rolling

29. d: Sharing

30. d: Coating

31. c: Accreditation

32. b: Heat transfer

33. b: Strategic planning

34. a: Total cost

35. : Acceptance sampling

36. : Authority

37. : Cost estimate

38. d: Remanufacturing

39. d: Cost reduction

40. a: Quality function deployment

41. a: Change management

42. : Aggregate planning

43. d: Pareto analysis

44. b: Change control

45. c: Project team

46. c: Quality Engineering

47. b: Chemical industry

48. c: Reboiler

49. b: Supply chain

50. a: Steering committee

51. d: Consortium

52. b: Quality management

53. d: Purchasing

54. a: Asset

55. b: Catalyst

56. : Zero Defects

57. c: Total cost of ownership

58. d: Economic order quantity

59. : Original equipment manufacturer

Commerce

1. d: Empowerment

2. d: Reverse auction

3. a: Common carrier

4. c: Cooperative

5. d: Case study

6. d: Computer security

7. : Technology

8. b: Goal

9. : Teamwork

10. : Good

11. a: Leadership

12. d: Microsoft

13. a: Total revenue

14. c: Fixed cost

15. : Complexity

16. d: Economic development

17. d: Antitrust

18. a: Bottom line

19. d: Market segmentation

20. b: Interest

21. a: Economy

22. d: Authorize.Net

23. b: WebSphere Commerce

24. : Logo

25. d: Board of directors

26. c: Market share

27. a: Economies of scale

28. a: Transaction cost

29. d: Merchant

30. c: Purchasing manager

31. : Statutory law

32. b: Budget

33. b: Evaluation

34. c: Raw material

35. : Trade

36. a: Silver

37. c: Online advertising

38. b: Trade show

39. c: Minimum wage

40. : Pizza Hut

41. : Stock

42. c: Property

43. c: Webvan

44. d: Payment card

45. d: Uniform Commercial Code

46. d: Merchandising

47. c: Mining

48. d: Consumer-to-consumer

49. c: Human resources

50. : PayPal

51. c: Mass production

52. a: Product line

53. d: Customer satisfaction

54. d: Pop-up ad

55. c: Level of service

56. a: Outsourcing

57. d: Organizational structure

58. a: Return on investment

59. b: Disney

Business ethics

1. a: Transocean

2. c: Electronic waste

3. d: Social networking

4. a: Collusion

5. d: Clayton Act

6. c: UN Global Compact

7. a: Corporation

8. : Toxic waste

9. a: Occupational Safety and Health Administration

10. c: Layoff

11. b: Accounting

12. c: Clean Water Act

13. a: Consumerism

14. d: Right to work

15. : Six Sigma

16. a: Coal

17. : Stanford Financial Group

18. b: Lanham Act

19. d: Kyoto Protocol

20. c: Workplace bullying

21. c: Micromanagement

22. d: Medicare fraud

23. d: Catholicism

24. b: New Deal

25. b: Junk bond

26. c: Global Fund

27. d: Disclaimer

28. : Enron

29. b: Patriot Act

30. c: East India

31. d: Utilitarianism

32. : Invisible hand

33. d: Pollution Prevention

34. b: Whistleblower

35. a: Cause-related marketing

36. c: Sexual harassment

37. a: Biofuel

38. d: Endangered Species Act

39. : Madoff

40. b: Energy policy

41. b: Skill

42. a: Ethics Resource Center

43. : Locus of control

44. a: Urban sprawl

45. c: Criminal law

46. d: Undue hardship

47. b: European Commission

48. c: Employee Polygraph Protection Act

49. : Partnership

50. c: Pure Food and Drug Act

51. c: Fair trade

52. c: Great Depression

53. : Organizational structure

54. a: Capitalism

55. b: Siemens

56. b: Arthur Andersen

57. : Internal control

58. d: Exxon Valdez

59. d: Ponzi scheme

Accounting

1. : Chart of accounts

2. d: Inventory

3. a: Payroll

4. c: Taxpayer

5. c: Debenture

6. d: Certified Management Accountant

7. : Ledger

8. b: Money

9. : Revenue recognition

10. b: Balanced scorecard

11. c: Articles of incorporation

12. b: Tax shelter

13. a: Tax rate

14. a: Income approach

15. b: Public company

16. a: Income tax

17. a: Net investment

18. b: Historical cost

19. b: Process Management

20. c: Property tax

21. b: Petty cash

22. a: Decentralization

23. c: Adjusting entries

24. b: C corporation

25. b: Subsidiary

26. c: Maturity date

27. b: Deposit insurance

28. d: Debt ratio

29. d: Financial Accounting Standards Board

30. d: Taxable income

31. c: Single Audit

32. c: Fixed asset

33. c: International Financial Reporting Standards

34. a: Contributed capital

35. d: Amortization

36. a: Minority interest

37. a: Cost of goods available for sale

38. a: General ledger

39. : Flowchart

40. : Financial Accounting Foundation

41. a: S corporation

42. d: Pension

43. d: Shareholder

44. c: Return on investment

45. a: Automated teller machine

46. : Sales

47. : Financial instrument

48. a: Operating lease

49. a: Accounting information system

50. b: Net realizable value

51. c: Going concern

52. a: Parent company

53. c: Debit card

54. a: Common stock

55. c: Revenue

56. : Investment center

57. : Internal auditing

58. : XBRL

59. a: Customer profitability

CPSIA information can be obtained
at www.ICGtesting.com
Printed in the USA
LVHW010153301019
635716LV00002B/89/P